WOMEN AND CHRISTIANITY

Mary T. Malone

Women and Christianity

VOLUME THREE:
FROM THE REFORMATION TO THE 21ST CENTURY

the columba press

First published in 2003 by
the columba press
55A Spruce Avenue, Stillorgan Industrial Park,
Blackrock, Co Dublin

Cover by Bill Bolger
Origination by The Columba Press
Printed in Ireland by Colour Books Ltd, Dublin

ISBN 1 85607 365 3

Contents

Dedication
To my parents
Ellen Agnes Malone (née Nixon) (1904-1987)
and
James Dominic Malone (1886-1958)
Their gentle, courageous, and loving spirits
still support our lives.

Introduction

The increasing visibility of women on the ecclesial and cultural scenes from the sixteenth century on adds a new complexity both of choice and analysis to Volume Three of *Women and Christianity*. On the one hand, sources for the history of women become relatively more available in ecclesiastical and secular documentation, making the choice of whom to include and whom to omit more arbitrary; on the other hand, the very familiarity of such women as Teresa of Avila and Mother Teresa of Calcutta makes the historical analysis of their real contributions at once more difficult and more important. Volume Three, *From the Reformation to the Twenty-first Century*, hopes to place such women in the context of their times, thus casting a more critical historical light on their lives. Without exception, the women gain in stature and interest from such analysis.

The period begins with the seismic event of the Reformation – or series of reformations – which challenged, with particular consequences for the lives of women, the meanings of the celibate priesthood and sacramental marriage, along with the multiple symbolic resonances these had created throughout the tradition. Both church ministry and marriage had then to be reconfigured, with paradoxical results for women. The Protestant return to biblical sources briefly offered women a glimpse of an expanding and inclusionary ecclesial and social role, but the newly articulated doctrine of the authoritative headship of men in family, church and society placed a definitive theological barrier in the path of women's aspirations to full participation and to leadership.

A new era had dawned, however, and the issue of women's

full participation and the possibilities of women's leadership was to haunt male leaders of church and state to our own day. The late medieval *querelle des femmes* began the long history of consistent challenges made by women themselves to the traditional understandings of subordination and confinement to the private sphere. These challengers included Renaissance women philosophers, women political theorists of the French Revolution, women founders of Religious communities, and finally feminist exegetes and theologians since the nineteenth century. One of the initiating reasons for the sixteenth century debate was the arrival on the scene of several women rulers, most notably, Elizabeth I of England. If women were designed by God, as the new Protestant theology taught, to be always subject to a male head, how then, it was asked, could a queen legitimately rule? Decades of intense discussion produced the image of the split woman, with a public face of some possible authority, and a private face of subordination. This public/private dilemma still bedevils ecclesiastical and social policy in a variety of ways, and, for example, constitutes one of the chief arguments against the ordination of women in the Roman Catholic Church.

The enormous expansion of European perspectives occasioned by the 'discovery' of the New World excited at once human greed, lust for power, and Christian missionary zeal. Subsequent 'missionary conquests' on all continents present us with conflicting stories of Christian heroism and utter brutality on many fronts. Women play a minor role in such exploits, but the life of women such as Marguerite Bourgeoys, who travelled alone from her native France to Canada on a ship with one hundred men, carrying absolutely nothing with her in order to 'test' God, demonstrates that Christian woman were continuing to create new opportunities for themselves despite all the continuing prescriptions on their lives. By the nineteenth century, Protestant and Catholic women missionaries were circling the globe in similar hair-raising journeys, while, at home, Quaker women exegetes were making even more startling assaults on traditional biblical understandings of women's Christian identities.

The educational innovations for women and girls created by generations of women religious, not to mention the extraordinary assortment of their other contributions in health and welfare, need to be highlighted and placed in proper context, after having been taken for granted by the Roman Catholic community for centuries as the normative reality of Catholic life. The brilliant originality and stubborn persistence of so many women founders, in the face of an often unwelcoming church, needs to be remembered, as well as the glorious heritage of service provided by such communities. The challenge to the historian lies in the abundance of a certain kind of necessarily spiritualised record, as each community strove to gain ecclesiastical recognition for its existence and work. The real genius of the women founders and their earliest followers is often buried beneath centuries of an imposed image of the 'holy foundress'.

The twentieth century expands the perspective in every direction, while the opening years of the twenty-first century offer an even more complex picture of the future of women Christians, as of Christianity itself. The closing chapters of Volume Three will focus on the global feminist challenge to Christianity, as women across the continents add a new breadth of vision and a new depth of challenge to traditional understandings of the lives and roles of Christian women. These challenges focus on a new reading of the old sources in the context of the contemporary experience of women. Among the topics that are at the centre of such exploration are spirituality, ethics, ecofeminism, and the multiple issues involved in the debate on the priestly ordination of women. The questions raised by the Christian women of today are breathtaking in their scope and complexity, but they have released the kind of renewed spiritual energy that will definitely carry women Christians through the twenty-first century.

Neither the author nor this volume would have survived without the support and counsel of many. I thank my family and friends for their ongoing encouragement and interest in the project. I am deeply grateful to the readers of the two published volumes for their generosity in making their appreciation known to me personally. I want to thank my Canadian friends for their avalanche of support whenever I arrive in my second and much loved home. From so many, I wish to name only a few. First of all to my cousin, Sister Miriam O'Leary OCD, and to Professor Keith Egan of Notre Dame, Indiana, many thanks for your essential help with the chapter on Teresa of Avila. Lastly a word of gratitude to Seán O Boyle of The Columba Press for many kindnesses, and to the editors at Novalis and Orbis for their continuing support.

CHAPTER ONE

Continuity and Change

As the sixteenth century begins, we rejoin the story of women in the context of religious and political turbulence in every corner of Europe, ecclesiastical corruption, the ongoing inquisition and the appalling witchcraze. At the same time, the period known as the Renaissance made sixteenth-century Europe one of the most glittering periods in historical memory, with its profusion of artists, architects, and scientific and literary geniuses of all kinds. Indeed, the very political and religious patrons (both women and men) of such artistic exuberance were often, at one and the same time, the patrons of the most vicious religious persecution imaginable. When the extraordinary watershed of the various religious reformations was added to the mix, accompanied by perhaps the most influential invention of all – the printing press – the basis was laid for one of the most complicated historical periods known to us. As usual, we remember the high points, and have tended to judge the period from the point of view of those at the pinnacle of political and religious power. The attempt to peer into this creative and destructive turbulence from the perspective of the majority who occupied the lower end of the social spectrum will cast a rather different light on the period. This new perspective was heralded by the intriguing question first posed by the feminist historian, Joan Kelly: 'Did women have a Renaissance?'[1]

Despite, or more likely because of, the multi-layered turbulence of the period, women were a central pre-occupation of religious leaders, philosophers and politicians. For more than one hundred years now, and it was to continue for another two hundred, the vociferous debate, called *la querelle des femmes*, had been ongoing. It had been initiated by that remarkable woman, Christine de Pizan, around 1400 and was taken up by philosophers and theologians, women and men, with vigour. Christine, born in Italy, had been brought by her mother to live with her father, the court astrologer to the French court of Charles V. She was married at fifteen and had three children in what appeared to be a very comfortable existence. Then disaster struck. Within five years, both husband and father had died and, at the age of twenty-five, Christine was burdened with the support of her family, her mother and the accumulated debts of both husband and father. She became France's first professional woman author, and one of the first women known to us who wrote to support herself. She appeared to be self-taught in a wide range of subjects and had access in her unusually privileged early life to a huge range of books.[2]

As a woman writer, Christine soon found that her first task was to prove that women could and should write and, to this end, she had to challenge centuries of religious and philosophical thought about the seductive dangers and imbecilic capacities of women's minds. She directed her attention to one of the best known medieval denigrators of women, Jean de Meung, and, for the first time in history, began to challenge centuries of teaching about women. As her work continued, she became depressed at the multiplicity of negative diatribes against women in literature and decided instead to consult her own experience. 'I finally decided that God formed a vile creature when he made woman, and I wondered how such a worthy artisan could have deigned to make such an abominable work ... the vessel and abode of every evil and vice.'[3]

Christine goes on to try to refute each negative statement, thus trying to disprove, both from her own experience and the supposed evidence of historical tales, the conventional wisdom about the nature of women. Among other falsehoods about women she tackles the supposed truth that women enjoy being raped, asserting that, on the contrary, 'rape is the greatest possible sorrow for them'.[4]

Christine has been described as the protofeminist, and in one sense she was. Hers was one of the first voices to take on the tradition from her own experience. Her agenda, however, was not the agenda of today's feminists. She wanted the taint of being the supposed cause of all evil taken from women, but she could see no reason whatever why women should not be subject to their husbands. Her contribution, though, began a three hundred-year intellectual battle of the sexes. The actual lives of women were minimally affected by such musings, but it is important to realise that such religious and philosophical writing constituted the background to the lives of women during one of the cruelest periods of women's historical journey. We will meet other participants in this 'querelle' as they argue about women's right to and capacity for education, and also women's ability and right to rule. Elizabeth I of England will be one of the most notable subjects of this discussion.

Christine was one of the very few women who, because of the peculiar circumstances of her life and her own literary and philosophical gifts, was enabled to perceive herself in the context of history, conceptualise her own situation, and devise societal solutions. Most women were forced to live in a state of ignorance about themselves and their history, and the minimal education they did receive was designed especially to reinforce societal and religious restraints on their behaviour. As Christine had discovered, the first task of a woman setting out on any kind of independent career was to prove her own humanity and her capacity for thought. It was the deliberate decision over centuries by church and society to exclude women from education that had led to this state of affairs. From the sixteenth century on, much of the struggle of women to gain an equal footing in society was directed toward achieving access to education.[5] What we know of women in this period, as in others, comes from the few privileged women who had gained such access, whether through convent or court, the two main avenues for women. Even here, women had to argue both for the right to an education and then to prove their capacity for something more than

stereotypical feminine activity. At the turn of the sixteenth century, two women, both named Isabel, demonstrated the amazing
capacities for women for both good and ill. These were Isabella
d'Este and Isabella of Castille. Isabella d'Este was at the centre of
Renaissance life in a way not previously seen. She influenced
popes, rulers, and artists and was known then and now as one of
the premier collectors of Renaissance art. She stopped at nothing
to get her way and through the story of her life, we get a glimpse
of the daily lives of the Renaissance popes that reveals more
than we really wish to know about them. Apart from their impressive beautification programmes, their influence on ecclesiastical life was anything but beneficent. Isabella lived through
the pontificates of some of the most corrupt and gifted men ever
to occupy the See of Peter. Sixtus IV (1471-1484) was a warlike
pope who appointed Torquemada as head of the Spanish
Inquisition and delighted in blessing canons and other warlike
equipment. Needing money to boost his war-chest, he was the
first to conceive the idea of granting indulgences for the dead,
thereby discovering an unending source of revenue through the
manipulation of the bereaved. The initiation of sermons describing purgatory in the most lurid detail ensured that the money
kept rolling in.

He is reputed to have 'lowered the moral tone' of the whole
of Europe, but his successor, Innocent VIII (1484-1492) was no
great improvement. Together these two popes had caused edicts
to be issued against the Jewish and Muslim populations of Spain,
offering deportation, forced conversion, or death. Thousands
fled, thousands more were forcibly made Christians and over
two thousand were burned at the stake. When he died, it was
with one of the most corrupt reputations for a pope to date, but
even worse was to come. Alexander VI Borgia was well known
as a murderer, adulterer and robber before he became pope and
the papacy did not improve his character. Of course he had
bought the papacy, and the cardinals knew that they were in the
clutches of the 'most savage wolf' that Christianity had yet seen.
There is no point in detailing the orgiastic nature of his papacy,

nor the devastation wrought by his son, Cesare, but as Martin Luther grew to manhood, he could not have lived in a church with a more corrupt leader. When Alexander died in 1503, probably poisoned by the same Cesare, it was universally believed that there was no point in praying for a man already damned.[6]

The corrupt lives of such (and many more) popes are remarkable only for the contrast with the exalted position they occupied in the life of the church. Isabella d'Este grew up in one such corrupt family. Her grandfather, Niccolo, had boasted that he had slept with eight hundred women, but he had his second wife executed for adultery. Fidelity was obviously a virtue required of wives but not of husbands. Isabella herself, born in 1474, seems to have grown up in a fairly loving and stable environment.[7] Early in her life she absorbed the beauty and colour of her surroundings in Ferrara, and later during her married life in Mantua, and thus began her career as an avid collector of art. Europe was being flooded with colour, exotic food and dress, and the cosmetic industry took a leap forward from which, one might say, it has never looked back. The fact that Isabella's brother, Alfonso married Lucrezia Borgia, beloved daughter of Pope Alexander VI, places the family d'Este at the centre of ecclesiastical and political affairs. Isabella herself was engaged at the age of six to one of the Gonzaga family of Mantua and married, aged 16, in 1490.

In contrast to most women of the past, we have extensive records for the life of Isabella, even down to her shopping lists for clothing, jewellery, perfumes, shoes, and silk underwear. The expenses of dressing as befitted one of her status are mind-boggling, and dressing and self-adornment seem to have absorbed hours of each day. From the time of her marriage, much of Isabella's time was taken up as a pawn in political and ecclesiastical affairs, though perhaps, in her case, pawn is not the right word as she soon became known as one of the most shrewd manipulators in her family's interests. Among her many trips were several to console her sister Beatrice, whose husband, Ludovico Sforza, was consistently unfaithful, and even managed to have

his many mistresses painted by none other that Leonardo da
Vinci. In the unceasing struggles of Pope Alexander VI to expand the papal states and prevent France from occupying Italy,
Isabella became a most successful negotiator, as she journeyed
from Ferrara to Mantua to Milan to Venice and eventually to
Rome, deceiving and being deceived, and conniving to further
the cause of whatever side her husband and family wished to
promote. To add to her responsibilities, she was the lone ruler of
Mantua as her hero husband, commander of the Italian forces,
spent most of his time on the battlefield. The powers assumed
by this young woman were astonishing – we are told that she
once ordered a local priest to stop preaching anti-Jewish sermons.

Nevertheless, her life as a negotiator was fraught with difficulty. Pope Alexander VI made deals with France in order to
divide Italy among his many children. Gianfrancesco, husband
of Isabella, went from being an Italian hero as he led his forces to
victory, to being despised by all for being caught on the wrong
side as his papal and royal masters manoeuvred to gain the most
financially advantageous position. It must have been well nigh
impossible for Isabella to keep pace with all these manoeuvres,
but the fact that she survived is one of the reasons why her name
is remembered. In the process, she befriended French kings,
popes, Holy Roman Emperors, foreign diplomats, and in turn,
the rulers of most of the great states of Italy. And all the time she
was collecting art and commissioning paintings and sculptures
from the growing numbers of artistic geniuses that peopled the
Italy of her day.

She finally gave birth to a son, Federico, in May 1500. His
godparents were Cesare Borgia and the Emperor Maximilian.
People wondered who the father was since her soldier husband
had rarely been at home. At age 2, the infant Federico was be-
trothed to the daughter of Cesare Borgia and one of his many
mistresses. If family relationships seem intertwined almost beyond unravelling, the situation of Italy itself at the beginning of
the sixteenth century was no less confusing. The French held
Milan; Cesare Borgia held the central states as papal territory;

and the rest was carved up between France and Spain, with the pope – and Isabella – engaging in constant rounds of negotiation to their own best advantage. Florence, Ferrara, Bologna and Genoa were linked to France, Naples was divided between France and Spain, and Venice remained more or less independent. Mantua, Isabella's own state, as a result of her own brilliant negotiating skill, was said to belong to Cesare Borgia, and therefore the pope, on Mondays and to Louis XII, the French king, on Tuesdays.[8]

At the turn of the sixteenth century, fittingly enough, Isabella made a decision that would have been impossible for many of her predecessors. She decided, after hearing of yet another act of public infidelity by her soldier husband, that she would become an independent woman. She decided to devote her attention completely to her art collecting and expanded her artistic acquaintances to include Michaelangelo, Leonardo da Vinci, Mantegna and many others. In 1499, Leonardo had visited Mantua to sketch her portrait, and produced one of the most famous portraits of the Renaissance, though the actual painting was never completed. Several letters survive testifying to Isabella's desire to have the portrait finished, but Leonardo proved to be an elusive proposition. Isabella also became known as a famous host, one of her most successful parties being the celebration of the engagement of Lucrezia Borgia to one of her brothers – a previous marriage to another brother having been annulled for reasons of alleged impotence. Isabella determined to outshine Lucrezia and the plotting towards this end included sending priests to Rome to spy on Lucrezia's trousseau collection and the reclothing of the archers, soldiers, and attendants in garments to outshine those of Lucrezia.

The horrific death of Alexander VI, whose soul was believed to have been taken by the devil, followed soon after by the death of his son, Cesare, seems to have sobered everyone temporarily. The new pope, Julius II, so-called after Julius Caesar, as Alexander had been named after Alexander the Great, almost managed to unite Italy and did manage to make some headway in cleaning up the pig-sty that was Rome. He is remembered, of course, for his bullying of Michaelangelo into painting the Sistine Chapel, as well as hiring Raphael and completing the building of St Peter's. Nevertheless, his three daughters had to be married off properly. Isabella's eldest daughter was married to a relative of the new pope, and some cardinalates were granted to cement the relationship. Meantime, Isabella's husband was engaged in a passionate and public affair with Lucrezia Borgia, and eventually suffered the fate of most of the men of his day, a life shattering case of syphilis. Since Isabella's son was now virtually fatherless, Pope Julius II offered to take him to live at the Vatican as his own son. Isabella agreed to part with her beloved Ercole on condition that no corporal punishment was ever used in his education. The family confusion was compounded by the pope's attack on Ferrara with the forces led by Isabella's brother and husband. The role of Isabella in this debacle is not known, but her husband, at least, suspected that she was not on his side. It is rare for a husband in that age to write as Gianfrancesco did about Isabella: 'We confess to having a wife who acts on her own opinions. She has demonstrated that on a number of occasions.'9

Pope Julius II was mourned when he died in 1513, more for his triumphs in war than his holiness. His successor, Leo X Medici, was a man after Isabella's own heart. Art was his religion, and one of his three sons is remembered as Lorenzo the Magnificent. Between them they made Rome the centre of the civilised world, but in a state of financial ruin. The fact that it remained in spiritual ruin seemed irrelevant to everyone. Savanarola, the prior of the Dominican house in Florence, had tried to preach reform in this regard but had paid with his life in the papacy of Alexander VI, having refused the bribe of a cardinal's hat. Isabella moved to Rome early in the papacy of Leo X. It is said that she was so busy sightseeing that she had no time to attend church on Sunday, but sent money to a convent instead. She had come prepared in both dress and attendants and was soon known as the 'Queen of Rome', while her young women attendants were favoured as the companions of the richest car-

dinals. Pope and husband were in conflict over Isabella's continued presence in Rome for Christmas, but to ensure her place at
his side, the pope issued a special papal decree. Her confessor
assured her that obedience to the pope took priority over her
obedience to her husband. As the world was in turbulence again
with the death of the French king, Pope Leo took on Machiavelli
as his chief advisor. The pope could have used good advice because, as Martin Luther nailed his ninety-five theses to the door
of Wittenberg cathedral in October 1517, the pope's one concern
was that he was completely without financial resources. In 1519,
Isabella's husband, Leonardo da Vinci, and Lucrezia Borgia all
died within months of each other. Isabella now took up permanent residence in Mantua and became a dedicated and accomplished ruler, never having lost her old skill of negotiation. She
was said to have been particularly skilled at making a series of
agreements with pope, king, emperor and several rulers, each
one nullifying the other. Her closing years remained as exciting
as ever, occupied as usual in maintaining all her diplomatic contacts. She survived a whole series of popes and also the horrific
siege of Rome in 1525, when thousands of women chose suicide
by jumping in the Tiber rather than rape by the emperor's soldiers. Thousands died in the ensuing sack of Rome, young nuns
were put up for auction, art treasures were either burned or ransacked and plague completed the devastation. The Italian
Renaissance was effectively ended.

For centuries afterwards, Italy remained a Hapsburg province,
but the papacy as institution survived. Pope Clement, who had
been a prisoner in the Castel San Angelo, escaped in disguise,
and stories of English envoys chasing the fleeing pope all over
Europe, in their search for a divorce for Henry VIII, present a
somewhat comic twist to an altogether tragic tale. When
Clement VII was allowed back into the Vatican in October 1528,
he found Rome four-fifths empty and destroyed. The emperor
now needed to make concessions to the pope, as the imperial
coronation was about to take place in Bologna. Among the invited
guests at this farcical event was Isabella d'Este, the 'First Lady of

the World'. A letter of Isabella describes the extraordinary event as these two powerful men, who hated each other fervently, met for the first time. The emperor kissed the foot, hand and lips of the pope and was in turn 'tenderly embraced by the Holy Father'. It was all a piece of shameless make-believe.[10] This was to be the last coronation of an emperor by a pope.

Isabella also survived Pope Clement, who died a bitter and hated old man. She set out, as she reached the comparative old age of sixty, to be reconciled with all her family and her enemies. Another portrait was painted by Titian and shows her as a majestic, self-contained woman. She is reported to have said before her death, 'I am a woman and I learned to live in a man's world.' She died on 13 February, 1539, having asked to be buried privately beside her husband. In the year of her death, French ambition turned across the Atlantic to the New World, and Elizabeth I of England, who was to crush the might of Spain, was just six years old. There is little trace in the life of Isabella d'Este of the other cataclysm that was to engulf Europe, namely the Protestant Reformation. The problems of Martin Luther in far-off Wittenberg seemed of little relevance in the Italy of Isabella d'Este.

The attention of the other Isabella was much more focused on the affairs of religion. Isabella of Castille was forty-one in 1492 as three events of world-shattering importance took place, events that were crucial to the development of western culture. First, on January 2, the armies of King Ferdinand and Queen Isabella conquered the city-state of Granada and restored it to Christendom. Granada was the last Muslim stronghold in Europe. Secondly, on March 31, Ferdinand and Isabella had signed the Edict of Expulsion, which was designed to rid Spain of the Jews. Thirdly, in August, Christopher Columbus was dispatched to find a new trade route to India and 'discovered' the Americas instead.[11] Together, Ferdinand of Aragon and Isabella of Castille were known as the 'Catholic kings'. Isabella was a deeply religious woman, fanatical in her zeal to rid her kingdom of all the enemies of Christianity. To this end she initiated and took part in vicious wars and cruel inquisitions.[12] Her motivations, nevertheless, were always religious and were usually guided by her confessor, Cardinal Ximenes. The mission of Columbus was to 'supervise the preserving and peopling of them [The Indies], because thereby our Lord God is served, his Holy Faith extended and our own realm increased'.[13] The return of Spain to the Catholic fold was the main task of the two 'Catholic Kings'. The eight hundred years of Moorish rule had been ended by the recapture of Granada and the news of this event set church bells pealing all over Europe. The Jews were next on the list of enemies of the Catholic faith; they were given the choice of deportation or baptism. The crusade mounted against them was chilling in its intensity, despite the fact that Jews had been full citizens of Spain for centuries. The same choice was offered to any remaining Muslims, despite their lengthy history as citizens and vast contributors to the art and wealth of Spain. Sentiments of pity or compassion seem never to have entered Isabella's heart. She saw herself as divinely destined to fulfil the role of God's vengeful crusader, and one of the main signs of God's favour was the uniting of the two ancient kingdoms of Aragon and Castille. Isabella, aged twenty-three, had handled her claim to the throne of Castille after the death of her half-brother, Henry IV, by immediately proclaiming herself Queen and having herself publicly crowned. Her behaviour was seen as quite uncharacteristic of her sex and even her absent husband was shocked. In a sense, the positions of wife and husband were mirror images of each other. Isabella was consort to Ferdinand, king of Aragon, while Ferdinand had to be content with being co-ruler with Isabella in Castille. Eventually, the two grew toward a unity of rule, which was able to move beyond the niceties of their respective claims.

There was nothing in Isabella's youth which seemed to have prepared her for a life of such determined power. Her education had been minimal and it is clear that she was not going to allow such a lapse in the lives of her own children. The great Spanish educator, Vives, was assigned the task of supervising the education of her daughter, Catherine of Aragon, and his specially commissioned text for this task became famous. We shall be visiting this text below. Isabella taught herself Latin, the language of diplomacy, and hired teachers to oversee her own development in the martial arts of riding and warfare. She came to be renowned for her fierce austerity mixed with an almost sentimental piety. In a world of courtly immorality, she held herself aloof and uncomprehending. Like Isabella d'Este, she dressed in the required jewelled robes for public occasions but, unlike her Italian namesake, she seems to have preferred austere dress in private – 'a simple dress of silk with three gold hem-bands'. Again, like Isabella d'Este, the Queen of Castille had to endure her husband's public infidelity, and she turned to prayer for help through these humiliating ordeals. Her chaste virtues became famous throughout her realms and, in the public mind, she became a kind of mystical figure, who was deemed worthy to have 'given birth to the Son of God'. She was seen to be a kind of second Virgin Mary, who, through her life of virtue, atoned for the sin of Eve. Such ascription of sanctity was characteristic not only of her lifetime, but continued long after her death, right up to the modern period. The saint-loving Pope John Paul II would dearly have loved to canonise Isabella, but global outrage prevented such an outcome.

Despite claiming the queenship of Castille, Ferdinand and Isabella had to fight a bitter civil war against the other claimants to the throne, especially Juana, daughter of Isabella's half-brother. Juana was engaged to the king of Portugal and thus the war expanded in its range and intensity. Isabella participated fully, thus upsetting what was seen as the natural order of things. In scenes reminiscent of many a modern ruler/husband and wife relationship, Isabella deferred ostentatiously to Ferdinand in public, but behind the scenes, she was a dynamo of energy. She is credited with founding the first travelling military hospital in Europe and set herself the task of supervising the building of roads and the organising of supplies. She also set herself in charge of the religious life of the military encampment, and attendance at daily Mass was required of all.

Isabella's history of miscarriages was attributed to her involvement in these military campaigns, but finally her son John
was born. This was an essential part of her plans for the future,
because though a daughter could succeed to Castille, Aragon,
under the Salic Law required a male heir. Such legal requirements were beyond the control even of Isabella. Her son died
young, however, and of her three daughters, only Catherine of
Aragon was to have future influence of any kind. In 1501 she
had been married to Arthur, Prince of Wales, son of Henry VII,
but the following year she was left a widow. Three years after
her mother's death in 1504, Catherine became a kind of ambassador between the English and Spanish courts, and finally on 11
June, 1509, Catherine of Aragon and Henry VIII were married.
As we have seen, Henry's envoys were chasing the papal envoys
around Europe after the sack of Rome in 1527 seeking a divorce
from Catherine. She died in her own bed on 7 January, 1536,
having written the previous evening to the man she still considered to be her husband, Henry VIII, to express her forgiveness
and that 'mine eyes desire you above all things'.[14]

These three women, Isabella d'Este, Isabella of Castille and
her daughter, Catherine of Aragon were extraordinary women,
and especially the first two were recognised in their time as
somehow upsetting the natural order of things. In the last
decades of the fifteenth century, and for the next several hundred years, there was a lively and public debate about the role of
women. Because the bible was seen as the final arbiter in this
debate – at least as far as women were concerned – this debate
was a religious debate, a Christian debate. In a very real sense,
however, two parallel debates were ongoing. One was a continuation of the debate originated by Christine de Pizan, where a
woman, for the first time, set out to answer the 'lies' that men
had created about women. This was continued by what might
be called Renaissance humanists, both women and men, who
even though Christian by designation, made more use of contemporary cultural exigencies. Included in this group are several
women exegetes of scripture such as Isotta Nogarola, who

raised many of the questions about the standard biblical teachings on women in the stories of Creation, Fall, Adam and Eve,
and the teachings of Jesus and Paul, that have become familiar
today. Included also would be the writings of such men as
Erasmus of Rotterdam and Juan de Vives, who used the scriptures to reassert, in a new context and with different emphasis,
the ancient teachings about the inferiority of women. Paradoxically, this humanist and somewhat secular debate, while acknowledging some inequalities in the treatment of women, and
allowing for some necessary freedoms, tended to add new restrictions lest such freedoms would be pushed too far.

The other strand of public debate belongs to the extremely
religious context of the early Reformation period. By returning
to the sources of early Christianity, the early Reformation unleashed a momentary new experience of liberation for women,
peasants and the oppressed. As usual, this core Christian message of salvation for all was heard by women and the poor, but
the social and ecclesiastical implications were quickly denied
them. This debate will occupy us in the next chapter. Again
paradoxically, the new oppressive teaching of the Reformation
about women, in its reassertion of the headship of men in family
and church settings, also opened doors to education, as the new
religious debates required of all a new sense of ownership and
articulacy about the faith.

The presence on the social scene of prominent women who
were becoming articulate about their own place in society, and
who publicly challenged traditional male teaching about their
roles, unleashed volumes of writing on the respective roles of
women and men, queens and kings, wives and husbands. A
new and public body of opinion that might reasonably be called
'feminist' grew steadily. Initially, the favoured new type of
woman was the 'virile' woman, who was able by sheer courage
and perseverance, and the exercise of 'unnatural virtue' to transcend the limitations of the prescribed roles of submission and
obedience. As Christine de Pizan had done, the records of the
past were mined for such women, some real, mostly fabulous,

and where a woman model did not exist, she was invented. As the debate continued, the spotlight turned more on the androgyne, the woman – and man – who were able to combine the best of both sexes. This debate was abstract, theoretical and rhetorical, and often bore little relationship to the reality of most women's lives, possibly because the room for manoeuvring any kind of social change was so limited. Actually, the aim of such writing was not social change, but the creation of a new awareness and a new counterpoint to the increasingly common misogynist writing of the era. In this it was successful. Women were provided with a new language, a new voice and a new argumentation. The best source of this new argumentation was the bible.

One of the first women known to us to engage in a public biblical debate about the role of women was Isotta Nogarola (1418-1466), who challenged the teachings of a distinguished Venetian humanist, Ludovico Foscarini, and laid the groundwork for much later writing.[15] This body of biblical exegesis by women in the fifteenth and sixteenth centuries was completely unknown after the religious reforms of the mid-sixteenth century, and would have been seen by both Protestant and Catholic reformers as the height of female arrogance and heresy. One of the main points of the debate was about the respective guilt of Adam and Eve for the Fall. Both accepted without question the greater weakness of Eve, but Isotta argued that this made Eve less guilty than Adam, who should have known better. She argued that Adam had received the command not to eat directly from God, and therefore, his punishment was the harsher. Ludovico argued that Eve had tempted Adam, and that therefore her sin was worse. Isotta disagreed, arguing that Eve just longed to know the difference between good and evil, and the desire to know is natural, whereas Adam wanted to be like God and sinned more from pride. Isotta was able to back her arguments with quotations from patristic sources, demonstrating that she had access to a good library, but little is known about her life. Isotta's work was known to Laura Cereta, a generation later, who died just at the turn of the sixteenth century. Laura was a distinguished mathematician as well as biblical student. Like many other women, she used study and writing to help recover her equilibrium after her husband's death. Laura's father was accused of writing her letters for her, because it was not thought possible that a woman should show such insight and learning. She turned such male criticism against the writers: 'Where there is greater wisdom, there is greater guilt'.[16]

Marguerite d'Angouleme, Queen of Navarre, who died in 1549, wrote the *Mirror of the Sinful Soul* in 1531. She was a Catholic, but was very impressed with the theology of Calvin. She accepted the Protestant teaching of *sola fides* and used her royal court to encourage a wide-ranging theological discussion. Unlike many other women of her day, she was familiar with the writings of Hildegard of Bingen and Mechtilde of Magdeburg, and used their inspiration to speak authoritatively about her own religious insights. She devoted her writings particularly to biblical passages about women and must have caused some theological terror in the hearts of reformers by such phrases as: 'But Lord, if you are my Father, may I think that I am your Mother?'[17] She based this on the saying of Jesus that those who do his will are his brother and sister and mother. (Mk 3:35) As the teaching and life of the Reformation became part of the religious landscape of Europe, such debates became much more dangerous, and led to accusations of heresy.

One of the best known writers and theologians of this early period was the famous humanist, Desiderius Erasmus (1467-1536), friend of Thomas More and correspondent with Martin Luther. Erasmus was recognised as an intellectual in his day. He devoted his attention to making the scriptures the core of Christian life, and to this end he wrote extensive annotations to the Vulgate in order to correct errors of translation and transmission. He was not comfortable in any of the religious groupings of the day – though he remained a Catholic – but belonged more to the international community of scholars.[18] Like most male scholars, Erasmus entered the debate about women and men in his discussion of marriage and motherhood. He is always ambiguous about women's spiritual equality with men. In his work, *The New Mother*, he argues with a strong supporter of women in the fictional person of Fabulla. She insists that it is not according to the laws of nature that women have been subordinated to men, but simply that the male is more aggressive. She adds that childbirth demands more of a woman and is more dangerous for her than war is for men. Women and men are spiritual equals, she insists, because both are created in the image of God, and this has more to do with minds than with bodies. Erasmus would like to agree, but shares the common feeling of his contemporaries that women, given a chance, will always push this equality too far, especially if they are not married. A woman's autonomy can never be separated from her physical being, her femaleness. Like most male authors of the day, Erasmus is much more interested in the sexuality of women than in their minds, and makes this the centre of his argumentation.

Erasmus, like many of his contemporaries, was not in favour of convents. In his day, many convents, rightly or wrongly, were regarded as nothing more than brothels. In line with the Protestant reformers, Erasmus would have preferred to see all women married and obeying fathers and husbands. The vows of a nun, he says elsewhere, contribute nothing to religion, and the veil is just a 'linen garment turned inside out'.[19] Erasmus likewise had great problems with women of learning, and saw such women as nothing more than a menace. In his work, called *The Abbot and the Learned Lady*, which many think is directed at Margaret Roper, the daughter of Thomas More, he argues against the study of Greek and Roman authors by women, because women are made for pleasure: 'It is not feminine to be brainy.' The female opponent in this argument insists that women are just as capable of intellectual development as men, and that women, like men, must respond to the vocation to which they are called. She goes on to confirm the worst fears of all reformers by declaring that, once properly educated, women will proceed to fill the same ecclesiastical roles as men: 'We'll preside in the theological schools, preach in the churches, and wear your mitres.' And in an argument that had been heard before, and which has been reiterated since, she insists that she is not speaking of real social and ecclesiastical change here, but pointing out the spiritual and intellectual sloth of contemporary men.[20]

Erasmus replies that the role of the husband in marriage is not one of dominance but always one of authority. In the 'service of love' that is marriage, all authority is in the hands of the husband. His role is to love the weaker sex, thus maintaining a society of equals between them. Just to show his ongoing ambivalence about the marriage relationship, he goes on to assert the need for dominance in men, because the woman is always politically subordinate, and he is her natural superior. The wife must put up with cruelty, knowing that she has brought it on herself, he says, and yet she is not to act as the man's servant. Nevertheless, her main task is his well being and, like many preachers before and since, he ends by resorting to paradox: 'A wife is never more a mistress than when she obeys her husband.' All through this work, Erasmus is arguing from the Pauline dictum that the husband is the head, despite the spiritual equality of the two. Such equality, however, can never be actualised in the contemporary social situation.[21]

In 1525, Juan Luis Vives wrote his *Instruction of a Christian Woman* for Catherine of Aragon. This was a book for royal women called to rule, of whom there seemed to be a growing number during the sixteenth century. He teaches that a woman should never regard herself as fit to rule. She is weak by nature, subordinate in marriage, and her main task is to safeguard her chastity. Eloquence of speech is never present in a woman and when she imagines herself to be eloquent, she is merely babbling. Her vision of life, both past and present, is to be learned entirely from men. The model woman of Vives is similar to the model of Erasmus. She is destined to live a double life, always subordinate but outwardly giving the impression that this is her choice. The words of Vives are directed at Mary, the daughter of

Catherine of Aragon, but also at Catherine herself. The fact that these two women were not prospering politically was abundant proof that God did not wish women to rule. It is clear, then, that such teaching by both Erasmus and Vives was responding more to the current ecclesiastical and political situations than to any real impetus for the advancement of women's social or spiritual equality.

Indeed, their words seem mild when compared with one of the most destructive documents of all time, which was being circulated then, namely the horrific *Malleus Maleficarum*. This document, written by the papal inquisitors, Heinrich Kramer and Jacob Sprenger in 1486, was a manual for witch-hunters, giving specific instructions on how to capture, try, torture, and execute a witch. Much of the rest of the document is a hate-filled tirade against women's sexuality, and the newly minted belief that women were copulating with the devil. In this document, the most feared realities of the Early Modern period come together – the image of 'woman' and the image of the devil. This devil is a Christian creation designed to explain the presence of unexplainable evil in the world. Likewise, the creation of the image of woman was an ancient ruse for both pagan and Christian philosophers, which enabled them to ignore the evidence before their eyes of real women, who did not fit into the required parameters. At the turn of the sixteenth century, these two came together in the minds of religious leaders and initiated a major holocaust of women, whose ferocity still lacks adequate explanation. Both women and men were accused of witchcraft and both women and men were burned, but in the imagination and theological teaching of the time, as well as in the imagination of the twenty-first century, the witch is a woman. It is the *Malleus Maleficarum* which is largely responsible for this image. Until the eighties of the last century, the general opinion of scholars was that the witches were old women who were making a nuisance of themselves and got what they deserved. The ferocious and sexually motivated violence against women seems to have escaped their notice.

The old pagan belief in witchcraft received its Christian baptism in 1484 when Pope Innocent VIII brought out an astonishing piece of papal writing, *Summa desiderantes*, which attempts
to find reasons for the epidemic of sexual anxiety that was apparently sweeping through Germany. Men were becoming im-
potent and women were unable to conceive. Witches were
blamed for this state of affairs. They were having sex with the
devil and casting spells on their neighbours.[22] The pope commissioned the Dominicans Kramer and Sprenger to deal with
the matter. The University of Cologne reluctantly endorsed their
efforts, and the *Malleus* quickly went through nineteen editions.
The witchcraze itself did not properly get under way until the
early sixteenth century, but before it was through, thousands of
women and children had been tortured and executed, and several German villages had been left with no women inhabitants.
What the *Malleus* particularly planted in the imaginations of
Christians in the sixteenth and seventeenth centuries was that
witches were women, and these women were setting out to
wreak havoc on male sexuality. Kramer and Sprenger themselves did not go much further in their search for an explanation
of the supposed satanic character of women, than the evidence
of woman's bent rib, and the weird invented etymology of the
Latin word for woman, *femina*, which indicated to them that
women had less faith than men, by their very nature. The ultimate proof of woman's evil is in their insatiable sexuality: 'All
witchcraft comes from carnal lust, which in woman is insatiable'.[23]

Several writers attempted to explain this new phenomenon,
among them Paracelsus in 1521.[24] He brought his skills as physi-
cian, theologian and philosopher to the task of trying to give the
scientific explanation of this new phenomenon. He set out to defend women, but any defence of women at this time was likely
to bring only more vicious condemnations. In fact, even the
most traditionally approved behaviour of women was easily
held against them. Since it was taught that women were incapable of chastity, any unmarried woman was seen to be fleeing

men in favour of sex with the devil. Any deformed child was understood as the product of sex between old women and the
devil. Once started, the cycle was inescapable. The witchcraze illustrates the complexity of this early modern period of Renaissance and Reformation, when beside the rebirth of philosophy
and theology, one must also place the almost universal belief in
witches and the harm they intentionally generated.

Paracelsus was trying to understand why the image of the
witch changed from the male or female (usually both revered
and feared) who was privy to secret, often inherited knowledge,
and the wisdom of the ages, and who understood the healing
and magical properties of herbs and potions, to that of the evil
woman copulating with the devil. The inquisitors had drawn,
for the first time in European history, a direct line between the
old pact with the devil and satanic sexuality. Paracelsus tried to
understand the nature of the female and to explain scientifically
the occurrence of occult phenomena. He tries to demystify them
and make them comprehensible. He believed in witches – indeed their existence was by now an article of faith – but despite
himself, everything returned to the sexuality of women, the fear
of birth deformities, and male impotence. The end result of his
'scientific' researches was even more devastating for women.
Whereas the inquisitors had put it all down to demonic possession combined with women's weakness, Paracelsus attributed
intentionality to women, and therefore direct culpability.

More recent writers have also tried to explain the existence of
the phenomenon of the witchcraze in the context of Renaissance,
Reformation, the discovery of new worlds, the creation of early
capitalism, and the new scholarly explorations. No one explanation suffices, but it is obvious that in the new world that was
being created by reformer, artist, religious leader and renaissance philosopher, the space allotted to women was narrowing
dramatically. It was a burst of misogyny without parallel in
Western history, says Anne Llewellyn Barstow.[25] She isolates
three ingredients that must be included in any analysis, noting that
attention to the victims is absent from most previous accounts.

These three ingredients are the predominance of women victims, the savagery of the trial and torturing process, and the
focus on the sexuality of the victims. Other issues such as the
ownership of property by women, family feuding, and the traditional position of the woman healer in the village are also relevant, but cannot be taken in isolation. As a feminist historian,
Barstow also recognises patriarchy as a historical category, visible all too clearly in the fact that all the judges were men, the tor-
turers and executioners were men, and even more ambiguously,
those who initiated the process and prayed over the final moments
were ordained men. Barstow, alone among commentators, also
questions the effect on villagers and townspeople of watching
daily executions – and witch-burning was intended as public
display – and tries to explore the reasons for and consequences
of this public and violent intimidation of citizens by church and
state. She questions the functioning of religious and political
power through the sadistic sexual torture of women, and dis-
covers signs of the effects of such terrorisation on the later behaviour of women and men.

Barstow works from the historical records in an attempt to
gain a more accurate insight into the actual numbers of women
accused and burned as witches. Earlier estimates had ranged
from several million to the trivialisation and denial of the reality.
The records of the inquisition, however, survive and give immediate entry into the appalling world of male Christian cruelty
against defenceless and mostly female victims. Barstow estimates from the examination of records in the precise geographical
boundaries of northern Europe that about two hundred thousand witches were burned to death in the early modern period,
that is from 1560 to 1760. Whatever way one analyses this information, it was a mass murder of women. Barstow also points out
that these numbers don't account for lynchings, those who died
under torture, or those simply murdered in prison. The devil
was conveniently blamed for looking after his own in such circumstances.

The fact that most of these witches were the poorest of the

poor, condemned to live as outcasts, surviving as best they could, adds another light on the quality of Christian life in the period of the most profound theological debate and conciliar reform. The newly beautified exterior of the Catholic churches and the new dignified simplicity of the Protestant houses of worship covered such appalling activity with the veneer of public respectability. The torture and execution of the Pappenheimer family in Bavaria gives some idea of the randomness of a witch-hunt, and the public nature of the executions by fire shows clearly that such public displays were intended as more than just punishment of the accused.[26] Young duke Maximilian of Bavaria, after an intensive Jesuit education, had become concerned about witchcraft in his dominions. His wife could not conceive and he feared that a curse had been put on the family. He called for a witch-hunt, and the Pappenheimer family was designated. Anna Pappenheimer was fifty-nine in 1600. She was the daughter of a gravedigger, and was married to an itinerant privy-cleaner. Despite the dire conditions of her life – members of both trades were treated as outcasts – she had managed to keep her family of seven children together. The unfortunate family was also seen as Lutheran in the Catholic Duchy of Bavaria.

The parents and two adult children were arrested and brought to Munich for trial. Anna was seen as particularly guilty and after repeated torture, she finally admitted to all the usual witch-like behaviour – night flying, sex with demon lovers, murdering children to make ointments from their bodies, and the use of this to murder other people on the devil's orders. The entire family was convicted of witchcraft. Thousands gathered to witness the spectacle, which was so gruesome as to make the reading of it hair-raising after four hundred years. The tortures will be abbreviated here, but the worst dimension was the public stripping of the four so that they could be burned with hot pincers, and then the cutting off of Anna's breasts. Pieces of her breasts were then stuffed into her mouth and into the mouths of her two adult children, while the younger children were forced to watch. The eventual burning, several hours later following more torture, must have come almost as a relief. The reader hopes that by now the four are only semi-conscious. The records describe the procession to the place of execution, and take pains to note the colour and dignified dress of political and ecclesiastical officials. Meanwhile church bells were rung to announce that once again the church had triumphed over Satan. The crowd sang hymns, and vendors sold their wares. We are informed that, after this event, there was little further unrest in Maximilian's dominions.

It is only feminist historians who initially asked the question of what it must have felt like to be a poor woman in such a crowd. It is doubtful whether the usual affirmations of the church that the gratuitous continuation of torture after the 'witch' and her family had been convicted, was to ensure her salvation, would have brought much comfort. The ferocity of the torture – most of which has been omitted here – points to these victims as wild demonic animals. In light of the graphic nature of such messages to women, the elegant and abstract discussion of the scholars about the natures of women and men seems almost obscene. Also, in light of such scenes, the outrageous expenditure and display of Isabella d'Este and the manic fervour of Isabella of Castille seem to cast very little light on the lives of ordinary women. The relatively rapid spread of reformation religious morality, though not, to my knowledge, related to such events, must have offered women some sense of shelter and assurance, as Protestant leaders affirmed the dignity of marriage. It would take several more decades before the reforming winds would touch the Catholic Church, and this will occupy us for the next few chapters.

CHAPTER TWO

Women and the Reformation

The story of the sixteenth-century Reformations used to be told as two separate tales, each distinct from and opposed to the other. The Protestant story was one of a necessary return to the sources of faith brought about by the abuse of papal power, corrupt clergy, and misled laity. The Roman Catholic story was one of continuous and unbroken fidelity to the original biblical revelation, with a few failures along the way, but with absolutely no need of the kind of reform envisaged by the Protestants. Each story thus described, as we now know, is but a caricature of the reality. Both Protestant and Catholic groups were much more diverse than later portrayed, and it was not until almost one hundred years later that the rigid lines of the two new streams of Christianity were clearly apparent. Both of the stereotypical stories focused, in particular, on questions of ministry and leadership, power and authority, all seen at the time as solely male centred questions. When the real and decisive presence of women is added to the mix, the story of the shattering of the Christian reality in the sixteenth century becomes even more complex. The fact that none of the reformers intended the division of Christianity, despite the later ascription of such ill intent to Martin Luther especially, necessitates the examination of the motivations of the reform initiators, and the willing adherence of their early followers.[1]

All commentators are pretty well agreed now that reform took place because people were religious rather than irreligious. All are equally agreed that the re-shaping of the Western conscience, occasioned by the Reformation, was a watershed event in the history of the West. It is recognised by feminist historians, though not universally by others, that such a reshaping did not include women as beneficiaries. The question of ministry was at the core of the Reformation, and though there was some initial sympathy with the inclusion of women in the new understanding of the 'priesthood of all the faithful', such sympathy was quickly dissipated as the new version of Christianity settled down. Nevertheless, women presented themselves as fully faithful members of the numerous new Christian groupings, and the new circumstances occasioned many debates. All sixteenth-century reformers discovered very quickly that a return to primitive Christianity was well-nigh impossible, so what resulted was several completely new versions of the early traditions, each claiming to be the sole authentic one. Each group also had to come face to face with the fact that women were present in the primitive Christian groups, sometimes quite prominently.

Reformers can never depend on others hearing the cry for reform in precisely the same way. Throughout Christian history, for the most part, reform was understood to entail primarily the reform of the clergy. One of the main reasons for this understanding was that the rest of the Christian population simply did not matter in the overall view of things. As we have seen over and over again, reform of the clergy almost always resulted in a further religious deprivation of women, seen almost universally as the great tempting enemies of the celibate clergy. The Protestant reformers, with their abolition of required celibacy, had a rare opportunity to reverse this trend. With a married clergy, women had to assume new roles, and an opportunity presented itself, seen immediately by many women, to create new ministerial involvements for women. The liberation of women, however, was never seen as a goal of the Reformation, and many historians agree that the end result meant, yet again, that women were even further removed, in all post-Reformation traditions, from a public ministerial role. It is necessary to return to trace the parameters of the reform, in a very limited way, in order to understand the implications for women.

Martin Luther's was not the first reforming voice in the West of the late Middle Ages. The names of John Wycliff (1330-1384) in England and Jan Hus (1370-1415) in Bohemia will always be associated with specific reforming programmes that seemed to strike a chord in the hearts of many ordinary believers. These included especially the right of access of all believers to the scriptures in their own language, and new interpretations of the Eucharist, including the right of the laity to receive communion under both the species of bread and wine. In England, the followers of Wycliff are usually associated with the Lollards, but at any rate, many people were greatly attracted to a version of Christianity that stood for the equal standing of clergy and laity. The Lollards claimed Wycliff's authority for their belief that Christ left apostolic power to 'every good true Christian man and woman living virtuously'.[2] Lollardy grew into a kind of family sect, with women taking on a leading role. Such Lollard women came to know the scriptures with some fluency, and were accused both of ignorance and sophistication in their use of the scriptures in public preaching. Either way, the use of scripture, even the very possession of the scriptures, by women was seen as heretical. Lollard women, therefore, memorised the scriptures and often pretended ignorance in order to avoid the fate of the heretic. Nevertheless, several women were burned to death in England, including Margery Baxter in Norfolk in 1428, and Agnes Grebhill in Kent in 1511.

The controversy about women's preaching had been of frequent occurrence since the time of the Beguines, but these women – and their supportive menfolk – had further difficulties with Christianity. They denied transubstantiation, derided the use of images and pilgrimages, and had great doubts about honouring the saints. They also emphasised the greater moral value of marriage over celibacy. When Agnes Grebhill was burned at the stake in 1511, such Lollard ideas had been circulating for several generations. The following year, in 1512, Joan Washingby from Coventry was also burnt at the stake. Her story is similar to later stories of recusants moving from safe-house to safe-house all over England in order to spread what she believed was the true faith. Their husbands and servants often accompanied these women and there is evidence of much mutual support. The early decades of the sixteenth century saw a strong drive against Lollard women and men, and many heresy proceedings are documented. The intense dislike of Catholic ceremonial and ritual is a new and astonishing part of such records. Images of saints were said to be nothing more than 'carpenter's chips', and Elizabeth Sampson from London declared that she 'could make as good bread' as the priest, since it was only ordinary bread, even God being unable to be in heaven and on earth at the same time.[3] Women were not in the majority among the Lollards, but those who were part of this very diverse group, certainly took on prominent roles. In the later decades of the sixteenth century, many Lollards recanted, but at least twelve women were executed for their beliefs in these areas of southern and central England, and reports of 'meddling' women are recorded for several decades. The learning of such women is said to have baffled their judges and was counted by the courts as unconscionable arrogance by those who should have stayed home to care for their families.[4]

The records of Lollardy are particularly important because they allow us to hear the voices of the 'common folk' in religious matters, and surely the task of any reformer is to present the new teaching in such a way as to appeal to people at all levels of the social spectrum. Martin Luther's revolutionary stance seemed, at first, to have accomplished this admirably, but the spiritual freedom proffered by Lutheranism did not entail the freedom of the lower classes from aristocratic control. Nevertheless, throughout the sixteenth century, hundreds of thousands of people became Protestant in its three main forms of Lutheran, Calvinist, and Anglican, and thousands more followed the radical reforming vision of the Anabaptists. The seventeenth century would see the further development of the Baptists, Congregationalists and Presbyterians, and in the eighteenth century, the Moravians and Methodists would add their own reforming visions. It is doubtful if anyone can keep pace with the hundreds of evangelical groups that began to emerge in England and North America as a result of the 'Great Awakenings', and such groups continue to develop. While at its onset, the common factor binding all the Protestant groups together was resistance to papal power, it is only the members of the most recently developed evangelical groups that continue to maintain this focus. Since the end of the nineteenth century, the ecumenical movement has been growing in range and sophistication, and most Christians are now aware that the original apparently united garment of Christendom will never again, nor could ever again be as one.[5] It was only gradually that people realised that it was possible for several expressions of Christianity to live together more or less peaceably, side by side. The Protestant Reformation is more than a religious story. From the beginning, the reformers were aware of the political dimensions of the reform, and as the reality of the break-up of Christianity became apparent, the huge social implications were also realised. As the Protestants rejected the sacramental nature of marriage, for example, it became necessary to institute state supervision of the marital relationship.

Germany was the epicentre of this event. For decades, the realisation had grown that enormous amounts of money were leaving Germany for Rome, and nothing seemed to be coming back in return. The Renaissance popes were perennially short of money, and it was one such crisis that finally precipitated the revolt of Luther. Pope Leo X (1513-1521) had inherited huge debts from his predecessor, Julius II, the one who had forced Michelangelo to paint the ceiling of the Sistine chapel. Leo was also an avid builder and was determined to have St Peter's completed during his reign. For this he needed endless sums of money. Away in Mainz, the young prince-Archbishop Albert was in breach of church rules in trying to maintain control of several episcopal sees at the same time. For this he needed papal dispensation, and for papal dispensation, he needed money. The preaching of a new indulgence seemed to solve both problems. An indulgence was understood as a voluntary gift from the

faithful to the church, in return for which they were promised
the remission of the temporal punishment of sin in purgatory.
Despite theological nuancing, the people thought they were
buying forgiveness and the money poured in, especially under
the gaze of the Dominican preacher, Tetzel. The city of
Wittenberg was part of Archbishop Albert's territory, and there
the young professor of scripture, Martin Luther, was becoming
increasingly distressed at the whole notion of the preaching and
sale of indulgences. On 31 October, 1517, his personal and theological frustration resulted in the famous ninety-five theses on
the door of Wittenberg cathedral, and so the drama began.
Martin Luther was thirty-four years of age and had led a deeply
troubled spiritual life.

His growing conviction that only faith mattered and that forgiveness was, above all, a gift, was about as far removed as possible from the idea of indulgences. Luther's great fear was that he
would come to hate the God that had been preached to him. As an
Augustinian friar he had devoted himself to the practices of religious life in order to find peace for his troubled soul, but no spiritual or ascetic exercise brought him the assurance of God's forgiveness and love. The realisation, from his bible study, that faith
alone was needed, brought him the freedom he had sought all his
life. From his questioning of indulgences grew his challenge to the
authority of Pope Leo X, and here, he touched a chord in the
German soul. Gradually, over the next few years, while still wear-
ing his Augustinian habit, Luther's thought developed. It was the
age of the pamphlet, and the fortuitous arrival of the printing
press guaranteed a much wider audience than had ever been possible before. Luther worked his way through justification by faith
alone, the meaning and number of the sacraments, and arrived at
the realisation that nothing short of the total moral and spiritual
reform of Christendom was possible. Almost naturally, in the absence of papal support, he turned to the German princes, and so
the Protestant Reformation was under way. Luther was excommunicated on 3 January, 1521, and by 1524, the lineaments of the
Lutheran Church were falling into place.

Luther saw himself as the first man free of papal authority, but almost immediately, the limits of this freedom for others became clear. The German peasantry, hearing the message of spiritual freedom, translated it into a message of social reform and revolted. The revolt, on Luther's urging, was put down with the utmost cruelty. As a result, many of the poor returned to Catholicism, but the impetus of Protestantism could not be halted. The arrival of the Turks into the heart of Europe kept the pope and his allies occupied for the next few years, and Lutheranism was thus given a breathing space to organise itself. His much-heralded doctrine of the priesthood of the laity did very little for the laity, as Luther had no intention of having a lay-run church. The princes took on the administrative task of the bishops, but were not given a say in the development of doctrine. In the German cities, the numbers of clergy dropped by two-thirds, and by degrees, the redistribution of parish and monastic land was regulated. The city of Wittenberg lost its claim to fame as the largest holder of relics in northern Europe. The cathedral was reported to own almost twenty thousand relics, including an entire skeleton of one of the Holy Innocents, a piece of the burning bush, and some of the Virgin Mary's breast milk. The destruction of this collection and others like it truly heralded the arrival of a new world.

As the Reformation radiated out from Wittenberg, the genius of men such as Melanchton, Zwingli, Bucer, Calvin and later Anabaptists such as Menno Simons helped to shape the new European religious experience in very specific directions. The authority of scripture and the authorisation of lay people to own, read and study the scriptures became central tenets of all forms of Protestantism. The new and quite distinct forms of ministry, adapted to the specific needs of each new grouping, all appealed to the New Testament for their justification. Above all, the shaping of new forms of prayer and worship enabled people to experience themselves as belonging to a new kind of Christianity. It would be impossible, and is, in fact, unnecessary to discuss even a small part of these developments here. The examination of the effect of the Reformation on the lives of women, however, will help to give an idea of how these new religious movements penetrated the daily life of a huge part of the West, and it is to this that we now turn our attention.

A chance survival of a piece of writing by a citizen of Strasbourg called Ursula Jost has provided us with a sense of what it was like to live through these turbulent times.[6] Ursula is rooted in the Christianity of medieval times but is integrally part of the new Christian movements, moving from Lutheran to Anabaptist in the course of a few years. In this one woman, we can discern in some small way, the personal faith journey that so often eludes us, as historians paint the larger picture. Ursula appears through her writing as an individual, a woman who had a definite relationship with God, who received messages from God for her community, and who expected to be heard by them. She was claiming a measure of authority in the institutional structures of the church and, judging by the popularity of her writing, she received the community's respect. The ability to testify publicly to her faith and her relationship with God, which had been denied most women in the past, was assumed by Ursula without question.[7]

Strasbourg was one of a handful of German cities that was really an independent state in all but name. Situated as a crossroads between France and Germany, it is no accident that its history was turbulent, controlled by successive and competing overlords. Strasbourg was also the site of an important Rhine crossing, and thus was situated in the midst of the commerce of goods and ideas. During the early years of the Reformation, some of the most important leaders were associated with the city. But in the first third of the sixteenth century, the leader was the former Lutheran lay minister, Melchior Hoffman, who was best known for his controversial reforming ideas. The twin influences on Hoffman's spirituality were apocalyptic faith and the charismatic gifts of the Holy Spirit, each being among the most destabilising forces in the Christian dispensation. Apocalyptic faith deals with the intense sense of present sinfulness accompanied by the consequent expectation of God's cleansing activity. The belief in the outpouring of the gifts of the Spirit leads, inevitably, to the democratising of the religious community, and a challenge to all leadership claiming a mediating power. Such beliefs lead to a highly intense form of Christian faith, and communities which distinguished very clearly between members and outsiders. Throughout the 1520s Melchior Hoffman was struggling with his newly acquired Lutheran faith, and when he finally broke with his community over the issue of the Real Presence of Christ in the Eucharist, he made his way to Strasbourg, where several varieties of Anabaptism were beginning to take root.

Hoffman was wholly taken up with reflection on the Last Days – a not unlikely thought in such turbulent times – and prophets and prophecy were central to his spiritual teaching. By 1530 he was part of the Anabaptist group in Strasbourg and shortly thereafter began publishing prophetic texts for the guidance of the community.[8] It is not at all surprising that he and many of his contemporaries felt that they were living through the last days of the church. What was new with Hoffman was that he felt that he had been singled out by God to interpret the community prophecy. It is in this context that the work of one of these community prophets, Ursula Jost, became public.

Prophecy, when read outside its immediate apocalyptic context, tends to seem a rather tame affair, and such is partly the case with Ursula's writing. Nevertheless, we get a clear sense of the choices facing the community and the necessity felt by them of distinguishing true and false leaders and divine spokespersons. We know almost nothing of Ursula's own spiritual journey, but through her words, we can read between the lines and trace the lineaments of her Christian faith. She was obviously responding to the new teaching about the priesthood of all the faithful, and the necessity of being open to the Spirit of God. Ursula's husband, Lienhard, was also a community prophet, and had spent some time in prison, apparently because of his prophetic activity. The prophetic visions of Ursula Jost took

place during the crucial years of 1524-1530, with the most continuous series occurring throughout the year 1525. They were
published, with other visionary works, by Hoffman in 1530 and
created quite a stir. In fact, shortly afterwards, he had to leave
Strasbourg because of such publishing work. There is no record
of anything untoward happening to Ursula at this time, but perhaps she was as little known to her contemporaries as she is to
us. Despite seventy-seven recorded visions, it is very difficult to
get a sense of her personality. After 1530, we hear nothing more
of her.[9]

Ursula Jost lived in a world and church that was dividing
right before her eyes. What must have added to the confusion of
everyone is that all these developing churches acknowledged
the same sacred texts and the same foundational events. It is the
interpretation of these events, and the practice of the by now fif-
teen-hundred-year-old faith, that led to the distinctions. Ursula
is very clear, in her visions, about the friends and enemies of her
new faith. Her friends are definitely the 'people of the common
sort', and her enemies include the rampaging Turks who were
warring in Europe at that time, and the traitorous clerics who do
nothing but lead the community into deception. In her own person, Ursula embodies the medieval Christian faith which she is
bent on rejecting. Her visions are dated according to the liturgical calendar and even the very act of visionary prophecy and its
symbolic structure is rooted in the past Catholic experience, and
was to disappear almost completely from the Protestant traditions. Even as Ursula was mediating God's voice to her community, religious attitudes were developing which rejected all such
mediation as unnecessary, and even sinful, in the face of the all-
embracing mediating events of the life of Christ. There was a
very brief window of opportunity for such prophetic activity as
Ursula's, and, under those circumstances, the survival of her
work is all the more remarkable. As the Anabaptist tradition
grew, it was the apocalyptic act of martyrdom which inspired
the community.

Ursula describes her visions as the opening up before her of

the 'glory of the Lord', and after the visions, the 'glory folded
back together again, moved away, and disappeared'. As we
have said, the visions follow the liturgical round from the feast
of St Michael, 29 September, 1524 through the seasonal celebrations of Advent, Christmas, Lent, Pentecost, Corpus Christi,
with many intervening feasts. She recognises Saturday as being
particularly devoted to the Virgin Mary. What distinguishes
Ursula from other medieval visionaries is the apparent lack of
effort. There is no mention of asceticism or unworthiness. The
presence of God simply appears, very often while she is lying in
her bed: 'Following this, still on my bed, I saw the glory of the
Lord come over me and appear to me in the form of a cloud. This
cloud filled the whole room. It separated or divided and opened
itself and I saw in it an inexpressible brightness, like the brilliance of the sun. In the brightness of the glory I saw a figure that
looked like a lattice, and in the spaces there appeared stars,
bright as burning candles.' Then in the lattice, God the Father
appears holding in his left hand 'what looked like a sphere'. God
addressed Ursula: 'If I withdrew my hand what would all of you
in the earth be? You would be altogether nothing.' (Vision 3)
This assurance of continuing divine protection is the main message of Ursula's prophecy. One is immediately reminded of the
vision of Julian of Norwich with God holding 'a little thing, the
size of a hazelnut on the palm'.[10]

The atmosphere of Ursula's writing, however, is mostly one
of dread. The Turks, described as 'black men', are leaving the
European mainland in 'troughs of blood'. (Vision 6) Cities are
being razed and the earth is covered with dead fish. There is
only darkness and downpours of sulphur and pitch. (Vision 32)
When Ursula has visions about the state of the church, it is the
'people of the common sort', 'each with his own scriptures' who
are at its heart. (Vision 20) On the other side are the prelates, described as 'goats' and 'toads, scorpions, spiders and serpents'.
(Vision 11, 47) Her visions also condemn 'scripture wizards',
and magicians who try to turn the Eucharist into an idol. (Vision
20) Her prelates often are being 'pushed into the darkness' by

the common people, or have their 'heads split open'. The pope meets a similar fate: 'Then in the glory of the Lord, the pope appeared in his triple crown. Then I saw that a rope was flung around his neck and he was dragged into the darkness.' (Vision 41) Ursula's horror of continuing Catholic eucharistic practice is revealed in a particularly graphic vision. She describes a 'horribly large and black man' who 'turned into complete darkness which descended into the earth. Dark shadowy tears sparkled behind the man and the darkness. The tears were full of floating communion wafers.' She goes on to describe the man 'in a white alb' worshipping the idol of the eucharistic host. (Vision 65)

If the Lollard disgust with Catholic liturgical ceremonial had not become known to us, it would be difficult to understand this visceral hatred of the Eucharist in someone like Ursula, who had, apparently, been baptised into the Catholic faith. When, however, such writing is also put in the context of the fierce religious wars and persecutions that were also part of the life of Christians of the 1520s, one can more easily understand how former associates could become deadly enemies. The viciousness of the period is also seen in Ursula's description of what seems to be the torture of the Anabaptist community. Vision 70 describes 'ferocious prominent men who were full of wrath', who had assembled their prisoners in a large hall. These people were 'ordered to be drawn up and then cruelly dropped on their faces at the feet of the tyrants'. There is evidence of such methods of torture from other records of the period. It is with some relief that one reads the concluding part of Vision 70: 'Then I saw the Spirit of God coming, leaping and dancing. He led the elect up the ladder with fulsome and exalted joy and jubilation.'

The prophetic visions of Ursula Jost are an invaluable testimony to the spiritual experience of one Christian woman at one of the great turning points of Western religious history. She sees herself as a leader, but different in no way from the 'people of the common sort'. She seems to be completely at home in the new church which is forming all around her, and in which she is participating fully. Ursula is harsh in her criticism of hypocritical and overfed clerics, both from the old Catholic tradition, but also from the more recent Lutherans. She is fully convinced of the rightness of her position and of her ability to discern the true from the false. There is no hesitation whatever in Ursula's use of her voice for the good of the church. Unlike mystics and visionaries of previous ages, she sees no need to engage in a rhetoric of self-diminishment for her own protection. There is no hint of a necessary purgation in order to make her worthy of the divine presence. In Ursula's day, suffering was ever-present, and a martyr church had very little need to speak of asceticism. The reality of dying for one's faith was ever-present.

On the other hand, one could not learn to be a mystic from the writing of Ursula Jost. Her work is not didactic in that sense. The Beguine mystics had written for the ongoing instruction of other women, and it is their ongoing reflection on the nature of the divine-human interaction that marks the difference between the mystic and the visionary. Ursula does not seem to reflect on her spiritual experience, but presents herself simply as a vehicle for her community. The people of Ursula's community in Strasbourg, and in many similar cities scattered across the face of Europe, were facing religious choices unimaginable even a few years before. It would take several more decades before the religious map of Europe would achieve some degree of stability, and even longer for some peace. The fortuitous survival of the writing of this transitional woman is a rare gift to later generations.

We are fortunate to have received a few other examples of women's involvement in these momentous events, and each one fills out the picture of the extraordinary changes that were under way, but also of the general expectation in the male leaders of the reform that the lives of women, from the perspective of marriage and the home, would not change significantly. This was not to be a social revolution for women, despite the brief window of opportunity for women such as Ursula. The life of Wibrandis Rosenblatt is one example of the commitment expected of the wife and mother in a reform family. Wibrandis married four church leaders in succession, accumulating all their children as the husbands died. In the process, the plague carried off the third husband, Capito, together with three of their children. In the same plague, the wife of the well known reformer, Martin Bucer, died, and Wibrandis and Bucer married for mutual support. Of the Bucer's thirteen children, only one was still surviving at the time of his marriage to Wibrandis. They had two more children and even adopted other parentless young relatives. All this took place when the Reformation was going through its earliest formative stages, and persecution, torture and even execution were constant threats. Wibrandis was exiled to England with her husband and huge family and she continued to care for them all after Martin Bucer died.[11] This is only one of dozens of similar incidents. The Anabaptists were victims of Lutheran and Catholic hatred and their lives were a tangle of nomadic wanderings, imprisonment, and negotiations with hostile authorities. The fidelity of women, men, and children to their new faith is astonishing.

As might be imagined, families were shattered during the Reformation period, with children and parents, husband and wives often choosing different paths, and sometimes betraying each other to the authorities. Such was the case with the sisters-in-law, Maria and Ursula van Beckum. Maria joined the Anabaptist community, and was driven from the family home by her mother, a staunch Catholic. Maria fled to Utrecht to her brother's home, but their mother was unrelenting and informed the police of her whereabouts. When the police came to arrest her, Maria appealed to her sister-in-law, Ursula to accompany her to prison, even though it is not at all clear that Ursula was an Anabaptist. The parents of both Maria and Ursula kept up a campaign against them, perhaps hoping to induce them to return to the Catholic faith.

The prisoners were interrogated by the Dominican inquisitor at Zwolle but he also failed to detach the young women from their new faith. They were, reportedly, both tenacious and theologically skilful. Their fate was inevitable, as in 1529, Emperor Charles V had decreed death to all unrepentant Anabaptists.

The key element in all Anabaptist interrogations was, of course, the subject of re-baptism. Both women are said to have replied that, as far as they were concerned, they had been baptised biblically only once. They denied the Real Presence of Christ in the Eucharist. The women surprised the inquisitors with their knowledge of subjects about which they were supposed to know nothing. Both Maria and Ursula were burned at the stake on 13 November, 1544. Maria's courage stayed with her to the end. She rebuked one of the soldiers who swore when the chain with which he was attaching her to the stake broke in his hands. She addressed the crowd, encouraging them to persevere and prayed God to forgive her executioners. Ursula was given the option of death by burning or death by the sword, but chose burning in solidarity with her sister-in-law. She too remained steadfast to the end. Both Lutherans and Anabaptists wrote hymns commemorating the courage of these two women.

The usual historical difficulties surround the re-telling of the stories of these extraordinary women. We are left with snippets of hymns, incidents of what appeared as intransigence to one community and courage to another, but very little biographical detail. The number of women martyrs in the Anabaptist community is an amazing testimony to the faith, loyalty and integrity of these women, and the occasional survival of details such as the fidelity of these two sisters-in-law towards each other adds unutterable poignancy to their story. Helene of Freyberg is another such woman, this time an 'extraordinary lay leader'.[13] In 1523, Helene inherited the castle and property at Munichau where she had been born. She married into the aristocracy and had four sons. In 1528, her name appears for the first time in the court records of the Tirol, announcing that she and her household had been rebaptised and had joined the Anabaptists. Local officials were ordered to confiscate her goods and property. Helene used her castle home to support Anabaptist preachers and to host meetings of the local Anabaptist community, thereby constituting her home as a house church. She visited the many Anabaptist prisoners in the area, and despite being closely

watched by officials, continued to do everything possible to promote her new faith. It seems that the authorities were puzzled
about her role in the movement, since they expected that only
men would exercise such prominent tasks. In 1529, Helene's
husband cleared his name, denying that he was a member of the
group. As the evidence against her accumulated, Helene fled to
Bavaria and was on the run for the next few years. By 1530, she
was settled in Constance and simply continued her organising
and housechurch activities.

Two years later, her property was again confiscated and she
was exiled. A public recantation was required of her, but she
continued to elude the authorities. She was seen as 'the primary
cause of so many people joining this movement'.[14] In 1535,
Helene was imprisoned and interrogated in Augsburg, about
the reasons for her abandonment of her husband and sons, and
her continued sheltering of and discussion with other Anabaptist
leaders. Helene's husband died in 1538 and her sons requested
the authorities to allow her to return to Augsburg. She died
there in 1545, having spent the last years of her life serving the
needs of her community. She took part in theological disputations, mediated between parties, sheltered travelling or fleeing
Anabaptist missionaries, and exercised a specific leadership role
in the community.

Towards the end of her life, some error on her part occasioned a public confession to her community and the text of this
remains extant. 'Especially I have sinned and become guilty concerning those in civil authority' she writes explaining that this
concerned her 'excessive conduct' and 'improper attitude'. The
whole thing remains a bit mysterious, but whatever occasioned
such a public confession, the strength of Helene's character
shines through. One wonders whether or not it was a case of
Helene's own leadership being questioned as the Anabaptist
community entered the settling down phase of its development.
As in all Christian reform movements, the freedom of the gospel
is never supposed to change the supposedly 'natural' subordination of women. Whatever the case, Helene was quite as capable

of dealing with such challenges as she was of leading the community. Such a redoubtable character would not have been easily subdued in any community.

One of the earliest activities of all aspects of the Protestant Reformation was the closing of monasteries and convents, the abandonment or actual destruction of shrines, images, relics and statues, and the sometimes enforced imposition of marriage instead of celibacy. There are not many records of women's response to such situations, but a brief glimpse is available in the life of Jeanne de Jussie, a nun of the Order of St Claire in Geneva. Jeanne wrote a spirited account of the 'Heresy of Geneva' between the years 1526 and 1535. In the end, Jeanne and her sisters had to leave Geneva because of its entirely hostile attitude to their monastic vocation. They settled in Annecy in France where Jeanne eventually became Abbess.[15] Sister Jeanne aimed to show that Catholic women were stronger and more loyal to their faith than men, since only one of their sisters left to marry whereas many priests and monks married disgracefully. All the other sisters, she reported, saw quite clearly the heretical nature of the new faith, even though many of their families were perverted. She tells of one Catholic wife who died suddenly of sadness when her new baby was forcibly baptised as a Protestant by the pastor. Many other women remained faithful, despite being beaten and tortured and showed themselves to be 'more than martyrs'. Three women were locked up for their refusal to attend the Protestant services, but they escaped through a window and went to Mass.

Meanwhile the convent was ransacked by 'Protestant men' who destroyed pieces of art and terrorised the nuns, but they did not succeed in persuading them to leave. Some Catholic women risked their lives by going to the convent to console the nuns for this invasion. By Good Friday 1533, Geneva seems to have been divided into two armed camps of Catholics and Protestants. Many Catholic wives were prepared to arm themselves and kill the heretic wives. Jeanne tells us that about several hundred Catholic women assembled to this end, accompanied by hundreds of children between the ages of twelve and fifteen, who were 'firmly decided to do a good deed with their mothers'. 'The women carried stones in their laps, and most of the children carried little rapiers ... others stones in their breast, hat and bonnet'.

After a Catholic man had been killed, the women turned on the wife of a Lutheran shouting: 'As the beginning of our war, let's throw this bitch in the Rhone.' Fortunately the woman escaped into a shop, but the Catholic women proceeded to destroy the shop and its contents. Meanwhile, the nuns of St Claire did not join this affray, but prayed fervently for the success of the Catholic women. It was reported that the 'heretics' were getting ready to march on the convent to force all the sisters to marry. In the end a truce was arranged and the day ended without further bloodshed.

The Protestant women are not portrayed as violent but as exceedingly aggravating, because they worked ostentatiously on feast days and continuously pestered the nuns to leave the convent. While Catholic processions were passing through the streets, Jeanne reports, the Protestant women sat sewing and spinning in their windows against the sabbath laws. They also did their laundry in the local river on Easter and Pentecost Sundays. This was seen as too much of a provocation and the Catholic women sent the clothes floating down the Rhone.

Another Lutheran woman persisted in coming to the convent to pour out her 'venom' against the nuns. She claimed that until then the commandments of God had not been truly taught and she said 'detestable words' against the sacrament. The nuns had to bar the door in her face, but she just kept on preaching to them. The city officials came to the convent several times to see if the sisters were being kept there by force, each time accompanied by Protestant women, who tried to tell the nuns about the joys of marriage. 'O poor creatures! If only you knew that it is good to be with a handsome husband, and how agreeable it is to God ... Thanks to God alone, I already have five handsome children, and I live salutarily.' The sisters replied by spitting on the spokeswoman.

Another time, the apothecary's wife who 'meddled in preaching' was brought to the convent. She disparaged the Virgin and the saints, praised marriage and denounced virginity, quoting St Paul to prove her points. When the nuns protested, the Protestant men said that the woman was holy and illuminated by God, and had won many people to the true faith of Lutheranism. By 1534, a new form of marriage service had been created, described by Sister Jeanne as being without solemnity or devotion and consisting of 'only their commandments to join together and multiply the world ... and some dissolute words that I do not write at all, for it is shameful to a chaste heart to think them.' For Sister Jeanne, the main fault of the 'heresy of Geneva' was the new praise of marriage for all, the deriding of the sacrament and the destruction of images.

Sister Jeanne is ably abetted in her resistance to the 'heretics' by the Mother Vicar of the convent. When the nuns were ordered to attend a public disputation about their faith, Mother Vicar led the resistance by saying that they were bound to lead a cloistered life, and that it was not the task of women to dispute publicly about the faith. She added that 'it is forbidden to uneducated people to meddle in interpreting Holy Scripture, and a woman has never been called to dispute or witness.' Mother Vicar, however, belied her words and publicly berated the visitors. When a town official asked her why the nuns wore such clothes, she replied that they liked them, and then asked him why he was dressed so pompously. When the Protestant leaders, Farel and Viret, came to dispute with the nuns, she set up such a racket of noise that she had to be removed from the room. She continued, however, to bang on the wall and cry out to the sisters not to listen, so distracting Farel that he forgot what he was talking about. After this experience they gave up on the project of converting the sisters.

Sister Jeanne shows the activity of women on both sides during the Reformation and pinpoints the new teaching on marriage and the abandonment of the whole monastic view of life as most offensive to herself, and most characteristic of the new teaching.

She is right in pointing out that, apart from freeing women from the 'false' teaching of monasticism, there is little new freedom for women. She underrates the new teaching on marriage, however, because it was this that changed not just the religious but also the social aspect of Europe in the ensuing years.

Until the Reformation, Christian teachers had distinguished for centuries between Christian life according to the commandments and the counsels of perfection. The former described a kind of minimalist requirement for the ordinary, and presumably married, believer, and assumed repentance for a life immersed in sexuality. The latter described the life of the monastic man and woman who had renounced the life of sexuality to practice the biblical counsels of poverty, chastity and obedience. Much of the writing focused particularly on women who had taken the vow of virginity, seemingly, according to patristic and later theologians, an act going against their very nature. It was more or less assumed that men were natural virgins, apart from the seductive presence of women. Judging by the virtual absence of writing on marriage, little was expected of married women, beyond subservience to their husbands and the availability of their bodies for the production of children. The writing of Augustine in this regard was seen as primary.

As we have seen,[16] marriage suffered much degrading comment during the Gregorian reforms and the attempts to deprive the clergy of the right to marry. Such writing did little to elevate marriage as a place of holiness for Christians, women in particular, despite the obvious need for some new theology to balance the previous theological anti-marriage blasts. Women, however, were seen as entirely necessary for the Reformation agenda by all the chief reformers, starting with Martin Luther. With the abolition of clerical celibacy, the fact that the vast majority of ministers and pastors would be married meant that a new theological persona appeared on the scene, the pastor's wife. Many historians assert that it is precisely here that the main influence of the Reformation is centred – on the domestic and religious reform of marriage.

Very early in his career, Luther ruled out the distinction between two kinds of Christianity and two classes of Christians.
There was only one kind of Christian, the baptised Christian. He
went on to affirm the sinful status of the Christian, despite justification by faith in Christ, while, at the same time, the freedom of
all from the necessity of engaging in good works to gain merit or
reward. Rather, what was required was joyful service for the
good of the world. The first and most important arena of this
service was the family. Even Moses did nothing but care for his
wife and children in a mundane way – this was now the essence
of holiness.[17] The family situated in the midst of worldly struggles, called upon all the best efforts of its members, and this is
what is required. Luther pointed out how the Catholics have entirely missed the point by pitching holiness in the arena of the
monastic life. For Luther, marriage is the school of faith, where
the ordinary proceedings of everyday life, washing, feeding,
teaching and burying the dead, are the means of holiness. No
other vocation is necessary. Both the housewife and the town
magistrate now have their vocation, rooted in their baptism and
not in some other kind of calling.

Much attention is lavished by all the reformers on the new
duties of the wife in this scenario. It is assumed that nothing
much will have changed in the role of the husband. The obedient wife, caring for her husband and children is engaged in
'golden, noble works'. The woman in labour should not be dis-
tracted by stories of the saints or their intercession, but should
concentrate only on doing God's will. Even if she dies in childbirth, she will still be doing the work of God. Luther's admiration for marriage knows no bounds – it is generally agreed that
his wife, Katherine von Bora, had an exceedingly civilising effect
on him – but he places it above all other states. 'The married
state is not only equal to all other states but pre-eminent over
them all, be they Kaiser, princes, bishops … for it is the common-
est, noblest state.' He goes further yet and makes of marriage a
Christian requirement for all.

Initially, then, Martin Luther thought very specifically about

the priesthood of all believers. There was no need for any distinction between the ordained and the lay. All are engaged in
the same task, the nurturing of the next generation, including
the task of teaching them. This requirement indicated the necessity of a literacy requirement for wives. If they were to hand on
the scriptures, then they had to be able to read them. Therefore,
there was a new emphasis on the necessity of at least a minimal
education for women. Luther saw such changes as quite dramatic
when compared with Catholic views of women: he called them
the 'despisers of women'. He even felt able to pardon women for
the sin of Eve because all were equally sinners. The ability to
give birth covers all the negative aspects of women. Such apparent liberality did not last, however, and very soon Luther joined
the ranks of the traditionalists with regard to women.

The Reformation placed women almost exclusively in the
realm of marriage, motherhood and childbearing, and since this
marriage was necessarily a culturally patriarchal institution, it
was essentially a union of two unequal people. The 'dreadful
madness of lust' that overcame men, and that was attributed to
the seductive nature of women, meant that marriage had to be
hedged around with very severe guidelines. All the reformers
equally call on the biblical evidence for the headship of the male
in society and marriage. The wife is naturally in subjection, and
it is the husband's duty to educate his wife towards goodness
and correct her when she fails. The wife was permitted to leave
her husband only when in danger of death from her husband's
behaviour. It is clear, then, that the reformers accepted without
question the right of the husband to use violence against his wife
almost to the point of death. Calvin wrote in 1559: 'We have a
special sympathy for poor women who are evilly and roughly
treated by their husbands', but this does not give them the right
to leave. A wife cannot interpret rough treatment, threats and
beatings as reasons for leaving – this is seen as normal within a
marriage. The wife should 'bear with patience the cross which
God has seen fit to place upon her, and meanwhile not to deviate
from the duty which she has before God to please her husband,

but to be faithful whatever happens'. Similar advice is to be found in all reform literature, little different from what had been handed on for centuries in the Christian tradition.

John Knox in Scotland was quite specific about the evil of women presuming beyond their subordinate status to assume rule in either household or state. This was contrary both to nature and scripture and was simply the usurpation of men's authority.[18] The Augsburg Confession of Lutheranism in 1530, one of the foundational documents of the tradition, focuses on marriage as a remedy for fornication. Nevertheless, there is a hint in Protestant writing that marriage is also for mutual love and comfort, and as we have seen, the wives of reformers contributed largely to this changing view by their fidelity and loyalty. 'What is more desirable', says Luther, 'than a happy and tranquil marriage, where there is mutual love and the most delightful union of souls?' Such mutual love, however, never moved beyond the belief in the natural subjection of women. Martin Bucer, one of the principal reformers, and husband of Wibrandis Rosenblatt, wrote: 'The true and entire purpose of marriage is that the spouses serve one another in all love and fidelity, that the woman be the aid and flesh of the man and the man the head and saviour of the woman.'

It is clear then, that the reformers found in marriage a marvellous comfort in the hurblyburly of the early years of the Reformation, and that they found remarkable women as wives who were able to cope with astonishingly turbulent marriages. Nothing in the Reformation, however, was aimed at the improvement of the social status of women. Nothing removed the necessity of submission. Nothing removed the husband's right to use violence against his wife, and, if anything, women were even more confined to the one choice of marriage in a now all-male led church. Two specific changes are significant for the development of later secular and ecclesiastical developments. First is the permission given, though in limited circumstances, for divorce and remarriage, which challenged centuries of Christian tradition. Likewise the refusal of the reformers to recognise marriage as a sacrament, and therefore the necessity of establishing secular guidelines for the celebration and public conduct of marriage, was a revolutionary change. As a result, marriage behaviour was monitored both by the new congregations and by the secular authorities. The Anabaptists insisted on very high standards of moral behaviour, and new respect for secular work brought a distinctly new demand for higher standards in public morality.[19]

Despite the increase in reflection on the roles of women during the Renaissance and the Reformation, there is still great difficulty in accessing the lives, loves, thoughts and beliefs of real women. The continued insistence on the subordinate role of women and their inability to rule meant also that the role of women in public discourse and writing was still greatly curtailed. Occasionally, however, solely through an accident of history, a document survives which throws some light on the real lives of ordinary women and men. Such a document is the correspondence of Magdalena and Balthasar, a married couple from Nuremberg in the second half of the sixteenth century.[20] There are 169 surviving letters between this merchant and his wife. He died in 1600 and she survived him by forty-two years. The Baumgartner family were neither peasant nor aristocrat, but part of the newly developing merchant class. They were lovers and business partners and the parents of one child, who died at the age of ten. Nuremberg, a free imperial city, was a merchants' town, situated between the rivers Main and Danube with immediate access to most of Europe. It had officially adopted the Lutheran faith in 1525, and though there were some complaints about Calvinist infiltration later in the century, the city magistrates managed to walk a fine line and keep the populace happy. Since 1525, all Catholic services had been banned, but the local religious houses were being allowed to die out quietly. The Dominican house lasted until 1543, the Cistercian until 1562 and the convent of St Clare and St Katherine until 1596. The few local Catholics were able to participate in the religious services in these houses without any fanfare. Towards the end of the century, the Italian mer-

chants complained that no provision was made for their participation in the Mass, but Nuremberg stood fast and pointed them to
the surrounding towns where Catholic Masses were plentiful.[21] It
seems that merchants of whatever nationality or religion mixed
with one another freely. Some of Balthasar's friends were Italian
Catholics. When, at the death of Pope Innocent IX in 1591,
Balthasar was in Lucca, he joined in the two days of fasting in
preparation for the new pope.

Neither Balthasar nor Magdalena comments much on the
institutional dimension of religion. Magdalena refers to a recent
ban on dancing, an activity she seemed to enjoy, and points out
that without dancing at weddings, the men only get drunker
than usual.[22] The personal side of their Lutheran faith shines
through every letter and there seems no doubt in the minds of
either one that God is the sovereign Lord of their lives – as is
central to Lutheran teaching. They pray constantly for each
other, and bow to God's will in success and failure, good health
and bad health. As Steven Ozment remarks, they believe in God
and purgative medicine.[23] Their lives seem completely free of
what has been called medieval superstition, still freely observable in other parts of Europe. In sixteen years of correspondence
and over one hundred letters, there is no mention whatever of
shrines, relics, witches or the devil.

What has replaced pilgrimages in the letters are the regular
visits, especially by Balthasar, to take the waters and engage in
the most appalling purgations in the spas at Lucca and elsewhere. Both Magdalena and Balthasar are completely preoccu-
pied by their state of health, or more correctly, both are endlessly
attentive to his health. He complains constantly of rheumatism
and all kinds of interior 'foulness'. The main remedy seems to be
bleeding, and the mention of 'bleeding calendars' and medical
pamphlets about the 'bleeding points' of the body show that this
was also a societal preoccupation. In 1584, Magdalena complains that she has to announce a death in every letter and she
often includes hair-raising details of illness in other families. She
describes, for example, a neighbour's child drinking whole bottles

of wine continually in order to stem the pain of a gangrenous foot.[24] Magdalena was wildly enthusiastic about the benefits of bleeding. In fact, it was often a reason for a travelling holiday. Whole groups travelled together to the best known centres, much like contemporary package holidays.

Even though there is ample evidence that this was a patriarchal marriage, with Balthasar, at least on paper, continually proclaiming his authority, it is clear too that both his wife and child took his authority lightly and knew how to deal with it to their own advantage. Husband and wife are at times open and loving in their relationship, at times aggrieved and frustrated with each other. He writes from Lucca during their betrothal, 'My honest, good, true, friendly, dearest, closest bride', and continues 'May it be God's will to keep us in his grace and help us soon to come happily together again in our little garden of joy.'[25] It is apparent that Balthasar is often absent during Christmas and the New Year, but he assures his wife that without her, his life is utterly boring.

Eventually Magdalena becomes his invaluable partner in their merchant business. He praises her shrewd business sense and entrusts her completely with the distribution and payment details of all the goods he sends home to Nuremberg from his travels. Sometimes his descriptions sound strangely familiar. He speaks of one route in particular as 'Murder Road' and outlines the dangers from highwaymen, mercenary soldiers, hostile townsfolk, and other unscrupulous bandits, not to mention weather, plague and famine. The Frankfurt Fairs seemed to be one of the main goals of the merchants' journeys. Here Balthasar describes the haggling – which he hated – and the final exchange of money, which brought on screaming, bickering and cursing. 'The longer I remain in Frankfurt, the more I suffer', he writes home.[26] The range of goods sent to Nuremberg from all over Europe is amazing – from 'bicoloured double taffeta' to endless casks of wine, from grains, artichokes and pumpkin seeds to Dutch cheeses, shoes and a German bible. Magdalena puts in a special request for quinces, pears and nuts, and complains happily that, since she has to taste all the wine to check for purity, she is often almost drunk on receipt of such consignments. Payment by the peasants is a constant problem, especially for such items as cheap knives and wine.

The great tragedy of their lives was the death of their son, 'little Balthasar' after only ten years. He was born at the end of 1584 and grew up alone with his mother for a good part of his young life. Understandably, when he begins adding his own notes to his mother's letters, these usually contain requests for gifts – for anything from celery to a horse, even a toy horse. His father uses gifts as bribes for good behaviour, and there is obvious conflict between the parents about the aloofness of the father's attitude. Without any apparent reason, the father occasionally threatens his son: 'Tell little Balthasar to be good, and that should I learn that he has been bad, I will bring him nothing but a good strong switch, and the next time I go away I will put him out to board with the schoolmaster'.[27] Little Balthasar was never in robust health, having been born with a neck deformity, and Magdalena's letters are full of his childhood ailments. She describes the attacks of worms, and the expulsion of three hundred of them after a cure of white Bohemian beer. By February 1592, the child is deteriorating, and despite fearsome purgatives and enemas, he showed no signs of recovery. In September, he asked his father one more time for a horse, but he was dead probably before the letter reached its destination. The autopsy showed an enlarged liver and kidneys, and the doctors marvelled that he had lived so long. Balthasar was again absent and Magdalena seems resigned when she writes to tell him the grim news. 'May God now keep him safe until we come to him', she writes. Later she pours out her grief to her husband for the 'short-lived joy' they have had from their son. 'Too early the clergy carried him away, too soon the bells were tolled for him.' By the end of the letter, however, she has returned to business, requesting another consignment of wine.

This correspondence is as close as we can get to the lives of an ordinary couple in late sixteenth- and early seventeenth-century

Europe. Despite the turbulence of the times, they seem to have lived a life that is not unfamiliar in many of its details. The settled nature of their Lutheran faith is surprising, but the early acceptance of Lutheranism by the city of Nuremberg, and its independent status, allowed space for a quieter and more consistent development than elsewhere. The couple's spirituality is distinctly different from their medieval ancestors. All their attention is focused on God and on God's sovereign power. They are sure of God's love and care, even though the capriciousness of God in granting and withholding his gifts sometimes raises questions in their minds. When the correspondence ends with the death of Balthasar in 1600 so does our knowledge of the family. We know that Magdalena outlived her husband by over forty years, living to the ripe old age of eighty-seven. She died on 14 February, 1642, and by then, the world had changed direction once again.

CHAPTER THREE

Teresa of Avila and Catholic Reform

For centuries, a commonplace in the search for reform had been
the demand for 'decent priests'. Even in such diverse personalities as Martin Luther, Ignatius of Loyola and Teresa of Avila,
this theme was one of a very few common strands. There is no
doubt that this was a major problem in the sixteenth-century
church. The complaints were endless and by mid-century, even
the papacy was beginning to take notice. It took some time for
the papacy to begin to set an example of what a good priest
might be. The acknowledged papal initiator of the Catholic reform in Rome, Paul III, pope from 1534-1549, had two illegitimate
children and several grandchildren, and his sister, Giulia Farnese
had been the mistress of Pope Alexander VI. The rot was everywhere. One bishop in Italy reported that he would be lucky if he
found two priests in his diocese who knew the words of absolu-
tion. A well-known proverb assured everyone that the profession of priest was the surest road to hell.[1]

So the search for decent priests and the problem of unworthy
priests had plagued the church for centuries, but somehow the
cries for reform were not heard at the centre. In the mid-sixteenth century, the papacy was, at last, listening to these cries,
but by then the reform had been set in motion by Martin Luther,
Ignatius Loyola and Teresa of Avila. It only awaited the papal
action of summoning the Council of Trent to make the Catholic
reform universal, and for a long time, many feared that this
papal initiative was never going to happen. As the great historian,
Jacob Burckhardt, remarked, it was the reformers, the mortal
enemies of the papacy, who in fact saved it.[2] Each of the three
reformers we have mentioned had experienced the problem of

63

unworthy and corrupt priests in different ways, and their response to the situation took very different tracks. Martin Luther, a
priest himself, concluded that celibacy constituted the main problem, and so established the Lutheran church with a married
priesthood. All subsequent Protestant reformers followed his example. Ignatius Loyola founded his own community of ordained
priests, which, as we shall see, was subsequently crucial to the
task of Catholic reform. Teresa of Avila constantly bemoaned the
lack of decent priests who could serve as spiritual directors for
herself and her Carmelite sisters. Her response was to join with
John of the Cross in reforming both male and female branches of
Carmel. All three, in their very different ways, contributed to
change the face of the church and the world for hundreds of years.

Before proceeding to explore the work of Catholic reform and,
in particular, the role of Teresa of Avila, it is worth commenting
on another strand of connection between the three reformers we
have mentioned. All three began their spiritual journey with
personal difficulties about the state of their souls. Martin Luther
feared that he might grow to hate the God whom he understood
to be making demands that he could not fulfil. His peace of soul
was dramatically restored, not in his endless attempts to carry
out what he later called Catholic 'works' such as penance and
pilgrimage, but in his discovery of the mystery of divine grace
given solely through faith in the one mediator, Jesus Christ. It
was in his apparent disobedience to the previous tradition and
especially to the leadership of the pope, that Martin Luther
found peace. On the contrary, it was through the strong assertion of the necessity of strict obedience that both Ignatius and
Teresa found the peace and central meaning of their different
vocations. Obedience to superiors, and ultimately to the pope
became the watchword of the Jesuits, and Teresa asserted over
and over again that it was only obedience that made her undertake tasks that were personally disagreeable, such as her writing. In this obedience, she found her peace of soul. Whether it
was through disobedience or obedience, the paths of the three
reformers were fraught with obstacles and opposition.

It is a commonplace by now in all histories of the sixteenth century reformations to say that the Catholic reform was not initiated by the Protestant reform, but given a certain edge and direction. Whatever the case of sixteenth century reform, it is true that the women mystics of the middle ages were persistent in their cries for reform, but continually rendered ineffective by ecclesiastical fear of women's Christian influence. It is also true that the initial reform work of both Teresa and Ignatius preceded the Protestant Reformation – indeed, they seemed remarkably unaware of the growth and significance of the work of Martin Luther and his followers. There were also other reformers on the scene, such as the new religious communities for priests, the Theatines and the Barnabites in Italy as well as groups of women such as those around Luisa Torelli, Angela Merici and Mary Ward. The next chapter will explore the work of these women, but it is important to mention them here in the context of the initial reforming attempts in the Catholic tradition.

It was the Council of Trent, however, which changed the face of the Catholic Church for the next four hundred years, and to which many still revert as offering the real face of the Roman Catholic Church. It was precisely the Roman-ness of the reform initiated by Trent that formed a Catholic tradition essentially distinct from much that had gone before – though it was professing an unbroken connection with the tradition – and it was the Council of Trent that laid the foundations of the Catholic tradition, precisely in its long-awaited reform of the priesthood.

Here, just an overview of the intentions and some accomplishments of the Council will suffice for our purposes, but it is essential to assert unequivocally that the Council of Trent saw no room whatever for any contribution to the church by women. The strict enclosure of nuns and the strict obedience of wives were essential to the Catholic reform platform. Nevertheless, it is remarkable that women, as so often before, undermined this dimension of the reform, in their unending efforts – and ultimately brilliant success – in harnessing the resources of an unwilling church to the accomplishment of their own religious goals. The post-Trent period saw the founding of several religious communities of women, which also were instrumental in changing the face of the church.

The reform of the Catholic tradition from its own substance was a continuation of the tradition of the Beguines, the Mendicant Orders and the women mystics and religious founders. These were among the groups who had kept the reforming impulse alive and who had found their ultimate meaning in their fidelity to the biblical tradition. So the church was not without resources when finally papal resistance to reform was no longer a possibility. Three dimensions of this continuing reform tradition, however, were essential to the institutional reforms codified at Trent. These were the active work of love in the caring for the poor and abandoned members of society, the so-called apostolates of education, preaching, healing and prayer, and finally the universal task of Christian self-realisation. All these groups saw that the journey inward was a prerequisite to the necessary public face of compassion, and these insights were characteristic of all the new communities. There were one or two reform-minded cardinals and bishops, but the greatest failure of ecclesiastical leaders was seen to be their non-residence in their appropriate sees, and therefore their complete ignoring of the tasks of pastoral care. The fifth Lateran Council (1512-1517) had made feeble attempts at reform, but aimed more at appearances than reality. Spain, as we have seen, had initiated its own reform through the untiring efforts of the Catholic kings, Ferdinand and Isabella, but even here, reform was aimed more at the crushing of heresy than at the reinvigoration of the Catholic tradition. Nevertheless, several reforming bishops from Spain eventually made distinctive contributions to the Council of Trent. It was one Spaniard, Ignatius of Loyola, who was subsequently considered to be of the greatest historical significance in the furtherance of Catholic reform.

Ignatius was born in 1491 and pursued the normal knightly life, including tonsure and the bestowal on him of a family benefice while still a child. His life, as is well known, was ultimately transformed by a bout of sickness after being wounded in battle, and the change in his life's journey was marked by the dramatic renunciation of the instruments of war and the rededication of his life to God. His path to becoming the ultimate churchman of his day was not without difficulty, and his spirituality was deepened by his time spent as pilgrim, hermit, student and finally, his ordination to the priesthood on 24 June, 1537. Along the way, both the constitutions of his new group, the Company of Jesus, and his handbook of holiness, *The Spiritual Exercises*, had been refined. The Jesuits, as they have always been commonly known, were formed by Ignatius into a highly centralised, patriarchal and hierarchical group, where the practice of obedience was central. Ignatius spoke of obedience as requiring that one be a 'corpse without will or feeling'. Even though Ignatius seems almost totally unacquainted with the works of Luther, it was the defence of the church against Protestantism which became the hallmark of Jesuit influence.

Now the church had its order of decent priests and eventually the Jesuits, with their commitment to education at all levels, became one of the main instruments of Catholic reform. Pope Paul IV, the reforming pope, and Ignatius of Loyola, the founder, did not always see eye to eye on the needs of the Catholic reform. The pope called Ignatius a tyrant and Ignatius feared Paul IV as 'God's wrath incarnate'. It had been a long tradition in monastic foundations that an order for women be formed, spontaneously or intentionally alongside a male order. Ignatius judged that such an arrangement would not be compatible with Jesuit commitments. His group had rejected many aspect of the old monastic life, such as group prayer, in order to free the members for the public work of the church. Ministry to women, with the notable exception of ministry to fallen women, was not to be part of this plan. Nevertheless Pope Paul III imposed an order on Ignatius to found a female branch in response to a request from Isabel Roser of Barcelona. This arrangement lasted only a year, but in 1555, the Infanta Juana, daughter of Charles V, was admitted to profession of 'scholastic' vows under a pseudonym, and was received temporarily into the order. It was to be a short-lived arrangement and the Jesuits remained resolutely male.

The expansion of the Jesuits was extraordinary. At the death of Ignatius in 1556, there were over one thousand members organised in twelve provinces. By the death of Lainez, his successor, in 1565, the Jesuits numbered well over three thousand in eighteen provinces. It was becoming an educational group and, especially at the upper levels of society, was to wield an amazing influence in Catholic reform right across Europe. Without the Jesuits, the reforms of Trent would have foundered with no local and effective infra-structure.

The universally feared Peter Caraffa was elected as Pope Paul IV in 1555 at the age of seventy-nine. He was variously known as a 'foul-mouthed southerner' born in the shadow of Vesuvius, or the chief instigator of Catholic reform. He chose for himself the old pagan title of Pontifex Maximus.[3] He was considered to be one of the most absolute misogynists to occupy the papal throne, for he regarded women as inferior to men in every way, according to the teaching of both Aristotle and Aquinas. The one woman to whom he showed any warmth was Queen Mary of England for exhuming and burning her father's 'heretical' corpse, and for attempting to restore Catholicism to England. Indeed, as commentators point out, it was Paul IV who, by his intransigence, sealed the fate of England's Catholics. The pope also launched his claim to ownership of England against the 'upstart' young queen, Elizabeth, she being twenty-five at the time, and he eighty. This time, his claims did not prevail.

Earlier, during the reign of Pope Paul III, but at the instigation of the then Cardinal Caraffa, the Roman Inquisition had been set up on 21 July, 1542. Caraffa's hatred of the Jews was well known, and towards Jews, women, 'sodomites', and heretics of any kind, the inquisition showed little mercy. Toward the end of his life in 1559, he inaugurated the *Index of Forbidden Books*, which together with the revised *Index* of Trent in 1564, effectively silenced intellectual, scientific, theological and cultural life for centuries. Even Teresa of Avila had to clear her shelves of many books, and one hundred years later, her sister Carmelite, Sor Juana Ines de la Cruz, as we shall see, had to rid her library of over three thousand books. We are told that over ten thousand books were burned in Venice and twelve thousand, including the Jewish Talmud, in Cremona.[4] Even for orthodox women and men writers, the act of self-censorship, so well known to women at all times in the church, took over as the most effective judge where the *Index* left off.

Given the state of Christianity in Rome throughout the early part of the sixteenth century – the reform-minded Cardinal Contarini considered the entire papal court and all the cardinals to be heretical – it is astonishing that the Council of Trent accomplished so much. When the Council was summoned by Pope Paul III, contemporaries remarked that the 'authors of the world's corruption' had gathered to reform the world.[5] There were several false starts. Initially only ten bishops were present and it took them six months to arrive. A second attempt brought even fewer bishops, in fact only the legates of the pope were present. Finally, 13 December, 1545 was named as the opening day and about thirty Roman and Italian bishops attended. No real theological debates occurred until a year later, and by then the anti-Protestant focus of the Council was clear. All realised that it was far too late to effect any kind of reconciliation, even though some attempts were still being made, and so Catholic thought was defined wholly in the spirit of continuous anathemas against the Protestant understanding of Christianity. The resulting renewed statement of the Catholic deposit of faith was remarkably effective, even though no attention was paid to the sometimes extraordinary differences of opinion among the Catholics themselves. All attention was focused on denying the legitimacy of Protestant approaches to Christian truth, especially around the doctrine of *sola fides*, and justification, the necessity of tradition as well as scripture, the numbering of the sacraments as no more nor less than seven, and the priority of the Latin texts of the scriptures over the Greek. Finally, it was asserted that the Mass was a sacrifice and could be celebrated only in Latin. In the final session, in 1563, the work of Catholic renewal was faced and there is now almost universal agreement that the work of Session 23 on the priesthood was perhaps the most significant of the whole Council. The command to every diocese to erect seminaries on the model of the Jesuit system, with the work of Aquinas as the main focus, was one of the most effective in terms of its influence on the ordinary Catholic. With the seminary, came generally better educated clergy and an amazing uniformity of teaching and preaching worldwide.

The cardinals, however, were not always engaged in the tough work of reform. There are accounts by the Secretary of the Council describing a banquet and ball organised for the visiting dignitaries by the Cardinal of Trent, Cristoforo Madruzzo. The cardinal was able to provide a meal with seventy-four different courses and wine that was over one hundred years old. As was the custom, after the feast, the cardinals were invited to join in the dancing, selected ladies having been included on the guest-list for this purpose. Several bishops, including the procurator fiscal of the Council, enjoyed the festivities. The archbishop of Palermo had been invited to open the ball, and 'all took place very honourably, with seemly modesty and Christian charity.'[6]

The Council of Trent was proclaimed on 26 January, 1564 by Pius IV, with the proviso that only the pope had the authority to interpret the teachings of the Council. Meantime, the Peace of Augsburg had been signed on 25 September, 1555, recognising the Protestant states of the Augsburg Confession. By now the face of Europe had been changed, and two separate Christian traditions set out to live side by side. This devastating fact left no time for Catholic reform to be implemented gradually or, in the time-honoured phrase, to be received by the people. Despite the new emphasis on pastoral care done by resident bishops and priests, the decrees of the Council of Trent were made obligatory on all by papal command from the centre. Hence, the adjective Roman which has ever since been attached to the Tridentine tradition.

Three reforming popes set the seal on Roman Catholicism. In 1566, Pius V, a strict, frugal and austere Dominican was elected. One of his first acts was to revive, yet again, and activate the Roman Inquisition, and again the burning of 'heretics' became a familiar addition to the work of reform. Pius was known to have a will of steel and it was his design that no believer would have the excuse of not knowing the doctrine of Trent and that no loophole by way of dispensation would exist for anyone. Now the whole paraphernalia of Catholic life was 'Roman' – Roman Missal, Roman Breviary, Roman Catechism, Roman Liturgy, Roman texts, and eventually, a new creation, Roman theology. Archbishop Charles Borromeo of Milan (1560-1584), with his new brand of harshness and determination, was presented as the ideal of the new Tridentine bishop. He devoted particular attention to the education, examination and continual visitation of the clergy who were trained in the three new seminaries that he had founded. It is extraordinary to think that such clerical education was entirely new in the church, and was to be the most effective instrument of reform. Besides, the education of clergy raised the whole question of education in the faith for everyone, and this concern was eventually to reach into the heart of even the smallest Catholic parish.

Turkish armies had been plaguing Europe for almost fifty years and their final defeat in 1571, at the Battle of Lepanto, seemed to set the divine seal of approval on Catholic reform. The fact that Pope Pius credited the victory to the recitation of the Rosary added another specifically Catholic aspect of Marian devotion to the new Catholic experience. Pope Gregory followed (1572-1585) and brought his skills as a Canon Lawyer to the process of reform. He chose to use papal nuncios as one of his main tools of reform, thus opening the doors to royal courts and state rulers. He reinforced the centrality of Roman thought by establishing seminaries in Rome for countries undergoing religious persecution, such as Ireland, England and Germany. Gregory also added a universal dimension to his reign by reforming the Julian calendar, bringing it into synchronicity with the astronomical year. Thus, in the year 1582, the month of October lost eleven days, ensuring that the feast day of Teresa of Avila would be celebrated, not on the day of her death, 4 October, but according to the new reckoning, on 15 October. It also ensured that in the correspondence of Magdalena and Balthasar mentioned in Chapter Two, Balthasar in Italy was living by the new system, while Magdalena, back in Germany, was still reckoning by the old method. It took about one hundred years for Protestant countries to adopt the Gregorian calendar, and it was only recently adopted by the Orthodox traditions.

Pope Sixtus V (1585-1590) set about the task of making Rome the model for the whole church, and to do this he had to tackle the Curia. He streamlined the central government of the church, fixing the number of cardinals at seventy. He also set out to beautify the city itself, laid out its streets, added the Dome to St Peter's, and replaced with the images of saints several of the ancient monuments to emperors and old Roman dignitaries. After three popes in the space of two years, the Spaniard, Clement VIII was elected (1592-1605). His effort was to try to bring personal holiness into the equation, as he acted the part of repentant pilgrim, ministering in hospitals and prisons. The Jubilee year of 1600 brought millions of believers to Rome and set an emotional seal on the increasingly central position of Rome. By 1600, the Catholic Church was the church of Trent, and a new power and self-confidence was apparent throughout the reformed Catholic world. The Roman Catholic Church began to assert itself and, in its attempts to establish an unbroken continuity with the church of antiquity, the new discipline of Church History was established. By now, it was clearly seen that the Protestant reformers asserted an essential discontinuity with hundreds of years of Christian life, while the Catholic Church reasserted its ongoing and unbroken claim to be the spokesperson for the whole of the Christian tradition.

The reform initiated by Trent was a mixture of moral severity and pious devotion, which eventually penetrated to the heart of the Catholic world. After the victory over the Turks at Lepanto, a new depth was apparent in devotion to the Virgin Mary, and the feast of the Holy Rosary was created as a commemoration. The rosary and other Marian devotions spread rapidly, as well as devotion to St Joseph, perhaps initiated by Teresa of Avila. With new emphases on the celebration of the Eucharist and the mystery of the Real Presence came a new focus on the tabernacle in churches, and on such rituals as the celebration of Bene-diction, where the people were blessed with the host exposed in a monstrance. More frequent communion was encouraged and many people had greater access to devotional retreats, pilgrim-ages and other ways of intensifying their inner spiritual life. The human person of Jesus became more central to these devotions, and participation in good works was encouraged. In a sense, the life of the convent and monastery had spilled out into the street, and many Catholics sought a life of Christian perfection. None of this happened overnight, but the psychological effects of the Council promoted a new optimism and will to reform in the Catholic parts of Europe. As we shall see, new religious orders for women and men flourished and the call of the foreign mis-sions added a romantic and adventurous strain to the faith. Several new martyr saints were created, in the normal propor-tion of five men to one woman, and these saints provided yet new models for piety. The foreign missions in the New World were a wonderful boost to Catholic morale, offering, as they did, a vision of millions of new souls to replace Protestant losses. The laity now seemed to have something to do, even if only vicari-ously.[7]

This movement of Catholic reform has been variously termed the 'Counter-Reformation' when opposition to Protestantism is being emphasised, and the 'Catholic Reform' when reform from its own Catholic substance and continuity with the past is being emphasised. Either way, the whole movement of reform was a masculinised performance, using, in the main, the imagery of war, military organisation and propaganda. The Catholic Kings of Spain had Christianised their subjects violently, and this vio-lence was apparent, not only in the virtual reforming reign of terror by Pope Paul IV in Europe, but also by the *conquistadores* in the New world. The fact that Mary Tudor's violent Catholic Restoration and the Roman Inquisition were endorsed by the papacy did not make them any less fearful. The Council of Trent wanted conformity of belief and uniformity of worship and one of the few dissenting voices to this programme belonged to women. The reform efforts of women were seen as hysterical and often fraudulent. Female piety was frowned on and several women mystics, known as the *alumbrados* were burned at the stake in Spain. New religious orders for men, such as the Theatines and Barnabites were founded especially for priests, and the understanding became universal that the work of the church could be done only by the ordained clergy. Several popes repeated the restrictions on the lives of nuns and the post-Trent church could only envisage the necessity of cloistered nuns in the life of the church. Indeed the repetition of the medieval laws on cloister had been one of the final acts of the Council, enacted as the bishops were coming to the end of their deliberations. The misogyny of the fourteenth century Boniface VIII was re-inforced, but it was harder to enforce in the sixteenth century. With such added restrictions as the *Index* the minds of women were cloistered as well as their bodies.[8] Both the Catholic and Protestant reforms reinforced male authority everywhere, whether family, town, church or state. As was by now traditional in a reform that focused especially on priests, the renewal of the clergy meant the oppression of women, as the two groups were always seen as antithetical. It was even suggested that women in their homes should keep their heads covered as a sign of their subjection. The only thing women had to offer, it was suggested, was hidden and silent prayer and subservience. Nothing more was needed. The marriage bonds were tightened by Trent, so that there was greater clerical control over all women. Poverty was seen as immoral and poor women, especially, were cor-ralled into a cheap labour force, thus becoming the first of the so-called 'deserving poor'. All reformers considered that the im-prisonment of the poor would be of benefit to society as a whole, especially if the poor were disciplined into hard work, the practice of religion, and respect for their betters.

So as the pope divided the world between Spain and Portugal, and as male missionaries set off to win souls for Christ, women were more and more confined to their quarters and few church leaders questioned these arrangements. The lives of many women, however, could not be so easily restricted to the parameters set for them by the reforming Catholic Church. Among these, perhaps the greatest was Teresa, who from her enclosed convent in Avila, managed to inject a completely new energy to a reform movement that was not clerically directed, and was not, at least initially, directed against the Protestants. Teresa, the third of twelve children, was born in Avila on 28 March, 1515, into a Spanish empire that was then becoming the greatest the world had ever seen. Being born into the first great world power with its vibrant sense of its own identity creates a certain kind of creative and energetic personality, and these qualities marked the life of Teresa. Her father was Don Alonso Sanchez de Cepeda who, after the death of his first wife left him with two young children, went on to marry Dona Beatriz de Ahumada, who was then only fifteen. Dona Beatriz died at the age of thirty-three in 1527 when Teresa was thirteen years of age. No wonder that it was reported that Teresa feared marriage much more then life in the convent.[9] The horizons of Spain had only recently expanded to include the whole New World, and a potential harvest of new church members presented itself to replace the growing losses in northern Europe, as well as the places only recently vacated by the Moors and the Jews. Teresa herself had Jewish antecedents, so there would have been an extra burden on the family, in the fervent atmosphere of contemporary Spain, to prove their Catholic loyalty. Whatever the reason, from a very early age, Teresa wanted to be part of it all, if not by being a missionary, then by being a martyr.

It was a close, loving and literate family and Teresa was surrounded by the books and romances that were the usual literature of the day. Teresa also chose other reading and was drawn to religious life after delving into the Letters of St Jerome, on the face of it a most unlikely source of monastic inspiration. By the age of twenty, Teresa had entered the local Carmelite Convent of the Incarnation, and was professed there in 1537. Shortly afterwards, Teresa began to be plagued by the ill-health that dogged her all her life. She became comatose, apparently after a failed local cure, and her grave was being prepared. Eventually, after a bout of paralysis that lasted for several years, Teresa recovered sufficiently to take up the daily round of her Carmelite community. Later she speaks of feeling well for three or four hours at a time, but her chronic ailments did not prevent her from leading the kind of vitally active life of travel and administration that the Council of Trent was most anxious to forbid for women.

In the highly fervent Catholic convent life of early sixteenth-century Spain, the occurrence of affective visionary and mystical experiences was expected, if not exactly encouraged for women. All through her later writings Teresa bemoans the lack of decent spiritual directors and the harmful presence of inexperienced and incompetent directors for the nuns. She speaks of the mistakes made by these men in the guidance of her own life. All the signs of a divided heart are present in her account of the first two decades of religious life, but eventually, her life fell into shape with her remarkable conversion experiences around her fortieth year. She moved from a life of indecision that was killing her, spiritually and bodily, to a life of complete dedication to God. The immediate sign of this new life was the intensity of her prayer, and the almost simultaneous realisation that such prayer demanded an appropriate atmosphere. It was this realisation that spurred her on to become one of the great convent reformers of all time.

The reform or re-founding of Carmel was begun from the time of her conversion in 1554, while Trent was in session. Her reforming intent owed little to the Council of Trent, but she was eventually to suffer greatly from the decrees of Trent about the religious activities of women. From Teresa's perspective at that time, freedom was the enemy of reform and the contemplative life, and she set her heart on restoring the primitive rule in all its strictness, with a very strong emphasis on obedience. Her own experience had led her to believe that it took steely determination to take on the demands of God in religious life, but her natural common sense and deep humanity kept her from the harshness that this reform might imply. The intensity of Teresa's prayer life startled and worried her directors and, as is normal in any reform movement, not all of those needing reform favoured Teresa's intervention. Teresa was therefore instructed to write down her vision of reform and her prayer experiences. Initially this task caused her great disturbance, but eventually, in a spirit of obedience, Teresa became a prolific writer of spiritual classics. The *Book of her Life* was written in 1562 and was followed by the *Way of Perfection*, and eventually by *The Book of Foundations*, and the *Interior Castle*. It was this writing which made her a household name across Spain, and helped to win support from the general public for a reform that was often hindered both by her brother and sister Carmelites as well as by ecclesiastical leaders. It was no accident that Teresa, like so many women writers before her, had to cloak herself in the 'rhetoric of protection'.[10] 'I write', she said, 'because I have been ordered to write, and these words are not mine but God's.'

The founding of St Joseph's, the first reformed Carmelite convent in Avila, reads like a spy novel. The town and the convents were in an uproar, and Teresa was being variously accused of innovations and immorality. Her frequent travel added the accusation of being a 'gadabout', and her life of mystical prayer left her always in danger of the attention of the Inquisition. It is not necessary here to list those who resisted and aided the reform, but among her strongest supporters were several aristocratic women, members of her own family, the General Superior of the Carmelites and a series of Papal Nuncios. It is true that a similar list could be drawn up of those who accused her, but eventually, the first convent of the reform was founded in 1562. Later, the year 1578 was a time of real diffi-

culty for Teresa as many of her supporters, including Rubeo the
Carmelite General and Gracian, the Apostolic Vicar, had either
died or been replaced. It was during this period that she was accused of being a 'restless gadabout', but also of being disobedient, contumacious, an inventor of evil doctrines, of travelling
against the prohibitions of Trent and of teaching in violation of
the apostle Paul's command to women to be silent. Teresa never
lost sight of her goal, and though her accusers connived against
her, she would never have survived without her natural as-
sertiveness and her spiritual strength.

During this period, Teresa was torn apart. Several of her sisters were bullied into giving false testimony against her. Several
were excommunicated. Even her most loyal supporters among
the nuns were confused and divided. Her friends, including
John of the Cross were either imprisoned or in hiding. She had
to resort to using coded messages in her letters to save her own
and others' reputation. Nevertheless, she held fast and eventually
permission was granted for Teresa's reform group to become a
separate Carmelite entity, henceforth known as the Discalced
Carmelites. A series of letters in 1578 give some indication of the
endless negotiations with church officials, local dignitaries and
even the royal court. Something of her charm and common
sense, as well as determination, comes through in a letter of
April, 1578, which was being carried by her brother Lorenzo to
the Vicar Gracian. After discussing the respective stances of
pope, king, archbishops, and Carmelite superiors, Teresa turns
her attention to more mundane things. She wants permission for
her brother to enter the convent in Seville in order to inspect a
new cooking stove, as she wishes to install a similar one in
Avila. 'If you were to read what they write about that stove, you
would not be surprised at our wanting one like it here', she
writes.[11] Her ability to turn effortlessly from the international
ecclesiastical scene to the affairs of the local convent and the well
being of her sisters is remarkable. These letters reveal too that
her health continues to plague her, especially her 'dreadfully
troublesome' head, which was apparently full of noises. Her let-

ters are peppered with references to her health, and the best
news usually amounts to no more than 'I am reasonably well'.

Late in 1567, Teresa had met John of the Cross in Medina. He
was twenty-five, she fifty-two, but they seemed to have understood each other and warmed to each other instantly, and he became the spiritual director she had always longed for. John was
born in Castile in 1542, and had studied with the Jesuits and
worked in a hospital for several years. He entered Carmel in
1563, attended the University of Salamanca and was ordained in
1567. The meeting of John and Teresa was a turning point in
both their lives. Both were dedicated to the reform of Carmel,
though John's involvement cost him even more dearly than did
that of Teresa. He had been kidnapped, imprisoned and tortured on two different occasions by his former brothers. John
was a learned mystic and is now recognised not only as one of
the great mystics of the West, but also an extraordinary lyric
poet. Like Teresa, John seemed capable of uniting both the mystical life and the life of administration and reform without too
great difficulty. He spent time as College Rector, Prior, Definitor
and Vicar-Provincial, as well as being confessor to Teresa and
the nuns of her convent from 1552 to 1557. It was during John's
imprisonment that he began to elaborate the mystical themes
that will forever be associated with his name, like the 'dark night
of the soul'. John's poetic gifts allowed him to push out the
boundaries of spiritual writing, tracing poetically the transitions
from meditation to contemplation, as Teresa had done in a more
conversational and even didactic manner. Today more than
ever, his insights into the human need to let God be God lend
depth and meaning to Christian spirituality.[12]

Once St Joseph's in Avila had been approved, Teresa set
about the task of founding as many Carmels as there were hairs
on her head, as the Father General had asked her to do in 1578.
Her travels brought her across the length and breadth of Spain
as she founded reformed Carmels for women and men from
Granada in the south to Burgos in the north. She was possessed
of a burning energy and often protested at the frustrations of

being female herself, and having to deal with women. She shuddered at the inanity of false devotion and flights of mystical fancy, and was willing to call on anyone skilled in contemplation for help. Her practical and sensible advice made abundant room for the heights of mystical prayer, but she had the keenest eye for dilettantes and those in search of adulation and divine consolation. On a trip to Alba de Tormes in October 1582, Teresa became ill and died. It was the month and year of the change from the Julian to the Gregorian calendar so her feast day is celebrated on the fifteenth of October rather then on the fourth. The same papal nuncio who referred to her as a 'restless gadabout' also complained that she 'teaches theology as though she were a doctor of the church'. Teresa was named a Doctor of the Church on 27 September, 1970, having been canonised in 1622 on the same day as Ignatius of Loyola, Francis Xavier and Philip Neri.

The mystical teaching of Teresa of Jesus (as she was known in her community) is contained in her main writings: *Life* (1565), *Way of Perfection* (1569), *Song of Songs* (1567), *Book of Foundations* (1573), *Interior Castle* (1577), as well as around four hundred letters, mostly dating from the last six years of her life, and a selection of occasional memoirs, and spiritual testimonies. Her works are written for her sisters, at the request or command of her superiors or directors. The style is conversational and very informal, without punctuation or formal arrangement. The purpose of all her writing is to lay the firmest of foundations for the new kind of spiritual life that she was advocating. She had the most intense feeling of God's presence, and after some bad advice and negative experiences in her early life, was convinced that contemplative abstractions were to be avoided. Teresa's prayer was rooted in a profound love of the humanity of Christ, and she felt that this was a permanent requirement for true contemplative prayer. From the year 1556, Teresa began to experience the visions and locutions that were to become an everyday part of her life.[13] Several years later, she felt herself enter more deeply into what is called in the gospel of John, the indwelling presence of God, and felt that it was no longer a question of sharing God's life but of God living in her. Like so many other mystics, such as Catherine of Siena, Teresa experienced a spiritual marriage on 18 November, 1572. This experience was traditionally associated with a turn toward outward ministry and this is true also for Teresa.

Like so many other women mystics, Teresa felt that her journey toward contemplation was available for all, although not essential for all. She was never elitist in her spirituality and corrected this wherever she found it among her sisters. Almost unfailingly, Teresa refers to God and Christ as 'His Majesty', which given the current political arrangements in Spain was not unusual. God was the supreme king, but was also her friend. Indeed friendship can be seen as key to her spiritual relationship. Her prayer, then, was a prayer of friendship that, in her case, progressed from friendship to mutual knowledge to union. Some words and phrases appear over and over again, such as 'drawing near', 'recollecting or centring' oneself, and the continual necessity of vocal prayer, to tame the 'wild horses' of the mind.

All agree that Teresa's most brilliant work is the *Interior Castle*. This work was undertaken to replace the book of her *Life*, which had been in the hands of the Inquisition for some time. Teresa was sixty two years of age, quite ill and still suffering severe 'noise and weakness' in her head, when her confessor ordered her to write this book for her sisters as a replacement for the earlier one. The bulk of the work was completed in two months during one of the most troubled times of her life. She describes seven dwelling places in the interior castle and the process of transition from one to the next. The first three mansions are for beginners, for those still relying on their own efforts; the last four are for those who have entered the supernatural realm and are experiencing what she had earlier called the indwelling of the Trinity. Prayer is the gate of entry and prayer activates the ongoing inward journey. The earlier stages focus a great deal on the necessity of self-knowledge, another common theme for women mystics, and the utilisation of every means possible to gain this knowledge. Over and over, Teresa reminds her sisters of the need for balance and guidance, and warns them against claiming too much for themselves or presuming that they are further on the journey than they really are.

The fourth dwelling represents the real turning point on the journey, in a sense, the move from meditation to the gift of contemplation. Love now becomes the central motivation, a love not marked by emotion, but by an intense desire to please God. She introduces one of her favourite mystical metaphors, again common to so many women mystics, that of water. For Teresa the real contrast in the spiritual journey was between the aqueduct, built with so much human ingenuity to convey water from the source to the consumers, and the spring, which just wells up effortlessly, filling every crevice. Teresa also delights in the image of the silk worm dying to produce a little white butterfly, and the analogy of marriage with all its stages of meeting, betrothal, and union. Her constant refrain is that love must never be idle, whether one experiences love as pain or delight. By the time the seventh dwelling is reached, the soul is experiencing a kind of co-naturality with God. Here again, Teresa joins with Mechtilde of Magdeburg, Marguerite Porete and Meister Eckhart, in the experience of the immensity of God and the nothingness of the spirit. The little white butterfly has come home.

Throughout this universally acknowledged gem of the spiritual life, Teresa comments on her noisy head, her poor memory, and her sense of being just a parrot, repeating what she has said before. She comments on her fear: it is 'terrible to be always frightened' (Third Dwelling 1.2), and on the unexpected trivialities that can send even the most advanced hurtling back to the beginning. She professes impatience with the cautious people who move one step at a time and encourages her sisters to have faith and jump. (Third Dwelling 2.7) From the fifth dwelling on, Teresa, admittedly, is searching for words. Human language is too coarse for what she needs to say, but she can feel the truth in the marrow of her bones. As she draws her sisters into the prayer of quiet, she hastens to remind them that this is not just a dreamy state. If they start languishing or swooning they should ask the prioress for more work and make sure they are eating and sleeping properly. (Fourth Dwelling 3,12; Fifth Dwelling 1, 1-3)

God's presence always leaves a certitude in one's being – one cannot mistake God for anything else. Besides, she adds, if one is in doubt about God's love, one need never be in doubt about loving one's neighbour. This is quite clear and a readily available test of one's fidelity. (Fifth Dwelling 3, 7) Teresa constantly berates herself for giving in to the prayer of abstraction at one period in her life as a result of bad advice. Even as she moves into the Sixth Dwelling, she is still harping on this theme. 'To be always withdrawn from corporeal things and enkindled in love is the trait of angelic spirits, not of those who live in mortal bodies.' She assures her sisters that she had attempted to do this. 'Afterward I saw clearly how wrong I had been, and I never stop regretting…'[14] In the tradition of so many mystics, Teresa hesitates as she approaches the final stages, because, as she says, 'others will think I know about it through experience'.[15] This is the experience of a God without limits, who brings the person to her own centre where God is to be found. Here faith becomes sight. Here, one always knows that God is present though the actual vision of God is not so clearly perceived. From Teresa's perspective, one of the most important consequences of arriving at this stage, it that now one is 'much more occupied than before with everything pertaining to the service of God'.[16] In her efforts to explain this, Teresa turns to one of the most confusing of biblical narratives. It is like having the two sisters, Martha and Mary living in the soul. While Martha still has to venture abroad to do all the work, Mary remains at the core. Nevertheless, one remains united like two candles or like rainwater falling into a river, or 'it is like what we have when a little stream enters the sea, there is no means of separating the two'. In what is almost her final comment of this spiritual classic, Teresa says: 'In sum, my sisters, what I conclude with is that we shouldn't build castles in the air'.[17]

The writing of the *Interior Castle* was a task that Teresa of Jesus started with a feeling of aversion, but ended with great happiness. She gives the impression that she knew she had written something that would survive and that was meant for everyone, because, as she insisted, no one needs permission to make this spiritual journey. The work of Teresa of Avila, the reformer, founder and teacher is now revered wherever people look for guidance on the spiritual quest. The church has deemed her writing and teaching worthy to be placed alongside the greatest teachers in Christianity. Had this openness been available in her lifetime, the history of the subsequent four hundred years would have to be written differently. The courageous open invitation to all women and men to pursue the call of God to the very boundaries of human existence would have expanded minds and hearts. On the contrary, it was caution and legalism that prevailed, as was evident even in Teresa's own life. Despite her visions, locutions and the evidence of her experience of the highest realms of prayer, it is Teresa's ability to cross the boundaries designed to restrict her contributions that continues to impress. She was intent on the transformation of the human and her life demonstrates clearly that this task can be accomplished in the most adverse of circumstances. Nevertheless, as everywhere in the Christian history of women, one cannot help wondering what might have been accomplished by, for and with women, if the sixteenth century, like all the preceding ones, had not again missed the opportunity of fully integrating women into its ecclesial vision.

This question must be asked again in the context of the life of another Carmelite woman who lived a century and a world away from the Spain of Teresa of Jesus. This is Sor Juana Ines de la Cruz who was born in Mexico in 1648, poet, intellectual, philosopher, and a woman for whom the church could find no place.[18] Her life – the little we know of it – shines like a glint of lightning in the otherwise historically womanless world of the *conquistadores*. The life of Sor Juana presents us with something of a mystery, because it is difficult to provide a context for her brilliant mind. From the age of six, she was able to read and write and seemingly badgered her mother for the chance to go to university. For an illegitimate, penniless child, the prospects were limited. Nevertheless her beauty and intellect attracted the attention of the viceregal court and in 1669 she entered the convent of San Geronimo in Mexico City. This was not necessarily because she had a vocation to religious life, but because of her aversion to marriage and her love of learning. The life of virginity, she discovered, was the only life that women and men could, theoretically, share equally. Like so many women before her, she felt that virginity could liberate her from the restraints of gender: 'I will never be a woman who will serve a man as wife,' and added, 'Given the total antipathy I felt towards marriage, I deemed convent life the least unsuitable and most honourable.' This choice would allow her to live alone and to 'have no obligatory occupation to inhibit the freedom of my studies'.[19] Sor Juana is reported to have observed the rule adequately, but all she really needed was a room of her own where she could pursue her studies in philosophy, her poetic writing, and her vast correspondence. She collected a library of thousands of books in Latin, Spanish and Portuguese, and read widely in medieval scholastic philosophy, and any Jesuit author she could find. She is said to have avoided theology for fear of the still very active inquisition. She became the quasi-poet laureate of Mexico and also wrote extensively for convent performances. Much of her poetic corpus consisted of erotic poetry and sexual satire. Eventually, the ecclesiastical authorities caught up with her, especially after the viceregal couple who supported her had been recalled to Spain. In 1691, she published her *Response* to their charges, which were really a result of clerical jealousy because of her popularity.

This *Response* is a kind of philosophical history of women and is startlingly original in places. It was to be her last prose text, and this time she could not avoid tackling the usual clerical arguments against women from scripture and theology. She likened herself to Catherine of Alexandria, another virgin

persecuted by the clergy for her learning, when she tried to
teach that gender is irrelevant in matters of intellect. She pointed
out that God gave women intellect to be used, and that it could
only be good for the church when women studied, taught, argued and wrote. She mined the writings of Aristotle and
Thomas Aquinas on natural law to point out the inadequacies of
the church's dealings with her. The central argument of Sor
Juana had to do with the 'inclination towards letters' that God
had implanted in her being, an inclination that could be ignored
only at her peril. She denied that the clergy could use her case to
argue against all women, using the rational norms of philosophy to punch holes in the ecclesiastical misuse of power against
women.

Sor Juana used all the resources of existing philosophy to
argue against the hermeneutical blindness of traditional philosophy about women. She lived in a fairly open Carmelite convent
of fifty nuns where, for twenty-seven years, she was archivist
and treasurer. She tells us that each cell had two storeys and that
each nun had five maids. Juana received many visitors and they
brought gifts of scientific instruments for her experiments, as
well as musical scores, art works, liturgical texts and books. This
self-taught woman in her convent cell engaged in an unprecedented amount of scholarly and literary activity and broke all
the conventional social and 'natural' norms about women. Her
cell became a laboratory, a library, a workshop and a studio and
was the most famous salon in the New World. The Viceroy's
wife took a special protective interest in her work, which was
understood by Sor Juana to be an attempt to prove that learning
in a woman was not the sin that the church supposed it to be.

In order to undermine her position, her bishop circulated
portions of her writings and his own queries under the pseudonym of Sor Filotea. He said that knowledge and speech are forbidden to women, and that from Juana's early reading of the
Song of Songs, her pattern of disobedience had been established.
This disobedience was even seen to have been initiated by her
mother who had dressed her as a boy so that she could study.

Both the bishop under his pseudonym in his attack, and Sor Juana in her response, argued more about the principal of a woman's learning than the actual content of her teaching and writing. Juana argued that the desire to know is a natural impulse implanted by God. If the bishop imposes silence on her, he will be destroying God's gift to her, and therefore her very nature. Her inclination to learning is part of the natural law for women, and is women's share in the eternal reason. Knowledge in women is their proper act and end. Juana argued against the institutional arrogance of sexism as it was being illustrated in her case and as it had been illustrated so often before, as for example in the case of Abelard against Heloise.

In the end, however, the power of the church prevailed. Sor Juana was silenced and ordered to dispose of her library of over three thousand books as well as all her other possessions. She ceased all scholarly activity in 1693 and died shortly afterwards in 1695. The scale of her learning continues to astonish and one is reminded of Hildegarde of Bingen. Sor Juana wished to acknowledge no other master than mute books, and wanted no other colleague but her inkwell. She accepted her silencing but interpreted it in her own way and took control of her silenced life to the best of her ability. We are given no reasons for her final capitulation, but with the departure of the viceregal couple, her main secular support had vanished. Her voice was silenced by the misogyny of the ecclesiastical establishment, but her intellect could not be destroyed. Over the space of more than three hundred years, it is the tragic and cruel silencing of Sor Juana that speaks loudly. She can truly be called the first New World feminist, and her *Response* to the cowardly bishop masquerading under the name of Sor Filotea, can truly be called the 'magna carta of intellectual liberty for women in America'.[20]

The ecclesiastical context within which both Teresa of Avila and Sor Juana lived was intentionally antithetical to their full inclusion in the life of the church. Teresa accomplished her goals through obedience, Juana through a life of disobedience. Each woman rooted her belief in her own interpretation of the tradition. The final obedience of Juana was an act of self-defence, intellectual and physical. In the following centuries, it was to be the genius of women to conceal their disobedience under a cloak of obedience. Over and over again, history presents us with women who could not accept the restricted place allotted them by ecclesiastical mandate, but were able to accomplish their ends under a cloak of obedience, which allowed them to survive and bring enormous richness to a church that failed fully to value their contribution. In the next chapter we will meet four such women.

CHAPTER FOUR

New Women's Communities:
Education and Health

The decrees of the Council of Trent, despite their authoritative imposition, took centuries to take hold in the ordinary life of the Catholic Church. Nevertheless, as the seventeenth century dawns, a new ferment is perceptible at many levels in church life. The exact quality of this ferment must be explored against a background of continuous vicious warfare across the face of Europe, and the continuation of many unreformed attitudes among the clergy, seen, for example, in the astonishing nepotism of the reforming pope, Urban VIII. At the same time, many of the old superstitions still governed the lives of the rural population, and as many reformers discovered, as the century progressed, most of the Catholic population of both town and country were largely ignorant of the most basic elements of their faith. It was to women that both Protestants and Catholics turned to remedy this situation, despite the fact that the seventeenth-century world saw a great decline in the influence of women generally. These reforming initiatives in education, and eventually many other forms of ministry, came not from the official levels, which in fact resisted the women at every turn, but from the newly awakened Christian devotion of a number of women and men who changed the face of the Catholic Church. The word 'devotion' is used here intentionally, as it became almost a code word for the personal appropriation of Tridentine renewal.

There were several obvious ingredients in this post-Trent ferment. One of the most fruitful was the revival of Catholic scholarship, even though such renewal took place within very sharply restricted parameters. Nevertheless, in the Counter-

Reformation atmosphere, the need arose to prove the antiquity of the positions put forward by the Catholics, and so the witnesses of the past were summoned forth in a revival (and in some cases the creation) of church history, hagiography, Canon Law, conciliar doctrine, and Patristic teaching. The ancient Fathers of the church were elevated to the position of 'Doctor' to add weight to their teaching. Thus a sound basis was sought for the Catholic re-emphasis of the main Tridentine doctrines of the Eucharistic Real Presence, the celibate priesthood, the sacrificial nature of the Mass, and the primacy of the pope. The normal historical accompaniment to this renewal, as far as women are concerned, is the reinforcing of ancient strictures about the private nature of women's church membership, and the irrelevance, and in fact negative quality of women's public contribution to church life. As one of the last acts of the Council of Trent – almost as the bishops were going out the door – the enforcement of cloister on all women religious was repeated in legislation that was to echo endlessly through the succeeding centuries.[1]

A new kind of Catholic (and anti-Protestant) piety begins to percolate through the cities and towns of what remained of Catholic Europe. As we have seen, some of this renewal was spurred on by the Carmelite reform, as it spread beyond the confines of Spain. Some was evoked as a result of the eucharistic emphasis and the founding of several eucharistic confraternities, which promoted devotion to the Eucharist and saw the restoration of Corpus Christi processions, and a new focus on the tabernacle before which a red light now drew attention to the mystery within. Rosary confraternities were also founded to promote the recitation of the rosary, and St Joseph was elevated to a position of new importance in the saintly pantheon.

A host of new Catholic preachers and reformers arose in Spain, Italy and eventually, France, to promote the new ingredients of Catholic reform piety. These were named over and over again as self-sanctification, apostolic works, and the all-embracing practice of charity. Men such as Philip Neri, the apostle of the city of Rome (1515-1595), and Pierre de Berulle, who founded the Congregation of the Oratory in 1611, added their voices to the growing influence of the Jesuits. What was characteristic of these three groups, and many similar ones, was that they were designed for priest membership only. The work of the church was now seen as exclusively men's work, and even more essentially, priestly work. Besides the promotion of a priestly spirituality, the education of boys was the main focus of these groups. By 1616, there were over three hundred Jesuit colleges for the education of young men, and such growth was also in evidence in the newly reformed mendicant groups. On 12 March, 1622, Pope Gregory XV celebrated in brilliant style the canonisations of Ignatius of Loyola, Teresa of Avila, Philip Neri and the Jesuit missionary, Francis Xavier. Some years later, the bodies of two women virgin martyrs were fortuitously discovered, and these were presented to the faithful as models of Tridentine spirituality. As in every age of the church, the saints provide a model of what is expected – active public life for men, and an enclosed or martyred virginal life for women. After the Council of Trent, there had been strong pressure for clerical marriage, but the papacy was adamant on the subject of celibacy, emphasising, to strengthen the point, that celibacy was a state superior to marriage.

Christian life in the first half of the seventeenth century, as well as the papacies of the three influential reforming popes, Paul V (1605-1621), Gregory XV (1621-1623) and Urban VIII (1623-1644), was carried on against a background of some of the most vicious warfare yet seen in Europe. The famous 'defenestration of Prague', when enraged Protestant delegates threw their Catholic counterparts out of the (ground floor) windows, initiated the horrific Thirty Years' War (1618-1648) which eventually dragged in the whole of Europe from Sweden to the Mediterranean and England to Russia. It was a religious war fought between the Protestant and Catholic defensive alliances, but political motives always predominated. The papacy disliked the growing power of the Spanish Empire and did not hesitate to call on Protestant soldiers to fight against Catholic Spain.

France had been ravaged by its own religious wars for decades previously as the Huguenot Henry of Navarre took the throne of France as Henry IV in 1589. It took him five years to free his own kingdom of France from the domination of the Spanish Catholic League, but he finally realised that only a Catholic monarch could unite France. In 1593, he renounced heresy and promised to practise Catholicism, remarking, it is said, 'Paris is worth a Mass.'

The Edict of Nantes was promulgated on 13 April, 1598, promoting, for the first time, the revolutionary idea that one state could house two religions. This is a landmark in the history of religious toleration and freedom, but it was centuries before the effects became perceptible. Catholicism remained the established religion of France, but the Huguenots were allowed to conduct their own services. Pope Clement VIII denounced it, saying that liberty was one of the greatest curses ever to befall the world.[2]

Finally, the Peace of Westphalia was inaugurated in 1648, which not only created the map of Europe for the next three hundred years, but also created a system of European states that had freed themselves from papal control. A new era was begun. The 1555 Peace of Augsburg was recognised, thereby recognising the legitimate existence of Protestantism and 1 January, 1624 was chosen as the date from which the ownership of church and other property would be reckoned. A modicum of peace descended on Europe, but memories forever bore the scars of horrific massacres, betrayals, and religious and political intrigue. New political problems would arise when debates over state toleration of religions would lead to princely absolutism, and new religious problems would haunt the churches as the secularisation of European arts, science and letters presented hitherto undreamt of challenges to theology and papal power. The stage was set for such problems as the reigning pope, Innocent X, condemned the Peace of Westphalia as 'null and void, accursed, and without any influence or result for past, present or future'. Europe paid no attention, as the pope was no longer a central political actor in the affairs of Western Europe.[3] It would take a late twentieth century pope to redress that situation.

The famous case of Galileo (1564-1642) is remembered as one of the main battlefields of the subsequent debate, and his trial before the Roman Inquisition is one of the most famous trials of history. Galileo had been a close friend of Pope Urban VIII and the two had often discussed the revolutionary hunch of Copernicus about the centrality of the sun and the movement of the earth. It was Galileo's brilliance in proving this hypothesis that brought him into the ambit of the inquisition, after the pope had turned against him. Galileo was relatively lucky in being allowed to spend the rest of his life under house arrest close by the convent where his beloved daughter, Sister Maria Celeste, was living as a nun. Because Galileo had never married Marina Gamba, the mother of his two daughters and one son, the girls had no worldly prospects, so they were consigned to the local convent before puberty. The son, Vincenzio, was legally declared legitimate. The correspondence between Galileo and Maria Celeste illustrates the close relationship between the two, and the father's reliance on his daughter's support and insight. The father's side of the correspondence was destroyed, apparently for the daughter's safety, but her letters survive to illustrate, not only the unpretentious nature of Galileo's brilliance, but also the marginal life of Maria Celeste. She spent her whole life in the convent in a state of near starvation, dependent on her father's generosity for the most basic necessities.[4] The correspondence, and the other writings of Galileo demonstrate well the marginalisation of scientific genius, but also the total neglect of women in convents, whether they were there by choice or through the demands of negative cultural assumptions about women. This semi-destitute state of convent women will appear again and again in the lives of seventeenth century women, as we shall see.

Throughout the seventeenth century, the traditional gender and social hierarchies endured. The days when women mystics could claim direct authority from God had come to an end. Such charismatic displays by women were distinctly unwelcome, and besides, women had been terrorised into silence by the appalling cruelty of the various witchcrazes in many parts of Europe. Nevertheless, the Tridentine church needed women to be the mothers of the new church. As the Protestants never ceased to point out, the vast majority of Christians, clergy included, were utterly ignorant of even the most basic elements of the faith. The various Protestant groups had to design a new programme of education from the ground up, rooted in scripture reading and various adaptations of Martin Luther's catechism. There was a greater sense of continuity in the Catholic community, because some segments of society has benefited from the presence of monastic communities of women and men in their areas. Now the problem of women loomed large before the Tridentine church. There was little or no communication between the public world of men and the private world of women. Both church and society were content to leave the social and ecclesiastical structures intact, but the demands of the Counter-Reformation raised new challenges in the area of the education of the faithful, and especially of women. Somehow, good Catholic mothers had to be created, mothers who in turn would become the teachers of their children. Yet again church reform managed to make more demands on women while, at the same time, restricting their activities even further.[5]

A generation before the Council of Trent was even envisaged such needs had been foreseen and tackled by a number of ingenious women in England, France and Italy. The story has yet to be told in anything like a complete version, but a continent-wide movement of women is perceptible from about the middle of the sixteenth century to the mid-seventeenth century. These were women, in the fashion of the late medieval Beguines, who were determined to transcend the invisibility of women's lives and exercise a public role in education, nursing and care of the poor. This was a religious impulse, wholly rooted in a gospel-inspired apostolic life, and wholly exercised in the most ingenious and creative ways. Before the Tridentine popes and bishops seemed to be aware of this destitute, deprived and ignorant section of society, several women, both aristocratic and peasant, had organised themselves to institute a comprehensive response to this social disaster. Both church and society were shocked at this unexpected and unheard of activity of women, and for the next hundred years did everything in their power to curtail the women's public active life. The problem was exacerbated by the fact that, as the seventeenth century dawned, the needs could no longer be ignored. Floods of destitute poor arrived in the cities, where they were either licensed to beg or criminalised. Women were being forced into prostitution in order to feed their families. As reform-minded bishops, such as Charles Borromeo of Milan, tried to implement the Tridentine programmes, they became aware of the enormity of the task of religious instruction in the face of almost universal ignorance. So there was eventually no doubt that a huge social and educational programme was needed, but the women, who had first discerned and responded to this need, were seen by the Counter-Reformation church as more of a hindrance than a help. Nevertheless, they were needed. It is this ambivalence about women in the face of monumental ecclesiastical needs that marks the one hundred years from mid-sixteenth to mid-seventeenth centuries.

Foremost among the first and most creative groups of women were the Ursulines, founded by Angela Merici in northern Italy as early as the 1530s. We know little of her early life beyond the fact that both her mother and sister died when Angela was still quite young, and that her early years were spent in the war-torn area around Venice. It is not, then, an accident that her young life was nourished by the heroic tales of the *Golden Legend*, or that the pictures of the Roman virgins Paula and Eustochium adorned the walls of the first Ursuline meeting room. Whatever kind of education Angela had, she was conscious of being part of a tradition of active, devoted virginal women, who were ready to dedicate their lives to God in the service of the gospel. She is said to have had an early vision of singing virgins ascending and descending a heavenly ladder

with the assurance that these would be her followers. Angela's
initial response to her sense of being called was to take a vow of
virginity and become a Franciscan Tertiary, that is a group of
women who clustered around the official Franciscan communities without entering the cloister. Angela established a home on
the Lago di Garda and organised a group of widows to care for
the sick and teach young women.[6] Angela's focus was always on
practical ways to help women toward a better sense of themselves as women, and to save them from the immorality and
poverty threatening them on all sides.

By 1530, the company of St Ursula was taking shape and a
simple rule was approved in 1534. Angela's vision was truly innovative. She planned a two-tier community of older, wiser,
more responsible women and a group of younger women who
would be guided by their elders. These two groups of older
widows and younger virgins each had their own leaders, with
special liaison personnel set up to communicate between the
two groups. For about the first one hundred years, the majority
of members were poor women living locally among those they
served. Angela herself took responsibility for the distribution of
alms and legacies, and demonstrated her excellent business
sense in setting up the corporate ownership of property so that
schools, orphanages and homes for prostitutes could be established. She sought the assistance of male attorneys and other
personnel when she herself did not possess the required expertise. When Angela died in 1540, it is said that one out of every
four families in Brescia had an Ursuline member.

The whole span of Angela's life preceded the Council of
Trent, so she herself did not have to face the challenge of cloister
that was re-introduced on 3 December, 1563 by Pius V in the
closing moments of the conciliar sessions. The real issue was not
the cloistering of religious women, but ecclesiastical control
over the mobility of women, their work, legacies and leadership.
This was a battle that Angela's daughters had to face. The
Ursulines spread rapidly. By 1620, there were sixty-five convents in France, and over three hundred on the eve of the

Revolution. Similar development occurred in Italy, where the Ursulines were linked especially with the reforming efforts of Bishop Charles Borromeo in Milan. The Bishop of Milan was seen as the model reformer in the Tridentine mode, which meant that he believed firmly in only one kind of religious life for women, namely the strictly cloistered kind. Nevertheless, he needed the expertise of the Ursuline sisters who, by now, were counted among the most creative educators of women in Italy. Together with the Congregation de Notre Dame, the Ursulines were putting their creative energies into the invention of a new kind of education, with proper training for teachers and better facilities for students. They still lived by the ancient apostolic ideal of identifying with the poor, thus helping them to help themselves. Nevertheless, the second generation of Ursulines was forced, both by their own relatives and by ecclesiastical pressure, to make some accommodation to the new rules. Angela's successor, Lucrezia Lodrone, imposed special clothing on the sisters, which then made it necessary to make strict distinctions between members and non-members.

In 1567, Bishop Borromeo wrote a rule for the Milan Ursulines, and suggested several modifications of their religious life, without imposing them. He needed them too badly for his massive educational programmes to lose these active dedicated women to the cloister. In 1566, the Ursulines were founding schools of Christian doctrine beside their hospitals, and many of the women were still living in their own homes. Angela Merici had always insisted on the voluntary nature of the Ursuline vow of virginity, but as the century wore on, the ecclesiastical strictures were against them. In Milan, the Ursulines became a diocesan group under the bishop's direction, despite the fact that Angela Merici had obtained a papal dispensation to be free of local episcopal authority. From this time on, the Milan Ursulines retained some of the original freedoms envisaged by Angela, but they were also cut off from the Ursuline development elsewhere. The episcopal designs of Bishop Borromeo prevented the Ursulines, as a whole, from having one cohesive and universal constitution.

The development of the French Ursulines shows the creativity of the group in claiming and retaining their authority, at least for a short period. In every area of the church, the Ursulines and the other new communities, had to learn, each in their own way, that the power of the Tridentine ecclesiastical institution was completely hostile to a public active apostolate for women. Angela Merici had demonstrated the brilliance of her vision by being able to claim the one space that was available to women in the public domain. She was one of the very first to be able to discern the church's need for specialised personnel to perform the practical tasks that would provide a support structure to the life of faith.[7] A generation before Trent, this woman of vision had a plan for the renewal of the church that was effective, all-inclusive and far-reaching in its ministerial goals. The ongoing misogynistic clerical attitudes completely blinded them, not only to the suffering of women and children, but also to the abilities of women to provide solutions. This institutional and canonical blindness postponed any real pastoral innovations for another three hundred years.

Nevertheless, the next generation of Ursulines in France, even though they never met Angela Merici, demonstrated that the same creativity and brilliance was apparently endemic in the group. At the same time, the Ursulines were just one group among many in the throngs of women teachers spreading across Europe in the early seventeenth century. The church and many of the ruling classes were terrified of these mobile, active and, in their own words, apostolic women. Some bishops forbade women to use the word apostolic to describe their activities, since this was a man's word to describe only the work of men. The intentional model of apostolic preaching adopted by the French Ursulines was, despite their great discretion, only calculated to inflame this fear. Nevertheless, for about thirty years the French Ursulines taught with vigour, intelligence and universally positive results throughout the whole of French territory.

The scene is set for us in 1616 when Mother Perette de Bermond, a charismatic and brilliant teacher, was sent by the

Ursulines of Lyons to establish a congregation at Moulins. The scene is described by the Ursuline historian:

> The Ursulines 'began to sing Vespers in the choir, to teach Christian doctrine, and to perform all the functions of Ursulines with so much profit and ardour that everyone flocked to the chapel on feast days and Sundays to hear the catechism that Mere Perette de Bermond gave there. The most respected people of the town were always among the first to arrive, and with such a crowd that it was necessary to turn some away; and seats were taken as at a sermon. This lasted until the year 1623, when the male superiors (with good reason, for this was an unusual thing) forbade the sisters to teach any longer in the church'.[8]

This public teaching, obviously seen by the people as the equivalent of preaching sermons, lasted for seven years. Then Mere Bermond and her companions were silenced. The unusual sight of women publicly proclaiming the Word of God in a church setting was recognised by all as a most unusual occurrence. The Ursulines themselves skirted the obvious difficulties as long as they could, referring to their work, as 'women's work' and 'domestic activities', but there is no doubt that they were claiming apostolic authority to preach the good news.

The French Ursulines had been founded by Françoise de Bermond in 1592, with twenty-four young women in a convent in Avignon, and then spread rapidly through the south of France. They were supported by a group of men engaged in similar work, called the Fathers of Christian Doctrine. In 1594, they received permission from Pope Clement VIII to teach young girls. Their reputation was greatly enhanced by the fact that, after the Edict of Nantes in 1598, Henry IV ordered the Huguenot aristocracy to send their daughters to be educated by the Ursulines, in the hope that thus they would return to Catholicism. Students flocked to the convents and there was no denying the excellence of their teaching, but many parents were shocked by the unusual freedom of the Ursuline lifestyle. These religious had abandoned the usual monastic practices of enclosed nuns with solemn vows, in order to leave themselves freer for their apostolate. Families who had used the convent as a repository for unmarriageable daughters – as Galileo had done – preferred to have their daughters in a setting where no one could change their minds. With the Ursulines – and other similar groups – the sisters always had access to their dowry, and with Angela Merici's emphasis on free and voluntary commitment, the freedom of these women seemed all too tempting. Family inheritance plans could be vastly disrupted by the return of unwanted daughters. Besides, the uncloistered life of the Ursuline sisters, led people to think that they were a group of repentant prostitutes.

The Ursulines, then, had to tread carefully, but their zeal for the spread of the gospel seemed to conquer all other fears. Wherever they could assemble a crowd they taught, whether it was in a church, a barn, or even a poultry yard. Their goal was not just to teach young girls but also to reform whole communities, and even the clergy themselves. The Ursulines were known as brilliant teachers who scaled their lessons to the age and experience of those they taught. On the other hand, in its thirst for orthodoxy, the church taught, following Trent, that the catechism should be taught literally word for word, without any explanation or departure from the text. The sisters not only entered into explanations, but even adapted their words to the idiom and dialect of the local community. There is no doubt that they were encountering village after village and town after town full of people who had literally been abandoned by the clergy, many of whom were still non-resident in their parishes. In Dijon, Anne de Vefure visited a monastery to reform the monks and teach them how to pray, and tried to urge the priests to teach the catechism. When the clergy retorted that they did not know how to do this, 'she freely and modestly showed them the method'.[9] The Ursuline writers record that their task was made all the more difficult because the clergy were so ignorant. They report 'the majority of those who approach these devout girls did not know the obligations of a Christian, nor even the commandments of God'. They were well aware that they were engaged in the primary evangelisation of town and country as if Christianity had never been known.

The transformation of the ignorant into the devout was plain to see. This is perhaps why the church tolerated this public activity for some time. By mid-century, as the clerical church began to pick up the pieces, the Ursulines and other teaching sisters were forced back into cloister to live under solemn vows, and the public teaching mission of the sisters was closed down. For the Ursulines, the practice of cloister was first enforced in Paris, and then gradually spread throughout France. There is no doubt that some of the sisters welcomed cloister, as it was presented to them as a 'more perfect state of life', but others resisted for as long as they could. This was, after all, not the vocation they had answered. Even within the cloister, some of the sisters continued to teach at the convent grille. In Paris, Sister Claude Anne taught the catechism to young girls in front of an audience which often included the future King Louis XIII and the papal nuncio, the future Pope Urban VIII.

Surviving documents of the Ursuline community show clearly that the sisters were well aware of the similarity of their work to male preaching. In fact they intentionally called up this image to add authority to their task of preaching the gospel. To their mind, there was little difference between what the Jesuits were doing and what they were doing. Mother Pommereu explained that the sisters, in their work, 'were associated with prelates, pastors and all others who act as spiritual guides'. The sisters brought their students to Christ and so were 'ministers of his blood and of his word'. Some of the listeners said that the words of the sisters touched them 'more than sermons'. Some of the sisters reminded their listeners of the 'preaching of Saint Paul'.[10]

In fact, the call to preaching was the motivation behind the vocation of many Ursulines. They felt themselves to be called to live the life of the apostles. One such was Marie de l'Incarnation, the great Canadian missionary, as we shall see in the next chapter, even though her biographer and son tried to diminish her calling. Antoinette Micolon began practising her preaching vocation when she saw her father taking interest on a loan. She felt herself forced to preach to him. As an Ursuline, she is reported to have assembled about sixty women in a large poultry yard, where she preached to them after Mass. 'And in order to be better heard, she raised herself above them, and standing on a chair, she spoke to them in the local dialect. ... It seemed that God put the words into her mouth, so appropriate and effective were they for the salvation of these poor peasant women'.[11] The rule of the French Ursulines eventually ordered them not to preach, thus depriving them of this very effective leadership, and depriving the church of such obvious gifts. The Ursulines knew they were treading on dangerous ground, but their literature is full of the image of preaching. All this activity was ended by the imposition of cloister, confining many of the sisters to a vocation and a life which they had not chosen. Some, as we shall see, brought their skill at teaching and preaching much further afield to the Canadian mission.

Angela Merici had inspired women to move beyond the traditional boundaries within which religious women had been confined. She changed the terms of the debate and had a vision which, when freely exercised, was seen to be of enormous benefit to the church. The women moved into a space that had been left vacant by ignorant and non-resident clergy. The Council of Trent set out to solve the problem of the clergy, but had no vision whatever of a public role for women. Even when the women showed clearly what they were capable of doing, they simply inspired fear and a desire for control in the church leadership. In future church legislation, the distinction between public preaching and private instruction was clearly made. The former was seen as the work of ordained men only; the latter was all that was allowed to women.

Eventually the whole of the Ursuline community was cloistered and confined to a ministry which was allowed to take place only within the bounds of the convent. Nevertheless, their ability to blur the distinction between teaching and preaching allowed them to expand their ministry, even within the confines of cloister. The challenge to such church confinement did not die down, however, as several other women felt themselves called to a public ministry in the church. Such a one was Mary Ward. What never fails to astonish about the life of Mary Ward is her courageous integrity in the face of intrigue, hostility and deliberate obfuscation on the part of church authorities and ecclesiastical enemies. She was one of very few women to make the trip to Rome in order to meet the pope personally and argue her case face to face. All who met her were impressed with her profound sincerity and evident holiness. She seems to have arrived in Rome like a whirlwind intending to blow all opposition from her way. What Mary failed to realise, however, was that the Roman mills of decision-making grind very slowly, and that the various elements of that huge bureaucracy seemed to work intentionally to foil each other's efforts. Mary Ward placed her trust absolutely in the pope himself, but in the end, the decision was not his to make. It was this aspect of Roman business that Mary never quite understood.[12]

Mary Ward was born in 1585 in Yorkshire in an England that was undergoing a renaissance in its political life, but that was becoming increasingly dangerous for its Catholic population. One year later, in 1586, Margaret Clitheroe was crushed to death in York for the treasonous crime of harbouring priests. The Yorkshire prisons were filled with people whose only crime was the possession of a rosary. The Bull of excommunication published by Pius V in 1570 against the 'bastard queen', Elizabeth I, sealed the fate of English Catholics. In 1580, the Jesuit mission to England had begun with the arrival of Robert Parsons and Edmund Campion, further raising the fear that Romish plots were afoot. In 1581, parliament retaliated with the Act of Persuasion, condemning anyone who was reconciled to Catholicism, while in 1585, another act targeted the Jesuits and all secular priests specifically as traitors. When, in November 1605, the Gunpowder Plot was discovered, anti-Catholic hysteria swept through England, understandably, and resulted in over-

flowing prisons, and over two hundred executions in the next
several years.[13] It was against this background that the young
Mary Ward conceived her vocation of working for the conversion of England, specifically by undertaking the Christian education of young women.

Mary's own childhood had been relatively carefree, though
she had been shifted from house to house in the interests of safety.
The Catholic landed gentry of Yorkshire constituted her environment and she grew up in houses where priests were illegally
sheltered, Mass was celebrated in ever-present fear of discovery
and betrayal, and contacts were constantly maintained with continental Catholics through various cloak-and-dagger arrangements. Almost all of the participants in the Gunpowder Plot
were relatives of Mary Ward's family, and her grandmother,
with whom she had spent part of her childhood, had spent fourteen years in jail for her faith. It is no surprise, then, that Mary
Ward's whole life is marked by fearlessness and a driving sense
of vocation that refused to countenance any of the obstacles in
her path. When she had been formed in a faith atmosphere that
accepted martyrdom as a distinct possibility, the opposition of
hostile clergy to her life plans seemed almost irrelevant.

In her early teens Mary's vocation made itself felt, and despite some family opposition, she persisted. Following such a
vocation entailed exile from her home and country and so, in
1606, Mary became a novice in the Community of Poor Clares in
St Omer, then in the Spanish Netherlands. This was not a happy
choice and after some hesitation and much bad advice, Mary returned to England and settled in London in 1609 at the age of
twenty-four. Here, through her prayer, she received the direction she sought, and her followers count these years as the
beginning of the Institute that was to be at the centre of Mary's
energies till her death. Her earliest companions all had familial
connections, and before long these accompanied Mary back to St
Omer where she opened her first house to work specifically
among the English migrants and their children. Success attended
this first establishment, and both postulants and students

flocked to St Omer from England. Within a few years, the familiar ecclesiastical resistance to such public apostolic efforts by
women began to make itself felt: the women should be enclosed,
they had no canonical status, there was no appropriate rule and
they wore no distinguishing habit. These complaints were to be
repeated endlessly, and with increasing ferocity throughout Mary
Ward's life.

In 1611, Mary received the insight that was to be her guiding
light and helped her to give a definitive shape to her new
Institute, now universally known as the English Ladies. Mary
became convinced that God wanted her group to take on the
character, intention and work of the Jesuit community. What the
Jesuits did for young men, the English Ladies would do for
young women. Since the Jesuits had received papal approval,
Mary saw no reason why her Institute could not receive similar
papal approbation. Little did she know then how much suffering and distress this was to bring to herself and her followers,
not just during her lifetime, but also for hundreds of years following. Had she known, however, anyone who comes to know
her life would have no doubt that Mary would have proceeded
with what she was convinced was God's plan for her. From this
time forward, Mary was harried by constant illness, and by the
hostility of those who resisted any attempt by women to assume
the vocation of 'Jesuitesses'. Mary's plans were quite specific –
what the Jesuits did, she and her companions would do. The
monastic elements of religious life would be reduced to facilitate
their public works of teaching, caring for prisoners, attending to
the sick and dying, all in an atmosphere of profound spiritual
freedom. It was not long before the first of many trivialising
names came to be attached to them – the 'galloping girls'. The
English ambassador to the Netherlands added his own version,
describing them as 'brain-sick English gentlewomen'.[14]

Over the next several years, Mary travelled widely founding
new houses in Liege (1616), Cologne (1620) and Trier (1621).
This travel took place against the backdrop of the Thirty Years'
War, and increasing financial worries, to the extent that some of

her sisters were dying from malnourishment. In 1621, Mary made the significant decision to go to Rome to gain approval for her work, and until her death, this was the main focus of all her efforts. Meanwhile her companions carried on the works of the Institute, often with brilliant success. As the community grew, the Jesuits began to distance themselves from Mary's project, stating that they were being made to look ridiculous by the novel claims of these women. Henceforth Mary was mired in a confusing web of personal admiration for her own integrity and holiness and institutional resistance to her projects. The two-month, 2000-mile, 30 miles a day walk to Rome was a hair-raising enterprise, but Mary and her companions arrived on Christmas Eve, 1621 and they had their first meeting with Pope Gregory XV on the day after Christmas.

Both the Pope and the Superior General of the Jesuits were favourably impressed by Mary and her group, but the opponents of her cause had arrived as well and the familiar complaints were now being aired. They included the following: the English Ladies called themselves religious but did not accept enclosure; they engaged in preaching against St Paul's specific commandment; since they were women, they were more prone to heresy; they were 'gadabouts', wandering to and fro across Europe; they had too many important friends working on their behalf; and they were a scandal and a disgrace to the Roman Church. Mary's response, whether from naïveté or integrity, was that they were only doing what the Jesuits did, so wherein lay the problem? It is remarkable that Mary, and many other women founders of the seventeenth century, simply refused to accept the cultural restrictions on a woman's life and work. It was precisely these restrictions, however, that ultimately brought about the suppression of the Institute.

Five years later, Mary was still in Rome, as the work of approving her Institute wound its tortuously slow way through the Congregation of Bishops and Regulars. In order to demonstrate the nature of their work to the Romans, Mary founded schools in Rome, Naples and Perugia, the last two attaining some real success. Meantime in Rome, Mary and her sisters struggled along on the edge of hunger and destitution, though Naples and Perugia were able to provide some relief. The poverty of these women is astonishing and it is likely that the illnesses that continually plagued Mary were seriously aggravated by lack of proper nourishment. Several of the Roman community had died simply from hunger. The new pope, Urban VIII (1623-1644), the one time friend and eventual judge of Galileo, consented to see Mary on 16 October 1624. Mary had presented several versions of her plan for her Institute, but now she simply asked the pope to 'approve on earth what had already been confirmed in heaven'.[15] Whereas such a request might have gained a favourable ear from a medieval pope, the seventeenth century pope simply assigned the task to the appropriate congregation of cardinals. There was, by now, much Roman opposition to the Institute, despite the practically unanimous favourable reports about their work. Powerful Roman groups, as well as the English secular clergy, saw that they could reduce Jesuit influence by delaying approval for Mary Ward's Jesuitesses. It was clear that the constant hostile reactions to the group were having its effect on the Jesuits, even as many, though not all, Jesuits worked hard to distance themselves. In 1624, Propaganda Fide voted to suppress the Institute, but the decree was not enforced. The following year, the Congregation of Bishops, after dozens of long-drawn out sessions, added their condemnation. The English Ladies were to disband and close all their schools. Again, this was not communicated to Mary Ward, and not enforced.

In the midst of the consequent confusion, Mary Ward set off for Munich and Liege in search of food and support, despite the fact that the houses in Rome and Perugia had been suppressed. The house in Naples survived by adopting tactics similar to the blurring tactics of the Ursulines. Amazingly, Mary went on to found new houses in Vienna and Pressburg and even journeyed to Prague to open a house there. The tide had turned, however, and despite Mary's astonishing and persistent efforts, and her success in garnering imperial and local episcopal support, the wheels in Rome were grinding towards suppression. In May 1629, Mary had another quasi-successful audience with the pope, and it was the papal lack of clarity in this instance, combined with Mary's unhesitating trust in papal support, that led to the final denouement.

From early in 1628, several decrees of suppression were communicated to the various houses of the Institute. None was communicated directly to Mary who was on the road again, awaiting word directly from the pope. The resulting confusion meant that Mary was continuing to write letters of direction to houses that had already received decrees of suppression. The criss-crossing of contradictory communication did Mary's cause little good, with one Cardinal speaking of the 'ever-mounting shamelessness of the Superior of the Jesuitesses'. When the final Bull of Suppression came, it seemed that only Mary was surprised. On 13 January, 1631, the Bull, *Pastoralis Romani Pontificis* decreed the total suppression of Mary Ward's Institute. The most bizarre accusations were uttered publicly, but none directly to Mary, and much of it was totally unknown by her. Hence, she was unable to respond to her accusers. All acknowledged the blameless lives of the English Ladies, even to the extent of calling them the 'mothers of the society of Jesus'. In the end, however, it was the perception of Mary's disobedience as she awaited word directly from the pope that worked most against her. Starting with St Omer in May 1630, the houses were closed one by one. On February 17, 1631, Mary Ward was arrested in Munich by order of the Inquisition and imprisoned with one companion in the dungeons of the local convent of Poor Clares. The decree had read: 'Take Mary Ward as a heretic, schismatic, and rebel to the Holy Church.' The arrest was conducted without a trial and the intention was to transport Mary (who was yet again ill and bedridden) to prison under cover of darkness. Mary, however, insisted on being taken in broad daylight, but was not allowed to say goodbye to her sisters. This 'monstrous heretic' was to be double-barred in prison, to be held incommunicado and to be guarded day and night. The Poor Clare sisters were said to be astonished when the monstrous heretic turned out to be a small, cheerful and humble woman. They did not implement the more horrific aspects of the inquisitional sentence and grew in respect for her during the two months of her imprisonment.

Mary's prison activities are a source of continuing astonishment at the courage and persistence of this intrepid woman. Mary's food, while in prison, was supplied by her sisters, and the wrapping of the food was used by her to carry on her communication with her Institute. The sisters now dressed as seculars, and many had taken private vows and continued to run their schools. Some left the community, saying they could not be part of an Institute founded by a heretic. Mary was kept well supplied with lemon juice and on the wrapping paper she wrote letters to her sisters while the Poor Clare nuns sang their office in the chapel. Mary seemed to blossom in prison and exhorted her companions to be merry in the face of all obstacles. On 14 April, Mary was set free and by March of the following year, she was back in Rome intent on getting another audience with the pope, who this time personally summoned her. The charge of heresy, the most shocking charge to Mary, was dropped, and she and her companions were allowed to live together in Rome.

Mary finally saw a copy of the Bull of Suppression. It must have filled her with despair. The Institute was to be 'suppressed, extinct, uprooted and abolished'. The reasons given were that the sisters had 'carried out works by no means suiting the weakness of their sex, womanly modesty, above all, virginal purity – works which men, who are most experienced in the knowledge of Sacred Scripture and the conduct of affairs, undertake with difficulty and not without great caution'. The groups are ordered to disband, lay aside their habits, their vows are abolished, all titles and offices are declared null, and the ladies themselves are not to gather, communicate or consult with each other on any temporal or spiritual matter.[16] The harshness of these decrees pale into insignificance before the fact that some of Mary's adversaries wanted her to be burned at the stake in Rome in the Campo dei Fiori where Giordano Bruno had been burned as a heretic thirty years earlier. Had Mary been in Rome, this is the fate that might also have been hers.

A house was procured for Mary and twenty-three of her followers in Rome, where they seem to have enjoyed the pope's favour. We know little of Mary's activities over the next five years – a prudent silence seems to have fallen over her activities. With the Bull of Suppression posted in all the main churches in the city, this seemed the wisest move, especially since there were many still trying to entrap her into making a false move. In Mary's letters at this time, code words are used to designate the pope and those around him and the very effective word 'silk' is used for money, something that again they were sorely lacking. English pilgrims to Rome flocked to the house, adding to the ire of the opposition. Mary became so ill that she was anointed, but to everyone's surprise she decided to go to Spa to seek a cure. With the pope's permission, she set out on the last of her major journeys, visiting friends and supporters along the way in Siena, Florence, Bologna, Milan, Vercelli and Turin, finally arriving in Paris in May 1638. This seriously ill woman had crossed the Alps in mid-winter and four of her party had died en route. Mary used the remainder of the trip to visit all her houses along the way, stopping in Paris, Spa, Liege, Cologne, Stavelot, Bonn, Antwerp and St Omer. It is said that Mary wept on leaving St Omer, only the second time that she was ever seen to weep. In May 1639, Mary arrived back in England and her journey was about to complete its circle.

A house was set up in London which quickly became a Catholic centre in this most dangerous of times for Catholics. Mary seemed to live a charmed life and it was not long until pupils were being despatched to her again. The Catholic rebellion in Ireland in 1641 brought on a frenzy of anti-Catholic activity in England. The London house was searched as often as four times a day. It seemed prudent to move again and this time Mary's journey took her home to Yorkshire. Mary was given a house in the country, but with the advance of Cromwell and his troops after his victory at Selby in 1644, Mary and her group moved into the city of York. On 11 July, York fell to Cromwell and Mary was allowed to return to their country house, now in a shambles after being occupied by over four hundred soldiers. A priest was smuggled in to celebrate Christmas, but it was clear by now that Mary Ward was dying. She named Barbara Babthorpe as her successor and died on 20 January 1645. Because the graves of Catholics were being vandalised by the soldiers, Mary was buried in the small Anglican church of St Thomas, with a large limestone slab placed on top to conceal her resting place. That is where the body of this incredibly persistent and holy woman lies to this day.

The life of Mary Ward shows up in stark detail the difficulty placed before intelligent and dedicated women who wished only to serve the church in the period after the Council of Trent. The situation was made even more confusing by Mary's well-intentioned but perhaps misplaced trust in the church leadership. No proof of heresy was ever offered to justify the judgement of the inquisition against her. Nothing ever motivated her beyond her longing to educate and catechise young women to take their place as good Christian mothers. For this purpose, her heart was set on having her Institute grow and flourish, and for this she needed ecclesiastical approval. The church of the time, however, had no use for dedication such as hers, and the prevailing emphasis on an all-male and all-priestly work force made Mary's vocation not only unnecessary, but positively offensive to most of the clergy. There were parameters within which a woman could serve God, but these were designed to remove women from the public scene in a cloister not only of body but also of mind and spirit. Mary Ward dedicated her whole life to the breaching of this boundary wall, and her efforts seemed to end in failure. Nevertheless, there are over four thousand women working in the church today, who claim Mary Ward as their founder. Even though the Bull of Suppression destroyed the First Institute, her followers maintained the essentials of Mary's vision. The rules of the Second Institute were approved by Pope Clement XI in 1703. In the kind of obfuscating move that seemed to bedevil the efforts of Mary Ward, Pope Benedict XV both approved the election of a Superior General and, at the same time, restored the Bull of 1631. In 1877, Pius IX finally granted approbation, but it was not until the beginning of the twentieth century that the members of the Institute were allowed to name Mary Ward as their founder. Now the English Ladies, as they continue to be called in Europe, and the Loreto sisters as they are known in North America can rejoice in their lives in an institute still brimming with the spirit and wisdom of Mary Ward. The spirituality of Mary Ward demonstrates, along with her inspiring life, the far-reaching insight of this woman 'with a mania for liberty' as one of her opponents described her.[17]

Angela Merici and Mary Ward were inspired by similar visions of the kind of apostolate that women could exercise in the church. In their separate ways and spheres, they were able to provide an example that would inspire thousands of women to follow the same path. The conviction of both of these women and their followers about the integrity and necessity of their God-given call was carried through with a single-minded and amazing zeal. In many ways, they were alone with their vision and had to use every spiritual and personal gift at their disposal to carry it through. The two other women to be studied, all too briefly, in this chapter, were partnered by like-minded clerics whose skills and vision interacted with their own to bring into being two distinctively different bodies of women. These partners were Jane de Chantal and Francis de Sales and Louise de Marillac and Vincent de Paul.

When one enters the world of Jane de Chantal and Francis de Sales, one is conscious of a complete change of mood. The power and curial connivings of Rome seem far removed, and there no longer seems to be the need for the long, lonely and turbulent battle of a Mary Ward. We now enter a scene rooted in mutual friendship, where the search for an authentic human and Christian existence, capable of being lived out wherever one finds oneself, is the hallmark of holiness. The friendship of Jane and Francis is the source of their spirituality, and though Francis had a formative influence on Jane's early life, their growing adult friendship became the mutually enriching centre of their lives.[18]

Jane Frances Fremyot, born in 1567, was the second child of a lawyer in Dijon. While she was still an infant, her mother died at the birth of her brother. Her father and an aunt raised them and both were given a solid and practical education, including knowledge of financial and legal affairs, which was to serve Jane well in later life. At the age of twenty, Jane married the Baron de Chantal and lived happily until his sudden death as the result of a freak accident. Jane, devastated with grief, was left to rear the surviving four of her six children, at the age of twenty-eight. Nine years later, just when her grief had turned into a deepening hunger for God, she and Francis de Sales met in 1604. Jane was now living with her father-in-law, and Francis was a young bishop whose reputation for church renewal and personal holiness was spreading across Europe. There was an immediate mutual attraction and Francis became her spiritual director.

Francis de Sales was the gifted first-born son of an aristocratic Savoyard family. He was educated by the Jesuits and, from an early age, had struggled with anxieties about his personal salvation, in a manner familiar from the lives of Ignatius of Loyola and Martin Luther. The resolution of the dilemma arrived at by Francis de Sales led him to undertake a spiritual journey significantly different from his predecessors. Francis decided that, whatever about his ultimate salvation, he could love God here and now, wherever he found himself, and that this option was open to everyone. He rejoiced in his radical human dependence on God, and realised that he was free to love and to enjoy the full human potential of each moment. As his studies continued at Padua and, with the help of a Jesuit spiritual director, Francis came to realise that the sufferings of Christ did not signify condemnation for humans, but an expression of love. His life thereafter was governed by the insight that God loves us and we are free to respond, and are responsible for acting on this love. A new note also appears in Francis' study of philosophy. He was haunted by the idea of beauty as one of the main instigators of the search for God. For him, the contemplation of goodness and beauty led inevitably to the contemplation of God.

With his father's initial disapproval and his mother's approval, Francis became a priest, despite the absence of a Tridentine seminary training. Francis was offered the post of provost of the Church of St Peter in Geneva, and assistant to the bishop who lived fifty miles to the south in Annecy. His aim was to bring Geneva, the home of Calvinism, back to the Catholic fold, but to do this by love and in a spirit of Christian peace. By 1602, Francis was Bishop of Geneva, and had launched his campaign of love, which was intended to form a community of the devout in Geneva. He was determined to inaugurate the Tridentine reforms, especially with regard to the education of the clergy and their moral reform. Spiritual direction constituted a central part of his programme, so it was not unusual that when they met during a Lenten series of sermons in Dijon, Jane would become one of the many who sought spiritual guidance from Francis.

Jane had been experiencing a call to live a more intense spiritual life, and the obvious solution seemed to be the religious life. This, of course, was impossible for Jane with her family responsibilities as parent and supervisor of both her father and father-in-law's properties. For six years the two friends grew in their understanding of each other, and eventually, in 1610, the Visitation was founded in Annecy. This was to be a community of women who wanted religious commitment, but who were unable or not desirous of joining an established monastic community. The Visitation offered such family-bound women a place where they could become 'daughters of prayer' in the context of a simplified monastic routine, but yet return to their families when their responsibilities necessitated this.[19] It was to be a community of love, gentleness, graciousness and tender concern for the poor and sick of the locality, who were visited and tended by the women. The Visitation also welcomed widows and offered a space for groups of women to stay for periods of retreat and reflection. The two friends had created a novel institution, which definitely suited the needs of Jane and her friends. Jane's youngest daughter stayed with her in the convent, and Jane herself moved in and out, arranging marriages for her other children and caring for her properties.

As the community grew, Jane became the superior, and together with Francis de Sales, was seen as a spiritual leader of the area, assuming her own role as spiritual director. Both carried on a huge correspondence which illustrates well the lineaments of a new Salesian spirituality, built on the insights and special gifts of both. Jane had extraordinary administrative skills, and was often impatient in her eagerness to see their plans adopted. Francis was less decisive, but devoted himself to his writing. Between 1608 and 1616, he laboured at his huge *Treatise on the Love of God*, a voluminous synthesis of the whole Christian past, and intended for wide circulation among all the faithful. Francis was also involved in public theological disputations, and kept up a busy schedule of diocesan visitation, spiritual direction, preaching, and frequent conferences for the sisters of the Visitation. It was inevitable that the success of the Visitation at Annecy would lead to requests for its expansion, and when the next convent was established in Lyons, the usual clamour about women moving freely in public inevitably arose. The Archbishop of Lyons was a strict enforcer of the decrees of the Council of Trent and practised the usual French rigidity with regard to Canon Law. As far as he was concerned, there was only one kind of religious life for women, and that was the official Tridentine version of a cloister, filled with women under solemn vow.

A lengthy correspondence took place between Francis, Bishop of Geneva, and Archbishop de Marquemont of Lyons. Francis explained his ideal for the Visitation – a group of women who had limited choice because of their family responsibilities. They would lead a mixed life, follow a simple monastic routine of prayer and community, and act on the responsibility of their life of love in visiting the sick, poor and indigent in the locality. Their vows would be simple, as was their dress, demeanour,

food and asceticism. Their feet would be shod but their hearts
bare. They would lead a perfect life of prayer and good works
following the example of the strong women of the gospels.[20]
Why should women who had family responsibilities or who did
not feel called to a strict monastic life be deprived of the opportunity of religious life? The archbishop wanted nothing but a
cloistered religious community, with solemn vows, which would
be called the Presentation and they would keep their good
works inside the convent. Francis replied with an abundance of
proof from the scriptures and tradition about the dignity of all
women:

> Woman ... no less than man, enjoys the favour of having
> been made in the image of God; the honour is done equally to
> both the sexes; their virtues are equal; to each of them is of-
> fered an equal reward, and, if they sin, a similar damnation. I
> would not want woman to say: I am frail, my condition is
> weak. This weakness is of the flesh, but virtue, which is
> strong and powerful, is seated in the soul.[21]

Francis went on to outline the history of women as widows and
virgins, and the capacity of all women to lead a life of perfection.
He pointed out that strict cloister was a relatively new phenomenon and its imposition deprived many women of following a
religious vocation. Besides, added Francis, the life of perfection
is interior, not exterior. All the cloister in the world will not
create the interior spirit, if it is not present. The archbishop's
reply was a foregone conclusion. These women are not true religious, they cannot be called nuns, and great scandal will be
caused. Besides the other monastic orders will start complaining
since we have imposed cloister on them. The Protestants will say
that we are bypassing Trent for our own convenience. He went
on to insist that the whole purpose of the Council was to prevent
novelties.[22]

The archbishop was not alone in his opposition, and the attitude of the parents of Lyons illustrates well the contemporary
attitudes towards women. When women were cloistered and
took solemn vows, they were legally considered to be non-persons,

having undergone a civil death. They could not return to their families and contract marriages. Parents who, for whatever reason, had daughters in convents did not want them coming back to cause legal wrangles and inheritance conundrums. The families of Lyons were wholly on the side of their archbishop in this debate. Francis responded: 'Ah, it is all about the dowries', but this dawning insight could not postpone the inevitable. The Visitation, allowed to keep its name, was transformed into a religious community with solemn vows and full enclosure. All visitation and travelling abroad had to cease, but they could still accept some older women and give retreats to laywomen. The daughters of the minor nobility of Lyons were not going to be allowed to intrude on family wealth, once they had been deposited in a convent. The archbishop knew the spirit of his people. Not many were willing to follow Francis de Sales on the path to freedom for all. It is interesting that, despite the reputation of Jane de Chantal, her voice is not heard in this debate. It was solved without appeal to Rome, but against the wishes of the cofounders. Vincent de Paul is reported to have said that the cloistering of the Visitation was a distortion of the original vision.[23]

This was then not just a spiritual debate about the role of women in the church, but a debate that spread across social, political and legal areas. No change in the position of women was envisaged in France or the rest of Europe at this time, despite all the insights of humanism and the Renaissance. The old phrase *aut maritus aut murus* was invoked again with regard to women – they were to be under the control of a husband or else cloistered. No other option was available. Even the holiness of Jane and Francis failed to change the terms of the debate, just as the exemplary lives of Angela Merici and Mary Ward and their followers were seen to be irrelevant to the centuries-long postponement of their dreams.

Nevertheless, when Pope Pius V gave approbation to the revised Visitation, it became an immediate success. By the end of the century, there were one hundred and fifty convents with over six thousand nuns. Francis did not live to see all of this. He died in Lyons in 1622 at the age of fifty-five. In 1616, the two friends had met and decided to 'let each other go' so that henceforth they would rely on God alone. They met again shortly before the death of Francis. Jane became the General Superior of the growing community.[24] In 1624, all the leaders of the community met to establish general regulations for the conduct of the group. Jane's letters of direction continue to inculcate the Salesian spirit of gentleness, tolerance and love. She offered a vision of great spiritual freedom and advised the local superiors of the communities to allow the members to grow in freedom and attain their own wisdom. Both Jane and Francis advocated a spacious liberty for all, and continually taught that God never invades human freedom. Jane was equally free in her advice about prayer: 'The great method of prayer is to have no method.' She advocated freedom of spirit here too, and urged her daughters to 'become pure capacity'.[25] This is not the place for a complete examination of the spirituality of Jane de Chantal; there will be a later chapter on women's spirituality.[26] Jane died in 1641, after one more joust with ecclesiastical authorities, this time conducted on her own. A system of convent visitations was to be established in order to supervise the internal dynamics of convent life. Jane resisted this mightily in order to preserve the integrity of the sisters' way of life. When she died she left eighty flourishing houses, which would continue to expand to all parts of the world.

Two other co-founders who were roughly contemporary with Jane de Chantal and Francis de Sales presented the church with a vision of a new kind of collaboration between women and men, but because of the dire social needs to which they were responding, their lives assumed quite a different trajectory. These were Louise de Marillac and Vincent de Paul. Seventeenth-century France presented a paradoxical face to the world. On the one hand, there was the grand design for France, formulated by Henry IV, and eventually realised by his grandson, Louis XIV, in the latter half of the century. This entailed making France the dominant force in Europe, a vision that included the domination of the Catholic Church. On the other hand, France was experiencing a 'climax of misery' with thousands of the desperately poor taking to the roads as a result of bad harvests, famine, plague, war, and total political neglect. Poverty became one of the most highly visible dimensions of French society when these despairing people began to converge on cities. Distinctions were made between the 'respectable poor' who were too proud to beg and the 'vagabond poor', who were seen to trade their human dignity for food. There were no adequate institutions to cope with such a mountain of misery and as the numbers grew, the poor began to be feared. Desperate people were being driven to desperate solutions. The few city institutions which did exist to care for children, often sold the children to beggars who proceeded to break their arms and legs in order to impress almsgivers. The aristocratic and political world of France had little will to attend to any of this, and by mid-century, the poor were being criminalised. In 1656, a royal edict forbade begging, and most beggars were expelled from Paris. The following year a huge round-up of the remaining poor took place, alms were forbidden, and thousands of non-working poor were incarcerated. It was the design of the State to punish poverty and make it invisible. One man, formerly a swineherd, now an ordained cleric, worked to change attitudes towards poverty forever. This was Vincent de Paul who preached to all and sundry that 'the poor are our masters' and that 'Christ is the poor'. Almost accidentally, Vincent met his most able cohort in this work, Louise de Marillac, whom Vincent always addressed by her married name, Mme. Le Gras.[27]

Vincent de Paul was born in Gascony in 1581, the third of six children in a hard-working peasant family. His early goal was clerical ordination as the most appropriate avenue to a rich benefice, which would enable him to contribute towards his family's welfare. He was ordained in September 1600 to what he considered to be a priestly career. From 1605-1607, Vincent mysteriously disappeared and no satisfactory explanation of his whereabouts has ever been discovered. In Paris, in 1608, he met

Pierre de Berulle, now the inspiration behind a huge renewal movement, and Berulle became his spiritual director. After a very rewarding experience in a poor parish, Vincent became chaplain and almoner to the Gondi family, and it was in this post that the event occurred that changed his life. A peasant on the estate asked Vincent to hear his confession, and this introduced him to a world to which he had been totally blind till then. He came to realise that there was a vast world of poor people, who besides their poverty were totally ignorant of the Christian faith. He encouraged some of his priest friends to conduct a mission, which was resoundingly successful, not only in the results in the lives of the peasants, but in the total change in the lives of the priests. Henceforth Vincent committed himself to a renewed priesthood, focused on the lives of the poor. In 1625, he founded the Congregation of the Missions, to gather priests together for the conversion of the countryside.

The good aristocratic Catholics were shocked to find such massive ignorance of the faith among the poor, and through preaching and hundreds of pamphlets, Vincent planned to keep on shocking them. 'If you have not fed the poor, you have killed them', he wrote. They were told that they were responsible for these abandoned people, and that they would be called to account for their neglect. His goal was the formation of a renewed social fabric, and he did not hesitate to use guilt as a motivator, and to promise future social benefits as a reward.[28]

An avalanche of projects followed. Earlier, Vincent had been appointed chaplain to the prisoners condemned to the galleys; now he founded orphanages, hospitals, asylums, workshops, training schools for servants, teacher-training institutes, legal aid for the galley prisoners, and even depots for the collection of goods, from food to furniture, for distribution to the poor. As the work progressed, Vincent noticed one outstanding fact – most of those who responded to his pleas for assistance were women. Charities were established where women co-ordinated this work and Vincent found the women much more accomplished at administration and economics than men. The women simply got on with the work, while the men fought for leadership. 'Men and women do not get along at all in matters of administration; the former want to take it over entirely, and the latter wont allow it. ... We had to get rid of the men. And I can bear this witness in favour of the women, that there is no fault to find in their administration, so careful and accurate are they.'[29] Eventually, wherever a mission was preached, a Charity was organised on a legal basis, with officers to co-ordinate fund-raising and distribution. Women from different ranks worked together and even organised a census of the poor in each area. When a Charity was founded in Paris in 1629, however, Vincent knew that the city ladies would not be willing to share the menial tasks. A young peasant woman, Marguerite Naseau met Vincent and offered to organise a group of peasant women who would be willing to do the work the ladies wished to avoid. Vincent said afterwards that Marguerite was the beginning of the Daughters of Charity. Since these were country girls, unaccustomed to city life, he knew that a training period would be necessary, and he asked Mme. Le Gras to undertake this in her home. So in the Daughters of Charity, the members and the founder appeared in reverse order.

Louise de Marillac was born in 1591 of an illustrious family. She was educated at the royal monastery of Poissy near Paris, where her aunt was a Dominican nun. Though always desirous of being a nun, Louise married Antoine Le Gras, who was personal secretary to Marie de Medici. It was a happy marriage, especially when Michel was born in 1613. On Pentecost Sunday, 1623, Louise felt assured by God that her desire to dedicate herself would eventually be fulfilled. In 1625, Antoine died. Sometime previously Louise and Vincent had met, and thus began a lasting friendship of two quite different personalities. Louise was intelligent, practical, decisive, and a brilliant organiser, but also she was scrupulous, diffident and in need of constant support in her spiritual life. Vincent moved slowly, with assurance, and his personality radiated peace. Throughout the year 1626, there are over thirty letters from Vincent to his new friend, where he urges her to moderate her anxieties and to live in peace and joy. In 1632, after a retreat, Louise began to realise her gifts and became more sure of herself. Thereafter, she assumed much greater responsibility in the various Vincentian projects and, in a short time, became the fulltime collaborator of Vincent. She assumed her old name, Louise de Marillac, and let go of the rigidity that had governed her spiritual life till then. In November 1633, the Congregation of the Daughters of Charity was founded. During the lifetime of Louise and Vincent, the Daughters numbered no more than two hundred, but the amount of work accomplished is astonishing. The ladies continued to provide the funding and the organising skills; the Daughters took to the streets, visiting homes, hospitals and prisons. Louise was brilliant at formation, and the Daughters were soon being asked to take over the hospitals where previously they had been just visitors.

The rule written for these first hospital sisters is totally comprehensive in its coverage of all aspects of nursing care – food, hygiene, dealings with doctors, care of the sick room, use of medicine, and dealings with the Ladies of Charity. The nursing and spiritual qualities needed were also outlined, and the constant exhortation was that 'in serving the poor, they were serving the Lord Jesus'.[30] The Daughters provided high quality care accompanied by deep concern and respect for each one. Other work followed in an avalanche, starting with foundlings. There had been a foundling home in Paris for over fifty years, but in all that time, not one infant had survived. By 1640, all the foundlings of Paris were the responsibility of Louise and her group, and true to her style, she created a whole new method of childcare, and initiated the first programme of foster care in France. Infant homes and trade schools followed, all designed with her extraordinary attention to detail. In 1639, a home for the galley convicts was founded and the Daughters began visiting the cells with food, and doing cleaning, washing and instructing the prisoners. Though often verbally and physically abused in this work, the Daughters never showed either fear or anger. As endless wars ravaged France, the sisters were sent to care for the sick on the battlefields, and to care for the refugees, who were again driven on to the roads of France. In one parish, the sisters were reported to be feeding about eight thousand people a day.

Care for the aged was another new venture. A hospice for twenty women and twenty men was established, elderly artisans who had been reduced to penury by the vicissitudes of life. Louise's creativity is again visible in the organisation of the hospice. The bodily and spiritual needs were obvious, but Louise insisted on pleasant surroundings, deep respect for each, and even provided occupational therapy. Local craftspeople were summoned to give workshops, and the elderly were allowed to sell the products and to keep a portion of the money in order to maintain their independence. Other sisters were sent out two by two to villages to educate country girls and to care for the village sick. Both Vincent and Louise always preferred a home-based ministry, rather than an institutional one, but the very success of the sisters resulted in the call to care for whole institutions. It was also the Daughters of Charity who, under the guidance of Louise, opened the first elementary schools in the archdiocese of Paris.

The amount of work done by this small group of sisters is astonishing, and between them, Vincent and Louise transformed the whole notion of Christian charity. Such work could not have been accomplished had it not been supported by a deep spirituality, and here again, both Vincent and Louise proved to be brilliant in the skills of spiritual formation. The study of the life of Christ and involvement in the yearly liturgical round are central to Louise's guidance, as well as a focus on the role of the Spirit in commemoration of her Pentecost experience in 1623. Almost four hundred letters of instruction survive from Louise to her first sisters and they show the movement from the personal spirituality of each sister to a 'mysticism of the group', where all would move forward together in mutual support.

It was the skill of Vincent de Paul, who was trained in Canon Law, which kept the Daughters of Charity from getting entangled in ecclesiastical battles about their status as religious. They took private vows, without witnesses, and took the form of a simple confraternity. Vincent taught them how to speak to bishops, insisting that they were poor, and because of their obviously necessary work had to be mobile. This meant that, if a bishop tried to interfere with their status, they could just leave the area. Louise, however, longed for centralisation, which would undoubtedly make leadership much simpler. When Vincent hesitated, Louise asked the Queen Mother to plead with the pope for the status of Superior General for herself. In 1655, this wish was granted. The Daughters of Charity showed no exterior sign of being religious – no bells, veils, grilles or habits. Inside the convent, however, they lived, prayed and acted as religious, and this 'holy deviousness' saved them from unnecessary episcopal interference. Louise instructed her Daughters: 'Your monastery is the house of the sick. The city streets are your cloister.'[31] Service to the poor was to take precedence over other spiritual practices and the sisters were instructed to 'leave God for God'. Gradually the nature of the community changed under the insistence of the bishops and the ladies who provided the money. The ministry of the Daughters became more institutionalised. By 1660, the Daughters ran three huge institutions in Paris alone, and throughout France bishops were crying out for their services. Eventually governments began to take over some of the services, but the Daughters persisted in their work. They join the other women of the seventeenth century who, in their zeal to live the Christian life, found themselves engaged in work that had been specifically denied to women by the Council of Trent.

The descendants of Louise and Vincent, who both died in 1660, now form a huge global family, and it is well nigh impossible to untangle all the connecting threads. Apart from the Daughters of Charity and the Vincentians, they include the community founded by Elizabeth Ann Seton (1774-1821) in the United States, their first native-born saint. We will encounter other descendants as the story of women continues, but the trail-blazing nature of the lives and work of these four women had incalculable influence on the future of Christian women in so many areas. Much of the rest of the story of Christian women will bear the marks of their influence.

CHAPTER FIVE

Women Missionaries to the New World

The modern world is deemed by many historians to have found its footing finally in the middle of the seventeenth century. It was a time of scientific and rational triumphs, and the balance was shifting from what God had revealed to what humanity was discovering. The vital issue at mid-century was the problem of authority, that is the relative authority of a series of male potent-ates successively in France, Spain, Portugal, England and Prussia. The traditional male power which lost most authority in this century was the papacy as old popes tried, mostly in vain, to compete with young and vibrant monarchs. Whenever authority became a political and religious issue, it was inevitable that the philosophical discussion of women's societal roles became a core concern, and that the results were never in favour of the ad-vancement of women. A new type of misogyny is evident every-where in the seventeenth century but, as always, the turbulence of the era gave women the opportunity to exploit the social dis-ruption to their own advantage. In the mid-seventeenth century, it was devout French women who seemed most ready to seize the opportunities offered, and the result was the unique spectacle of women missionaries setting out for the Canadian mission-field, at first in a trickle, but later in a flood. The Canadian mission was unique in this regard as none of the other far-flung mission-ary enterprises were open to the presence of women. It is, there-fore, with the Canadian mission field that we will be dealing in this chapter, but first it will be necessary to take a brief look at the state of religion in the France that was their motherland.[1]

The 1648 Peace of Westphalia signalled the demise of the political power and international prestige of institutional religion.

Nevertheless, it was also at this period that the Christian Church stretched its borders and power in unimaginable directions geographically speaking, and deepened its hold on human hearts everywhere in its domains in the practices of piety. Religious pluralism was now a reality and each religious group began, slowly but surely, to direct its attention to the religious development of its own members. Even though some key elements of the Catholic Christian tradition – revelation, scripture, the miraculous, prophecy – were being challenged by the growing authority of 'pure reason', nevertheless, the Tridentine reforms were taking root at local level. As the Protestants had earlier realised, the Catholics now saw that women were key to development at this level, as it was in the family that the faith of a lifetime was initially nourished. Thus it was that the education of women became a central preoccupation of the church, not however to broaden the social and religious roles of women, but to anchor them more truly at the centre of family life. Once again, it was the women religious who resisted this endeavour as they felt called in directions never envisaged for them by the male church leadership. From the devotional ferment of Old France came the courageous and far-seeing women missionaries of New France as it took root in the Canadian wilderness.

One of the most vigorous of the new rulers was Louis XIV of France. Cardinal Mazarin had laid well the foundations of French royal power so that when Louis XIV came of age in 1659, a new kind of absolute kingship was possible. The kind of national unity envisaged by Louis entailed complete uniformity in his domains, and to this end, penal laws were enacted against the Protestants and the Edict of Nantes was revoked. Thousands of 'dissenters' were sent to the galleys or, if lucky, were able to flee the country. The absolutism of the king created monumental problems with the papacy but, nevertheless, the reign of Louis XIV brought Catholicism new prestige throughout his dominions. The principles of the Gallican church were re-articulated in 1682 asserting the independence of the king within his own realms and upholding the right of taxation of the Gallican church. Further, the Gallican principles limited the pope's authority by asserting the superiority of general councils, thus depriving the pope of the right to define matters of faith without the consent of the church. All bishops, priests, and seminarians in France had to sign these articles and swear to uphold them.

The advent of Jansenism seemed almost inevitable in this atmosphere of political and religious extremism. Cornelius Jansen, who died in 1638, had revived some of the extremist elements of the ancient faith of Augustine of Hippo. It was an elitist faith, in its affirmation of human fallibility and inadequacy before God and the limited number of those who were capable of receiving the necessary divine grace. The whole doctrine smacked of predestination and was violently opposed to what was perceived as the weakness at the core of Jesuit teaching on the love and compassion of God. The Jesuits were accused of 'putting cushions under the elbows of sinners', and even the suggestion of a loving God led to accusations of pride and weak faith. Even though Jansenism was condemned by Pope Clement XI, its effects were ubiquitous. The whole of France and much of the rest of Europe were drawn into the debate, and the end result, as well as enormous partisan bitterness, was that most ordinary people felt even more unworthy about their participation in Catholic life than heretofore.[2] One of the eventual outcomes of the Jansenist debate, though it was not the only cause, was the suppression of the Jesuits, first by Louis XV, and then by Pope Clement XIV in 1773. The Catholic Church could not cope with too many powerful influences, and the expulsion of the Jesuits, for no really convincing reason, at least removed one power group from an increasingly complex European equation. Ironically, it was among the new non-Catholic powers of Prussia and Russia, that the Jesuits found shelter.

It was against this European backdrop of absolutist struggles and local parish piety that the missionary movement developed in the Catholic Church. The great Christian mission enterprise had begun at the end of the fifteenth century with the discovery of the 'West Indies' by Christopher Columbus in 1492 and of the real India by Vasco de Gama in 1497. This opening up of the world to east and west occasioned a momentous opening of the European mind and the vision of the creation of a world Christian empire. The discovery of the Thomas Christians in southern India compensated, to some extent, for the failure to discover the great imaginary Christian empire of the legendary Prester John. In May 1493, Pope Alexander VI drew a line on the map from north to south to the west of the Azores and allotted the west to Spain and the east to Portugal. This action indicates the remarkable mindset of Christianity, the papacy and the whole of Europe of the period. Europe owned the world, its religion was Christianity, and the pope was the appointed ruler. Such Catholic confidence was soon to be dashed, if only by the development of the naval forces of the Protestant nations.

Though the pope had claimed the world for the church, not everyone in this world was seen to be of equal value. The astonishingly rapid conquests in the Americas were not accompanied by any tinge of Christian compassion, and the old Aristotelian belief that some people were naturally designed for slavery led to the grading of humanity into categories of humanity and subhumanity. From the Catholic perspective – initially the whole missionary enterprise was Catholic – choices were made to the effect that subhuman people were not deserving of full Christian membership. This led to the founding of semi-Christian, non-eucharistic church membership for most non-Europeans, and to the banning of any kind of indigenous ministry. With the exception of the voices of Antonio de Montesinos and Bartolomeo de Las Casas, few voices were raised to dispute this arrangement. This missionary enterprise was a wholly male enterprise, indicating yet again the European belief that the functioning of the Christian church had no need of female participation.[3]

By the mid-seventeenth century the English colonies on the east coast of North America were settling. The oldest colony, Virginia, was Anglican, the Catholics were in Maryland, and New England was Puritan. By 1646, eighteen European languages were to be heard along the Hudson and most European

Christian churches had been transplanted to the New World.[4]
This was mission by colonisation and constituted, at least in
Puritan minds, a great new and holy experiment. The intention
had been to start afresh, away from the temptations and capitul-
ations of the Old World. A new democracy was to be created
where all would be equally welcomed. No democratic vision,
however, included women in its grand design, and so the restrictions of the Old World on the religious lives of women were
enacted with even greater force. The fate of Anne Hutchinson,
the 'American Jezebel', will be explored in the next chapter.
Here it is sufficient to point out how her life reveals very dramatically the extremely restrictive attitudes to women's religious
life in the Massachusetts Bay colony. Anne gathered women in
her house on Sunday afternoons to discuss the morning's sermon. Such behaviour was seen as laudatory in a minister's wife,
but when Anne began to adopt for the women the notions of
democracy and access to the Spirit of God that were seen as normal for the men of the colony, an outburst of rage by the male
leaders caused her to be excommunicated and expelled from the
colony. Anne Hutchinson was only one of a number of women
in the colony who tried to participate in the reformulation of
Puritan life and doctrine, but it was soon made plain that the
contributions of women were not only unnecessary, but also
downright dangerous.[5]

It is all the more remarkable, then, that the history of the
Catholic mission in Canada should illustrate that women were
central and essential to the story, not because of a change in male
attitudes, but because of the enormous courage and initiative of
a handful of French *dévotes*. Canada was a virtually unknown
wilderness at the beginning of the seventeenth century. In 1534,
Jacques Cartier had traversed the river systems, claiming the
country, and naming it New France. Quebec City was founded
in 1608 and on 24 June, 1615, a Roman Catholic Mass was celebrated for the first time on the island that is now part of the city
of Montreal.[6] The French set out to evangelise the three main
native tribes of Huron, Algonquin and Iroquois, against a back-

ground of constant tribal warfare. Though many male religious orders participated, the Jesuits were soon the dominant group, having arrived in Canada in 1632. By 1650 the Jesuit mission was over and the names of several Jesuit martyrs are revered throughout Canada to this day. Despite the courage and sanctity of the missionaries, the encounter with entirely different cultures was fraught with difficulties not encountered before. Besides, the aims of Britain and France, the colonising nations, often ran counter to the evangelising aims of the missionaries. In reality this encounter was only the beginning of the tragic story of the gradual disenfranchisement of the native peoples, which is part of the shameful history of North American colonisation.[7]

At the same time, a remarkable resurgence was taking place among French women, which would lead to the first large-scale participation of women in the church's missionary work. The whole enterprise seems to have started with a vision experienced by the remarkable Ursuline woman, Marie de l'Incarnation. In December 1633, in her convent at Tours, she felt called to Canada as a missionary, and two years later this was reaffirmed in a second vision that assured her she was to go and found a convent in Canada. By 1639 the plans were complete and three Ursulines, together with three nursing sisters, were ready to set out for New France. The trip was facilitated by Mme. de la Peltrie, who felt herself compelled to give her whole fortune for the furtherance of the Canadian mission, and this happy coincidence was taken as an added confirmation of the visions of Marie de l'Incarnation. There seems to have been some friction among the sisters about which rule to follow, and Marie was determined to have a unified Ursuline rule approved before departure. She was more or less successful in this and determined to resist every episcopal act of interference to the 'limits of obedience'.[8]

Marie had described her original impulse to her spiritual director as the vision of an 'afflicted place' and was so determined to respond that she said she was ready to risk a thousand lives. Little did she know the harsh regime that was ahead of her in a country that was just beginning to be known in Europe. The reports in the *Jesuit Relations* that had been arriving in France for a decade now, cannot have been other than terrifying to this first small group of women missionaries to leave Europe for the New World. Their initial aim was to convert 'those dear savages', to educate them, and eventually to attract some of them to the Ursuline community. Marie, despite being a visionary and mystic, was a very practical educator. Everything had to be invented as this first group of sisters worked solely on their own initiative, without any blueprints or role models. The sisters called winter their 'harvest time', as the various native groups left their young girls with the sisters for the duration of the harsh snows. Marie and her sisters washed, fed, nursed and taught these girls and intended, from the start, to integrate the daughters of the French colonists with the young native women. Marie learned several native languages and taught these to the daughters of New France. Marie also wrote a dictionary of Algonquian languages, a book of sacred history in Algonquian and an Iroquois catechism and book of prayers. The Huron men were as welcome as their wives and children and one of Marie's companions, Mère Joseph, was treated by these men as their mother confessor. Their work was endlessly interrupted by native warfare and Marie wrote all the details back home about several Huron women killed in the Iroquois wars.

As we shall see, it was the desire of each group of women missionaries to integrate the native children and women with the French women and children of the colony. Though the initial efforts succeeded, Marie's fears of episcopal interference proved to be well founded. As a result of pressure from the colonists, the sisters had to set aside a special place for the French girls who could pay for their education. Eventually, a succession of bishops insisted that the missionary sisters take on the customs, dress and rule of their home communities. During Marie's lifetime, some resistance was possible, but after her death, the sisters of the colony in Quebec were as enclosed and restricted as their sisters in France. It is clear from her correspondence that

Marie realised that the native girls were not suited to the type of cloister that was being required, and also that the young women of the colony needed extra protection in the wild and unruly life of the new colony.[9] When Marie died in 1667, Quebec had become a city and the Ursuline students were becoming the first ladies of New France. With these developments, the mission to the native groups was postponed for several decades. No Ursuline convents were founded at that time from Quebec, owing to the turbulence of the political scene.

Much of the information about the Ursuline mission and the founding of Quebec City is derived from the correspondence of Marie. She is said to have written about twenty thousand letters, of which three hundred survive. It is clear that, in the spirit of the Gallican church of the time, there is some confusion between French culture and Christian tradition; nevertheless, the desire of Marie and her sisters to serve the whole colony is obvious in every word she writes.[10] She can also be a strong critic of her own countrymen, especially the merchants: 'I mentioned to you in another letter a cross which I told you was more painful to me than all the hostilities of the Iroquois. Here is what it is. There are some Frenchmen in this country so low and without fear of God, that they lose all our new Christians by giving them strong drink such as wine and *eau de vie* in order to get beaver skins.'[11] This was in 1662. A few years later, she records the growth of the colony in both numbers and scandals: 'It is true that many people are arriving from France and that the country is becoming very populated. But in the midst of the honest people come also a great many bad ones of both sexes, who cause many scandals. It would have been much better for this new church to have few good Christians than to have such a large number give us so much trouble.' She goes on to denounce again the trade in alcohol, which continues despite having been named a mortal sin by the bishops. Such behaviour, she says, will inflame the 'savage nations' to unite in opposition to the colonists. Marie and her sisters exerted every effort to stem the tide of corruption that was accompanying the foundation of New France, but the limited success of their efforts in this area is writ large on the subsequent history of the colony.

Much of our information about Marie de l'Incarnation comes from the biography written by her son, Claude Martin. He had been the recipient of many of her letters and had been close to her, despite their lengthy separation. As a biographer, Claude had to choose a central theme for his mother's life, and he chose to describe her as a supporter of male reformers. It is clear that Marie did not see herself this way, but the strength and holy in-dependence of her character – 'to the limits of obedience' – had to be modified for public consumption. We know that, as a young woman, Marie loved to attend sermons, and to pass on to others what she had learned. 'I spoke out loud,' she said, 'telling them what the preacher had preached, and adding my own thoughts which rendered me eloquent.'[12] She saw herself as a preacher's mouthpiece, but also as a preacher in her own right. When Claude set out to write his mother's biography, he also described her as a preacher, but made clear distinctions between the preaching tasks of women and men. He took a lengthy di-gression to explain the difference between preaching and teach-ing. He began by citing all the usual objections to preaching by women: the association of 'public' women with a lack of mod-esty, the sinful propensities of women in speech, the natural weakness of women, the unwillingness of public opinion to ac-cept women in positions of authority, and the association of preaching with the priesthood, an office definitely prohibited to women. For this reason, women, he said, could not be called simply apostles, a title reserved for men only, but they could be called apostolic women. Hence, Claude confined his mother's activity to a restricted area not recognised by Marie or by the other Ursuline missionaries. He used Teresa of Avila's descrip-tion of women supporting men through their prayers, to de-scribe his mother's missionary activities, even though he knew that the activities of the Ursulines missionaries were much more extensive than this, especially in the early days of the Quebec mission. He describes the Ursulines as 'angels and guardian spirits ... who entreated heaven to send them apostles...'[13] In this way, her son reduced the heroism of Marie and her sisters to the acceptable level of conventional French and ecclesiastical thought about appropriate feminine behaviour. He downplayed the apostolic activity of the missionaries in the interests of emphasising their apostolic spirit, thus ensuring that the women missionaries were always seen as subordinate to the male missionaries.

Such re-formulating of women's missionary contribution was common in the French church of the time, despite the contradictory factual and written evidence. Another necessary distinction was that between public preaching and private teaching, and it is important to remember that these distinctions were made by the supporters of women, such as Claude Martin. In such writing, the public activity of the women of the early church such as Magdalene or Priscilla was also reformulated as private activity, so that it could be clearly distinguished from the public activity of the apostles. Even such private teaching as the women were supposed to be doing was to be confined to simple matters, and certainly not to lofty doctrines, as the Archbishop of Bordeaux explained to the Ursulines of his diocese. He had instructed the sisters in 1609, to adhere strictly to Cardinal Bellarmine's catechism of the Council of Trent, without any personal interpolations or attempts at explanation. This rote form of teaching was to be followed in every Ursuline convent and therefore every personal charismatic initiative or impulse to preach was forestalled. Into this narrow model, the heroic activities of the Quebec Ursulines were confined by their European male supporters, in order that the public would accept even this limited role. It is a gift for the genuine history of women that at least some of the letters of Marie de l'Incarnation survive, giving a real sense of the harshness and heroism of the frontier activity of these women founders of the Canadian church.

The vision of another French woman missionary to New France was by no means constricted by these continental musings about the roles of women in the church. Marguerite

Bourgeoys (1620-1700) came from an affluent family in Troyes, where, as a young woman, she joined a lay association of the Congregation de Notre Dame. Soon she became the leader of the large group of 'externe' sisters attached to the cloistered community, whose leader was Mother Louise de Chomedey, sister of Paul de Chomedey, the founder of Montreal. Within a few years, Marguerite herself was to become known as the 'mother of the church of Montreal'.[14] Paul de Chomedey was not interested in sponsoring nuns to travel from France to Montreal, but on Marguerite's insistence, he accepted her on condition that she travel alone. As Marguerite hesitated and sought advice about the wisdom of travelling as a lone woman on a ship with several hundred men on a voyage that would take at least three months, a vision of the Blessed Virgin assured her that this was her destiny. She was so reassured by this vision that she determined to trust God entirely and set out for Canada without a single penny and nothing but a 'little package under her arm'. She began her missionary life as she intended to continue it and turned her attention to her male travelling companions. They appeared, at the end of the journey, to be cleansed from their former ways as 'dirty linen going through a laundry'.

Marguerite, still a laywoman, longed for the deeper commitment of religious life. In France, she had been refused by two communities, but her spiritual director, Antoine Gendret, had complete faith in her. He had taught her that there were three ways of life open to women, the reclusive and penitent life in imitation of Mary Magdalene, the cloistered life of service in imitation of Martha, and finally the active outgoing life in imitation of the *vie voyagère* of the mother of Jesus illustrated in her visit to her cousin Elizabeth. This last was the pattern of outgoing lay activity envisaged by Marguerite in Montreal. It was to be a life without the traditional trappings of religious communities, where the poor would be as welcome as the rich, and which, far from just being tolerated for women, was positively enjoined on them by the example of Mary.[15]

Marguerite arrived in Montreal in 1653. For four years she

did whatever work was necessary in the Chomedey household, though she was never considered to be a servant. As she had done on board ship, she continued to care for the soldiers, doing their washing, nursing and feeding them, and always instructing them in the ways of salvation. Her desire to found a school was thwarted by the severity of the climate and the high rate of infant mortality, which was depriving the small colony of its children. Eventually in 1658, she was given a stable for the purposes of founding a school for the 'instruction of the girls of Montreal'. This was her first school and immediately the need for teachers became apparent. Marguerite returned to France to recruit more teachers, and returned the following year with four teachers, engaged on civil contract, but agreeing to live in obedience and chastity for the duration of their service. This was the first free school in North America. Marguerite was expecting the nuns from Troyes to come to run the schools but, because of a change in the governance of the colony, this plan was abandoned. Eventually, the colony was placed directly under the governance of the French monarchy. By 1669, Marguerite was building a much larger house for what was now the first non-cloistered teaching Order in North America, the Congregation de Notre Dame. There was, by now, a sister community in Montreal, the Hotel-Dieu community of nursing sisters, and both communities sought official approbation for their life and work. After another trip to France in search of more teachers, Marguerite returned with both royal and ecclesiastical approbation for her work as a secular sister. The approbation from Bishop Laval of Montreal was given to the women 'on condition that they do not in the future aspire to the religious life'.[16]

The work flourished in the communities springing up along the banks of the Saint Lawrence River, and schools, workshops and missions were rapidly founded. There was also, in the mission of Montagne, a school for native girls who were to be taught and raised 'in the French manner'. Marguerite was by now universally regarded as a saint and the community benefited greatly from her reputation. Her original ideas about the life of the com-

munity prevailed initially, but it was gradually revealed that all
was not well among her companions. Marguerite's willingness
to take on any work was distressing to some of her sisters.
Particularly upsetting was Marguerite's sponsoring of the *filles
du roi*. These were young French orphans who had been shipped
out to the colony to serve as wives in the community.
Marguerite took care of these girls, educated them, and served
as a kind of matchmaker for the colony 'for the sake of creating
families'. She admits that this work did not please her sisters as
they felt abandoned by her and deprived of her leadership at a
very crucial time. During Marguerite's lifetime, the Congregation
de Notre Dame continued to be involved in a multiplicity of
works, but after her resignation in 1693, the work of the community was concentrated in the schools. In one sense, this was an
inevitable development in the growing colony. In another sense,
it was perceived by the bishop and others as an attempt by the
sisters to 'act the ladies' and move beyond their former roles as
maids of all work.[17]

Marguerite was much distressed by these developments, and
though by now old and weak, she offered her services to keep
the abandoned institutions going. Her offer was refused. Other
changes gradually crept in. Marguerite had been determined
that the sisters would earn their own way by doing laundry and
needlework, especially for the churches. She had always insisted
that the schools would be free, and she had always refused the
offer of foundation money from wealthy parents. The lack of
women in the colony had meant that there was no shortage of
work, but it also meant that after working in the schools and
missions during the day, the sisters had to stay up most of the
night to do the work that supported them. As a result, their way
of life was often desperately poor and their diet meagre. One of
their principal clients was the Sulpician seminary, whose superior
was a great admirer of the sisters. He wrote that the sisters,
through the work of their own hands, were able to build or pur-
chase several large properties in the Montreal area. This was
true, and some of the sisters began to wonder why they could

not begin to enjoy some of the fruits of their labour. Marguerite was outraged at this suggestion and saw it as backsliding in their commitment. She railed against her sisters for their wish to abandon the 'little life' where all had been equal. Now divisions among the sisters were occurring, and some of them were being treated as servants of the others. She mourned the loss of the spirit of poverty in the desire of some sisters to have 'mattresses and sheets and lots of utensils, and to live unlike the simple folk, and to have all sorts of comforts which the local people do not have'. The old strictness of life was disappearing and Marguerite was sure that this would result in a weakening of the their commitment to God.[18]

It seemed, however, that the growing colony did not wish the sisters to live in such dire straits, and the voice of Marguerite was seen as saintly, but a voice from the past. Montreal in the 1690s was growing in confidence and wealth. The daughters of the rulers and merchants needed an education suited to their place in the colony, and the colony rejoiced when the new convent was 'one of the best built in town'. The congregation was seen as one of the main institutions of the colony and no other voice was heard accusing it of backsliding. It was taking its appropriate place in the growing city. Marguerite's inspiration had come from the French Catholic Reformation. Many of the new sisters were now Canadian, and their inspiration came from the needs of this fast developing new colony. Like many other similar congregations, it was being shaped primarily by forces outside itself. The desire of the original sisters to teach the native children and found missions in the native communities also ran into difficulties, partly because of the inter-tribal wars. Marguerite had taught that Mary had received both shepherds and kings and that the sisters, likewise, should receive all, and that their preference should be for the poor. In the school curriculum, she insisted that all girls should be taught how to support themselves by the work of their own hands, so that all could make an honest living. Many of these ideas also fell by the wayside in the forward-looking Montreal of the eighteenth century.

Nevertheless Marguerite's ideas brought a new kind of religious community for women to the New World. She had spent much of her life defending the notion of sisters on the move wherever their work called them. She had insisted that her sisters learn to travel by horse and canoe and become accustomed to a life of wandering. 'We are asked why we prefer to be "wanderers" rather than cloistered, the cloister being a protection for persons of our sex ... Why do we go on missions which put us in danger of suffering greatly and even of being captured, killed, or burned by the Indians? There are signs that the Blessed Virgin has been pleased that there is a company of women to honour the life she led in the world and that this company be formed in Montreal. Further, the Blessed Virgin was never cloistered...'[19] When Marguerite died in 1700, there were about fifty sisters. Ecclesiastical law dictated that the number be kept below eighty until the 1840s, when Bishop Bourget removed this limit. By the mid-twentieth century, there were over six thousand sisters in Quebec and thirty five thousand worldwide. Two saintly women are particularly remembered in Quebec tradition as being influenced by the life of Marguerite Bourgeoys. These are Jeanne le Ber and Kateri Tekakwitha.

Jeanne le Ber was the daughter of a very wealthy and successful businessman in Montreal. He had made a fortune in the fur and fish trade between Canada and Europe and was one of the first importer/exporters to exploit the riches and needs of both Old and New France. Jeanne had been educated by Marguerite Bourgeoys personally, and when Marguerite had to return to Europe in search of more teachers, Jeanne was sent to the Ursulines in Quebec City. Here was a privileged young woman who profited from the presence of two saintly founders in her new country. Jeanne's spiritual life was thrown into confusion when one of her new friends, a follower of Marguerite Bourgeoys, died suddenly. She made a vow of chastity, and following the example of many young women throughout the history of Christianity, she lived as a recluse in her parents' home. After ten years, she felt that God was asking more of her, and

she offered to rebuild one of Marguerite's convents in return for
being allowed to live nearby in an anchoritic cell. This was one
of Marguerite's first large convents, and when it had burned to
the ground, Marguerite had seen this as God's judgement on the
sisters' departure from a life of poverty. Now an apparent bene-
diction from God seemed to authorise the rebuilding of the convent, and the anchorhold where Jeanne le Ber wished to spend
the rest of her days. This was to be the first such anchorhold in
North America, and signalled the fact that much of the Christian
tradition of the old world was to make its way to the new, even
though the recluse tradition had not been popular in Europe for
several hundred years.

The enclosing of Jeanne, the daughter of the richest man in
Montreal in her anchorhold was a significant event for the
whole colony. There is a remarkable contemporary description:
'The feast of Our Lady of the Snows fell on a Friday that fifth of
August1695. Solemn vespers were chanted in the parish church,
after which a procession was formed, headed by the clergy ...
Quitting forever the home of her childhood, breaking asunder
the last and closest ties that bound her to earth, she followed the
clergy, accompanied by her father and several other relatives. It
was a striking scene ... Dollier de Casson blessed the cell and, as
she knelt before him, exhorted Jeanne le Ber to persevere therein
... He then led her to the threshold, and she passed calmly into
her new abode, closing and fastening the door while the choir
chanted the litany of the Blessed Virgin.' It is a scene set in this
barely forty-year-old colony that could have been lifted straight
out of thirteen-century Europe. Jeanne, the first anchoress of the
New World, lived on in her cell for almost twenty years until her
death in 1715. Her time was spent in prayer, needlework, reading and extraordinarily intricate embroidery, samples of which
can be seen in the Motherhouse of the Congregation de Notre
Dame in Montreal to this day.[20]

Kateri Tekakwitha is the first native-born saint of the New
World, daughter of an Algonquin Christian mother and a
Mohawk father from the Iroquois nation. Kateri's family as well

as Kateri herself suffered the tragic fate of imported diseases brought from Europe to the New World. Her father, mother and brother died in a smallpox epidemic, and Kateri herself became partially blind and severely disfigured in the same disaster, which killed thousands of her tribes-people. Kateri made her contact with Christianity through the Jesuits, and one of these, Père Cholenec, later wrote her life. She had been immediately attracted to Christianity, and after several months of instruction, was received into the church on Easter Sunday, 1676. This was not an easy decision. As Kateri approached the church for her reception, she was showered with stones, treated with contempt, and even the children hooted at her in derision, whenever she appeared.

Kateri, in search of Christian support, escaped from her home and eventually came to Caughnawaga near Montreal. As her family came in search of her, Kateri had to flee again to the mission of Sault Ste Marie in northern Ontario. In 1679, Kateri became the first native woman of North America to consecrate herself to a life of virginity. Again, here in the wilderness of the New World, an ancient Christian drama was enacted. Kateri's family were determined that she would marry, having known no other destiny for a young woman. They considered that her virtue should make her an excellent catch for 'some able hunter who would bring abundance to her cabin'. When the local priest seemed to take the family's side, Kateri is said to have responded: 'Ah, Father, I am not any longer my own. I have given myself entirely to Jesus Christ, and it is not possible to change masters. The poverty with which I am threatened gives me no uneasiness. So little is needed to supply the necessities of this wretched life, that my labour can furnish it.'

During the following year, still all alone in her desire to live a life of virginity, Kateri came into contact with Marguerite Bourgeoys' community and realised that Christianity had structures to facilitate such a life as she desired. This was the first time she had seen nuns and was overjoyed and reconfirmed in her life choice. She made her vows on the feast of the Annunciation.

Kateri lived a life of strict asceticism, imitating the ancient desert ascetics, of whom she had never heard. The bravery of the Iroquois in the face of physical hardship and suffering partly inspired her choice of a life in imitation of the crucifixion. It is no surprise that she died within a short time, in 1681. The fame of her holiness spread through the native villages, and many people were reported to have been miraculously cured. Kateri Tekakwitha has been continuously venerated among the First Nations still living along the borders of what is now Canada and the United States, and her miracle-working fame surpasses that of any of the other early women Christian founders in the New World.[21]

Jeanne Mance (1606-1673) was, perhaps more than any of the other women studied here, one of the true founders of Montreal. She was the daughter of an attorney in Langres and had gained valuable nursing experience on the front lines during the Thirty Years' War. Jeanne was summoned to New France by a dream, similar to many reported by the other early missionaries. Her friends and advisors thought she was either joking or seeking attention, but at the age of thirty-six, Jeanne arrived in the New World in 1642 to be co-founder with Paul de Chomedey of the settlement of Montreal. She had come equipped with sufficient money to found the first hospital in New France, designed to care for both native Indians and French settlers. It is no wonder that this first small group saw themselves as the 'New Israelites' as they stepped ashore at Ville Marie, Montreal, having canoed from the settlement at Quebec. Paul de Chomedey organised a fraternity of five brothers and sisters who 'pledged to help one another, to serve the others where they needed their help, to attend to the sick ...' This was a lay community formed for the exigencies of the moment. The land was not yet cleared and was covered in forests, which made the endless travels of the women and men both dangerous and exhausting. Eventually, a small chapel was built and the Eucharist was reserved there. The annals then record a charming and probably unique story: 'Since our "Israelites" did not have enough oil to keep a light burning day and night in front of the altar, they decided to put a jar of fine glass filled with insects called fire-flies, who live only during the summer. The glass seemed as bright and shiny during the night as if there were many little candles inside.'

For thirty years, Jeanne Mance worked as part of this unique female-male lay community. As the hospital, l'Hotel-Dieu, expanded, Jeanne brought from Dieppe the Hospital sisters of Saint Joseph to help with the work and was also instrumental in persuading Paul de Chomedey to allow Marguerite Bourgeoys to follow her dream of coming to work in New France. Jeanne also served as the treasurer of Ville Marie, as the settlement was called and showed distinctive and sometimes controversial leadership in her handling of the funds. One of her most controversial decisions was the transfer of funds from the hospital to the military defence of the colony, arguing that if the colony ceased to exist, the hospitals would be of no use. When Jeanne Mance died in 1673, the hospital system was well established and continues in Canada to this day.[22]

Like Kateri Tekakwitha and Jeanne le Ber, Marguerite d'Youville was born in the New World in 1701, the daughter of a French officer. She was educated by the Ursulines in Quebec and then married a Montreal merchant who was involved in the illegal trading of alcohol with the native tribes. During the next eight years, she bore six children, of whom only two survived. When Marguerite was twenty-nine, her husband died suddenly and she and the family were left in destitution. She supported herself and her young children by sewing – anything from army tents to ball gowns. Marguerite's own poverty made her aware of the destitution all around her, and her life began to be one of care for the poor, sick and even of the prisoners. She shared her meagre resources with those in need and did not hesitate to beg in order to get funds for the burial of the abandoned poor. By degrees, other women joined with Marguerite and in 1738, four of them formed themselves into a new community for the one goal of serving the poor.[23] The small group initially met with intense hostility rooted in the memory of Marguerite's previous life as wife to a man who made his money selling liquor to the natives. They were stoned in the streets and greeted with obscenities as they made their way to church. They were accused of continuing the illegal liquor trade and some priests even refused them communion. The favoured humiliating epithet of the populace was *soeurs grises*, the drunken sisters, but the followers of Marguerite d'Youville have become known in Canada as the *Grey Nuns*.

By 1747, the Grey Nuns had taken charge of the General Hospital of Montreal, replacing a group of Brothers, who left them with a huge debt. The French/English war for this corner of the New World was raging all around them, but the Grey Nuns continued their work of serving the poor, especially the elderly, retarded women and men, and eventually prostitutes, who could choose the Grey Nuns in preference to prison. Such work did not improve their reputation with the people, who still preferred the retiring, cloistered, and supposedly more ladylike behaviour of the nuns in Europe. Marguerite's reputation took another beating when, after finding a dead baby in a snowdrift, the Grey Nuns opened an orphanage for abandoned babies. The further radical inclusivity of Marguerite's vision was clearly demonstrated by her determination to nurse all those involved in the military conflict. In her hospital, she opened special wards for the participants, English, French, Algonquin, Huron, Montagnais, and Iroquois. She hid escaped prisoners of all kinds in the convent cellars and helped them to escape. In one remembered incident, Marguerite paid a huge ransom to free an English prisoner, who was about to be tortured for information. The freed prisoner, John, became a valued associate of Madame d'Youville. In one cloak and dagger incident, four English soldiers scaled the convent walls hotly pursued by the French and Indian regiments. A blind Indian, already rescued, smelled their presence and reported them. As the French were entering the convent compound, they were met by a group of Grey Nuns departing with Madame d'Youville's blessing. These were the soldiers, who duly escaped and John later returned with the nuns' habits and cloaks.

Marguerite d'Youville was considered a traitor by all, because she insisted on helping all, regardless of their allegiance. Her life, and the lives of the nuns, were therefore in constant danger. She is one of the most consistent witnesses in Christian history to this determination to live the inclusive gospel message without any exceptions whatever. Her life is full of similar hair-raising incidents, such as hiding soldiers from one group under the tents she was sewing, as the other group came to arrest them. Marguerite died in 1771 leaving a thriving community behind her. In recognition of her universal care of all, in the most dangerous situations, she was named by Pope John XXIII as 'The Mother of Universal Charity', and was beatified in 1959.

The lives of several Jesuits and other martyred male missionaries have been well remembered and celebrated by the ecclesiastical recognition of canonisation. Their lives are testimony to the courage and faith required of these early missionaries to the New World. Such courage, faith and universal love was also in evidence in the women missionaries, but, because of their subsequent history of semi-cloister in imitation of the European pattern, the stories of the women were forgotten and neglected for many years, sometimes even by their own followers. It is appropriate that the names of the women and men, whose names now adorn the streets, churches, squares and monuments of Quebec and Montreal, be remembered for their real contributions to the founding of Canada. The ongoing contributions of the followers of these women will be explored in a later chapter.[24]

Before leaving the stories of these remarkable women, it is necessary to comment on one of their unique contributions, and that is the virtual invention of schooling and education for young women. Initially, religious life for women had been designed to promote the sanctification of the women in a life of retirement from the world. This cloistered life of virginity was seen as the peak of womanly perfection, going some way to atone for the permanent damage done to all women and the whole human race by Eve and all her daughters. This doctrine was repeated endlessly. It is therefore, almost easy to understand

the horror of contemporary believers when post-Tridentine religious women sought a much more active role in the church and
in the world. As we have seen, they had many predecessors in
this vision of a life of active compassion but, since the history of
women recorded only the women of church-prescribed holiness
and obedience, the more active and flamboyant women were
quickly forgotten. In every age of the church, holiness had a political as well as a spiritual face. In both Old and New France, the
roles adopted by women in the Catholic Reformation challenged the accepted beliefs about women in radical ways. The
choosing of public roles by women was seen as provocative and
alarming, despite the obvious necessity and utility of the work
they were performing – serving the poor and sick, assisting the
elderly and unwanted, and almost without exception, attempting to provide an education for young girls, both in the religious
sense of learning the Christian faith, but also in the secular sense
of preparing them for motherhood and for self-supporting
work. Society, again almost without exception, resisted these efforts or, given the obvious needs, co-opted them to fit the conventional womanly profile. The most radical of these new tasks
was that of education. There was little or no pattern of universal
education, and certainly no model for female literacy, education
and apprenticeship. The women then had to invent female education from scratch, and what might be called a battle royal
ensued for the next three hundred years, as generations of
women's educational communities attempted to make the education of women as significant as that of men.

The first problem to be overcome by the women was the task
of proving that they could be good contemplative nuns as well
as active teaching women. The women founders and their clerical advisors prescribed a 'composed' outward appearance so
that 'there is nothing which can alienate or disgust, or estrange
or by its excess intimidate the scholars'.[25] There were to be no
more raptures and ecstasies: 'How would it be to find an
Ursuline lifted up from the earth and out of her senses when she
was supposed to be teaching catechism or serving the children.'[26]

The women founders, however, were as determined to be seen as proper religious, as they were determined to be allowed to act as their public vocation required. 'It is not an association of schoolmistresses that I plan to create,' said the Ursuline, Anne de Xainctonge. These women were intentionally constructing a new form of religious life, whose parameters became increasingly clear to them, even though the male ecclesiastical leaders seem never to have understood the implications of the new system.

The women founders knew that they had to discard, to some extent, at least four of the traditional monastic practices in order to facilitate their new active and public life. These were cloister, the recitation of the Divine Office, the traditional monastic practice of asceticism and the traditional religious habit. Lengthy argumentation continued through the succeeding centuries on all these points. Perhaps the most successful front was that of the Divine Office. The women succeeded in showing that their voices, needed for daylong teaching in large classrooms of unruly children, could not also be used in daily chanting of the Divine Office. Their new life was to be apostolic, even if the women could not be called apostles. Their practical and spiritual life and manner had to be such as to attract students. The cornerstone of their spirituality was expressed in the phrase 'leave God for God'.

There had always been some minimal forms of education for young girls, but it was always seen as inferior to that of boys and much more easily dispensable. Women's illiteracy was almost universal, and in fact literacy was not desirable, below certain social classes. There was no agreed curriculum for girls and women, except what was required to make the girls into good Christian mothers.

The new idea of some continuous schooling in organised classrooms following a more or less standard curriculum was totally new. Besides, the teachers were not trained, and often no better educated, initially, than their students. The women learned by observing the male teachers, especially the Jesuits, more or less surreptitiously. That women should study the same subject matter was a cause of dispute for centuries, philosophy being seen the most alarming addition to the women's curriculum. This, however, is jumping ahead. At the beginning, the skills of crowd management were as necessary as the skills of literacy. The women evolved their own systems, dividing the classes by age and experience, organising competitions, providing benches of reward under a statue of Mary, and benches of punishment at the back of the room. All the women founders resisted corporal punishment and opted instead for a variety of shaming and rewarding mechanisms. A kind of pattern of classroom behaviour evolved forbidding shouting, anger, bullying, name-calling, striking or fighting. The teachers were encouraged to study the students and learn to know their natures, likes, talents, capacity and inclinations, and then educate them accordingly. In contrast to the rote memorisation of the time, the students were to have the subject explained to them before they were required to learn it. Results were soon apparent. 'Their teaching is marked with exactitude and gentleness. They can be understood by the youngest and the oldest alike.'[27]

The teaching sisters began to produce their own methodology. Gifted teachers were circulated to other schools to pass on their skills. New curricula, even new catechisms were written. The standard Tridentine Bellarmine catechism was basic, but was adapted by the sisters to their own purposes, and one of these purposes was to avoid awkward topics such as the sixth commandment about chastity. The women teachers added illustrations and stories to make the material understandable, but often, in desperation, had to resort to the usual rote learning. It is clear that the congregations helped each other, sharing whatever was found to be effective. At every turn, however, the creativity of the women was stifled by external regulations and expectations, and, as the founders died, the styles of the different groups became institutionalised. Any departure from the original pattern was seen as disobedience and disloyalty, and by the end of the seventeenth century a new form of rigidity had set in.

Nevertheless, each group now had its own inbuilt education system for its own members. All the nuns were expected to be literate and knowledgeable and capable of communicating the basic subjects. The students were taught to read and write and do basic calculations, but also to walk properly, write letters, speak well and behave appropriately, whether at school, in public, in church or at home. The teaching of reading and writing to young women was resisted, but, as the nuns insisted, it led to the expansion of the schools as new materials like desks, books, pens and the like were required. The teaching of writing to young women drew a special wrath on the nuns. Writing was a masculine act. Writing by women turned the world upside down, and besides it would lead to the women engaging in unlawful liaisons. 'Writing and even reading should be forbidden to all women. This would be the way to confine their ideas and to enclose them in the useful work of the household, and also to inspire them with respect for the first sex, which would be instructed in these same skills with all the more care since the second sex is being neglected.'[28] It was also feared that reading and writing 'would encourage the servant class in an idleness which is scarcely fitting for domestic life'.

Nevertheless, the new education, limited though it was, continued and eventually was accepted as the minimum required by everyone. Parents began to accept reading and writing as essential skills for their children, even though there were always some hostile observers who accused the nuns of perverting the social control aims of schooling. In 1752, a visitor to Montreal accused the nuns of 'spreading a slow poison … in so far as the educated girl acts the lady, and is affected, and wants to be established in the city and to marry a businessman; and considers as beneath her the estate into which she was born'. Next to reading and writing, the nuns valued what was called 'handwork'. This was seen as the very essence of femininity, of the distaff side of the race, and once trained in handwork a girl need never be idle. Authoritative voices like that of Fenelon added their approval: 'The strong woman spins, she stays in her house, she is silent, she believes, and she obeys.' Even such handwork was to be simple and never raised to the professional level of fancy embroidery.

Two added principles became embedded in this elementary system of education: girls and women should be taught only by women, and all such women should be unmarried. Throughout the seventeenth century in both Old and New Worlds, the education of young girls became a social necessity. As the numbers of women's religious communities grew, the numbers of students grew proportionately. The church began to be feminised and democratised in some sense, not so much in teaching or decision-making, but by sheer volume of numbers. A norm of 'good motherhood' was created and a new style of home piety that would prevail for centuries. At this stage, the education of women was simply planting seeds for the future, but women were becoming their own agents of change, even in the very restricted scope allowed to them. Throughout the century, schools, hospitals, and orphanages proliferated, all through the initiative of women. They started from nowhere, a situation as true for the Old World as it was for the New, and changed the face of cities, towns, villages and homes. By the end of the seventeenth century it was widely recognised that the education of young girls was a worthy religious vocation. This was a situation brought about by the sheer numbers and enthusiasm of the women themselves. All the initiative lay with them and every woman founder had to face down the active resistance of both lay and church leaders. By the dawn of the nineteenth century such women had made themselves indispensable to the church.

CHAPTER SIX

Protestant Women:
Philosophers, Missionaries and Mystics

The eighteenth century has been designated the Age of Enlightenment by historians, and most discussion of the period has focused on the upsurge of reason rather than faith as the dominant characteristic of the age. Nevertheless, the Age of Enlightenment carried within itself distinctive movements of faith that have been just as influential in the sphere of religion. As we have seen, all such movements, in the history of the West, take their name and motivational force from a male dominant perspective and this age is similar. The Age of Enlightenment was rooted in the enlightenment of men, but not necessarily of women, except in its earliest stages. In fact, once the logic of the Age of Enlightenment became rooted in the Christian culture of the West, the position of women was even further reduced. This held true in both the religious and secular spheres. Despite the obvious differences between secular Enlightenment and religious faith, both movements followed similar trajectories where women were concerned, going from initial grudging participation to the customary demotion of women to the private spheres of church and state, and for precisely identical reasons, this time with an eighteenth century twist. The convulsion that was the French Revolution ended the century with totally unsuspected challenges for all the citizens of Europe and the wider world.

One of the hallmarks of the Enlightenment was the questioning of the limits placed by religious faith on the minds of men. The minds of women came to be of interest only when some women assumed that such a discussion included them. Initially, the pleasures of rational conversation in delightful social settings designed by women, constituted one of the new pleasures of Enlightenment culture. These *salons* were centres of avid discussion about the rights of citizens, slaves, Jews, commoners, the colonised, but not of women. When such a topic arose, the ancient 'truths' about the necessary subordination of women because of their feebleness of mind and questionable ethics were invoked. Philosophers of the age, such as John Locke, were of the opinion that 'every man has an equal right to natural freedom', but such rights were not to include women, who had no *natural* right to freedom, though occasional concessions might be made for exceptional women. There was no doubt, however, that such freedom as might be granted to women, would always be a concession granted by men. Freedom for women, which, if it included her involvement in the government of the state, heralded the end of good government. Women, it was asserted, were suited only for dependence, and when they attempted independence, universal disorder was the result. The philosopher Hegel volunteered his unique reason for such assertions, saying that women were incapable of thinking and acting according to the dictates of universality.[1] Two other outstanding supporters of the Enlightenment, Voltaire and Rousseau, though bitter opponents on everything else, yet agreed on this one subject. They both saw a woman who adopted a stance of reason as a 'scourge to her husband and children' and 'always trying to make a man of herself'. The realm of reason was and was to remain a male realm. The revered Enlightenment philosopher, Immanuel Kant, added his opinion that such women might as well wear beards, because 'painful pondering' was contradictory to the nature of women.[2]

All through the eighteenth century, even though many women presided over salons attended regularly by such philosophers, and often rivalled them in the quality of their reasoning, nevertheless, the women realised that in order to gain acceptance in their society, they would also have to emphasise the 'feminine' virtues of being a good wife and mother. One is reminded of Hilary Clinton in much more recent times having to engage in the gymnastics of cookie-making in order to win acceptance from the part of the American public which disapproved of women having careers on a similar level to their husband's. Throughout the whole eighteenth century, despite some initial acceptance of women thinkers, such observations about the natural irrationality of women gained in bitterness and volume, with the sole aim of denying to women any participation in education. A new chapter was added to the writing on women – praise of her domesticity. As men of the middle classes became more involved in the political and industrial life of the state, they saw their domestic comforts disappearing. They compared the turbulence of their public life with the necessary tranquillity of the home, well run and organised by the reformed and domesticated wife. As domesticity was glorified, so other choices of women were condemned and the women who made them vilified. Jean Jacques Rousseau led a crusade for breast-feeding, asserting that the original sin consisted in women's refusal to breast-feed their babies.[3] As we shall see, there were women like Mary Wollstonecraft who wrote on women's behalf, defending the 'bluestockings' as learned women were nicknamed. Despite their brilliance, the effect of their writings was minimal in changing social mores, but they have left us a strong signal of the continuity of women's protest against their enforced privatisation.

Throughout the eighteenth century, the church was faced with one of the greatest crises of its history. It was an age of old, ineffectual popes faced with young and vigorous rulers, inspired by the tenets of the Enlightenment. The eighteenth-century Roman Catholic Church, despite the exuberance of its baroque art, had less influence on the public affairs of European states than at any previous time. The Protestant churches, less centralised, and less reliant on tradition, were able to face the Enlightenment challenge with more energy, but even so, the influence of Protestant leaders waned considerably. It was not until the explosion of the First and Second Great Awakenings in parts of the American States, that Protestant energies were released. On the other hand, the scholarly developments in the

study of scripture and church history on the European continent, while vastly contributing to the restoration of Christian
scholarship, likewise served to diminish the devotional faith of
many in the inerrancy of the scriptures, and the unbroken holiness of the tradition.

In 1713, an attempt was made to put an end to decades of
Catholic feuding between Jansenists and their main rivals, the
Jesuits, by the publication of the papal bull *Unigenitus*, by Pope
Clement XI. It was a monumentally divisive document, serving
only to add confusion to confusion, and amply illustrating the
distance between the Enlightenment ideals of rational debate
and the spirit of the papacy. While no one would deny the necessity of challenging Enlightenment questioning of the validity of
a scripture-based faith, the pope chose to bypass the debate and
forbid almost all scripture reading to Catholics. In its place stood
only and always an unquestioning obedience to the pope. This
did not end the religious disputes, however, and the whole of
France was divided on the issue of what was called 'ultramontanism'. Sixty years later, in a move which served more than
anything else to illustrate the weakness of the papacy, Pope
Clement XIV, on 21 July 1773, dissolved the Jesuits, confiscated
their property, and commanded that no future pope should ever
recall them. The condemnation of both parties to the Jansenist
debate did nothing to heal the wounds that the original disagreement had occasioned.[4] This was a dispute that had disrupted
normal Catholic life for decades, not only in France, but also
throughout the Catholic world. The dispute was carried abroad
by missionaries and even centuries later its echoes were to be
found wherever Catholics gathered. The Jansenist debate carried
into the later centuries resonances of the old extremist tendencies
faced by Augustine in Hippo when confronting the Donatists.
The harsh, self-righteous and judgemental nature of the original
Jansenist position has continued to echo in the Catholic tradition
whenever it feels itself confronted by modernity. The alternative
stance adopted by the Catholic Church in the succeeding years
of the eighteenth century and right into the nineteenth and

twentieth centuries was to retreat from such confrontation to concentrate on its own certainties.

The Protestant world had been fighting for survival right up to the Peace of Westphalia in 1648. The question of mission did not arise in communities where survival and maintenance were the issues. The chosen emphasis on the ruler as responsible for the religion of his domains led, inevitably, to a regional Protestantism. Throughout the seventeenth century, however, England and Holland began to challenge the dominance of Spain and Portugal on the high seas. Just at the dawn of the eighteenth century, in 1701, the Anglican Society for the propagation of the faith was founded.[5] Its main work was to be ministry to Anglicans in the West Indies and the Americas, but the need for a mission to 'Indians and Negroes' began to be formulated. Eventually, through the preaching of Cotton Mather (1663-1728) in Boston about an eternal universal gospel, and of Jonathan Edwards (1703-1756), later President of Princeton University about a 'worldwide concert of prayer', the notion of mission became central to the experience of American Protestantism. By 1800, it was clear that the New World of the Americas and the West Indies would become both Christian and a world where the white man could impose his will. Eventually such developments were hastened not only by the upheaval of the French Revolution, but also by the invention of steam and electricity, which vastly facilitated travel and aroused in the West a new thirst for travel. The growth of Christianity to the East was much more complicated and far less clear as to its outcome.

Church history of the eighteenth century was largely an attempt to respond to the new form of political power, namely the enlightened despot. This was a new kind of kingly rule, no longer based on the divine right of kings but on rationalism. The best ruler was the one who had access to the best advice. Rationalist philosophers came to the fore and the chief obstacles to their influence were seen to be the clergy, the old feudal aristocracies, and the monasteries. Rulers with absolutist dreams freely intervened in church affairs, suppressing monasteries, and opening the world to what was presented as a new freedom of thought. The Age of Reason, however, was more characterised by the pattern of its thinking than by any new creative thought.[6] The age was secular in spirit and faced every aspect of traditional thought with a spirit of scepticism. Thus the intellectual and religious patterns of thought and behaviour, that had dominated Europe since the time of the great councils, were gradually weakened. The autonomy of the mind of man (*sic*) was invoked rather than divine revelation and a new belief in the infinite capacity of human beings for unending progress was articulated on all sides. The new philosophers and scientists were greeted as the heroes of the age – in England, Locke, Newton and Hume, in France, Voltaire and Diderot, to name but the most influential thinkers. The emphasis was always on free discussion rather than the explicit content, and the whole was dominated by a few cardinal rules. Reason was the new and marvellous tool and the world of nature was given unparalleled authority. Natural law was the ruler of all, and it was in the court of nature that all truth was tested. It was an age fascinated by the 'order of nature' and by man's (*sic*) natural ability to substitute reason for the submission of thought demanded by revelation and doctrine.[7] Such recourse to reason is brilliantly illustrated in the *Encyclopedia* of Diderot.

Despite merciless criticism of the church and all ancient systems of thought and belief, the Enlightenment was curiously conservative. These middle class men were looking for stability, not novelty. They abhorred disorder, and the greatest disorder of all was the attempt by women to join the circle of those distinguished by the use of reason. Despite the adoption of Deism as the characteristic belief of the Enlightenment, that is a profession of faith in the God of Nature, the Great Mathematician, the Prime Mover, the philosophers of the age did not hesitate to appeal to the traditions of Christian thought when they needed to put women firmly in the place assigned to them by both God and nature. For fifty years, Voltaire was the most powerful influence on European thought. A confirmed deist, he attacked miracles, prophecy, the authority of scriptures and the authority of the clergy, and all pretensions by women to be included as rational thinkers. The Catholic response was to attempt censorship, but this was utterly futile. Without the Jesuits, the Catholic community was left without intellectual defenders.

In Germany, the Enlightenment took a different form. While the emphasis on reason predominated, and disbelief was rife, there was also a movement of reform. Protestant scholars applied the new rational principles to a study of the scriptures, to an exploration of the origins of Christian history, and to a study of the person of Jesus. In the long run, though these theological movements were to have a powerful influence on the churches, they served also to disillusion the ordinary believer. It was in response to such intellectual movements that German Pietism was born, and that eventually the revivalist movements of the two Great Awakenings took place in the American States. The preaching of such men as Jonathan Edwards was given credit for this revival. The churches experienced phenomenal growth and were galvanised into action. Edwards preached an emotional invitation to repentance, urged people to resist the evil of slavery and called on all to engage in the education necessary to become familiar with the scriptures. Enormous difficulties ensued when the early theological preachers were replaced by men who relied more on emotion than content, and established groups such as the Presbyterians and Baptists became deeply divided and fragmented.

Before exploring the participation in these revivalist groups, it is necessary to return to the Age of Enlightenment in order to explore the contributions of women. The women we are concerned with here are Protestant women philosophers, many of them more noted for their secularism than for their faith. The voice of Catholic women intellectuals will not be heard at all for several more centuries, until opportunities for education are finally made available to them. Women who were in a position to have access to education were often the daughters or wives of professors, ministers, or teachers. Some few were themselves teachers. There is space to discuss only a handful of these women, but the range of their authoritative writing is impressive under such very restrictive circumstances. Damaris Cudworth Masham (1659-1708) was the daughter of a prominent member of the Platonist school at Cambridge.[8] She was denied the opportunity of higher education for herself, but she grew up in an atmosphere of philosophical discussion. Her philosophical pursuits were encouraged not only by her father but also by her romantic attachment to the philosopher John Locke. When she eventually married Sir Francis Masham in 1685, Locke continued to live in the household, and Isaac Newton was a frequent visitor. Her writings are an exploration of the relationship between faith and reason in Christian theology, epistemology and morality. In 1696 she wrote *A discourse concerning the love of God*, and in 1705, *Occasional thoughts in reference to a Virtuous or Christian Life*. She also corresponded with both Leibnitz and Locke, and Locke wrote to commend her learning: 'The lady herself is so well versed in theological and philosophical studies, and of such an original mind, that you will not find many men to whom she is not superior in wealth of knowledge and ability to profit by it.' In this letter, Locke also points out that she has ruined her eyes through reading. Masham is at pains to point out that no revelation can be contrary to reason. There is no room for absurdities in religion. If God is rational, then, so should good Christians be. Reason, however, is not enough, as we need religion to steady us, especially in the area of morality. For Masham, religion is the knowledge of how to please God. Perhaps as a comment on contemporary styles of religious teaching, she points out that rote learning of religion makes Christianity look ridiculous. She strongly objects to the deplorable state of education for women. This alone is the cause of widespread impiety in both women and children, because faith must be understood, not just handed on by habit. Girls are caught, she points out, between silly fathers and ignorant mothers and are not taught to think and reason properly. Most men, she says, don't want knowledge, but neither will they allow women to have access to it.

The moral double standard draws her particular wrath, especially the widespread view that chastity is the main virtue of women. For her, this is a kind of minimalism that simply serves to lower women's proper self-esteem. According to the gospels, she points out, both sexes should be chaste. She is outraged by the fact that a failure in chastity is seen as a peccadillo in a young man but as infamy in a woman. Men are not following Jesus Christ in this but simply setting their own norms for their own convenience. True virtue is according to the gospels and right reason, not just in accord with social or Christian convention. Masham argues for love as the core of morality, love of all creatures and of God. One cannot exist without the other. Masham points out the atomising tendencies of male thought, and tries instead to bring together faith, reason, love and pleasure. 'For as by the existence of the creatures, we come to know there is a creator; so by their loveliness it is that we come to know that of their author, and to love him.' It is obvious that Masham is writing for an exclusive circle of upper class women and men, but even here, her writings seem to have had little influence. Nevertheless Damaris Cudworth Masham represents another in a long line of women who raised her voice to plead for proper education for women and an end to the double standard of morality.

The name of Belle van Zuylens is perhaps a little better known.[9] She used the name of Therese Levasseur as a pseudonym to commemorate the servant and sexual partner of Jean Jacques Rousseau. Rousseau had disowned his own five children, despite posing – and being remembered – as one of the great European educators. The children were taken from Therese and sent to an orphanage and the two subsequently separated. His suicide was always blamed on Therese Levasseur, and by no less a person than Madame de Stael, whom we shall meet later. Belle wrote a pamphlet in defence of Therese's reputation, but Madame de Stael bought all the copies to prevent its circulation in a peculiar eighteenth-century form of censorship. Belle also set out to prove the hollowness at the heart of Rousseau's theories of education. His educational plan based on a return to nature was very popular, but van Zuylens pointed out that his supposed equality was concerned with men only and was based on the 'natural inequality' of women. This is just using a return to nature to promote discrimination between the sexes. Such differences as exist between the sexes are not merely 'natural' and inevitable, but the consequence of social inequality and discrimination over the centuries.

Belle van Zuylens was one of the few critics of Rousseau's prescribed inferior role for Sophie in his educational 'classic', *Emile*. She accused Rousseau of being fundamentally anti-woman, using a sentimentalised form of ignorance to demean them. For her, the virtual imprisonment of women in the household without any recourse to proper education was the chief cause of the oppression of women. Belle was entering dangerous territory here. Christianity and most social and theological commentators, as well as Enlightenment philosophers, rooted their prescription of the inferiority of women in their biological role. When Belle moved beyond this to blame women's inferiority on the social construction of difference by men, it was a daring move, and it brought the wrath of both church and state on her head.

'I have no talent for subordination,' declared van Zuylens to James Boswell. 'To be free has ever been my most ardent wish, to be free and to shake off the etiquette.' In her novel, *Three Women*, she conducts an elaborate imaginary experiment with twins, a boy and a girl, where the boy is given a girl's name and vice versa. She is trying to imagine a life without the imposition of social convention and theological prescription, as she experiments mentally with a woman's life beyond social convention. She seeks the origins of the woman's 'self' and tries to move beyond the boundaries of a prescribed identity. For Belle, it all ended in insanity. One might call it an experiment too far, but the ingenuity of this eighteenth-century woman is impressive as she raises questions that need all the skills of twentieth-century psychotherapy to explore. She describes herself as being 'now foolish then wise' as she tries to 'get rid of the veils education has cast over our minds'. The task of exploring the implications of sexual difference for women and men still waits explorers with the bravery of Belle van Zuylens, and an extra dose of the wisdom that was available to her at that time.

The final woman in our brief list of women philosophers is better known but perhaps a little less courageous than Belle van Zuylens, namely Mary Wollstonecraft (1759-1797).[10] Mary's aim in life was to encourage women to practise self-governance and to achieve it herself. Her life-long battle against her impetuous emotional life was a constant source of discouragement and seemed to be a kind of embodied contradiction to the personal stability that she was trying to accomplish. Her society saw women as the link, which separates the superior male from the inferior beast, and Wollstonecraft sought a more equitable evaluation for women. To this end, she took on the leading male theorists of the age, especially Rousseau, but there is always some tension in her thought as she tries to negotiate the perilous waters of sexual difference and its implications.

Her own turbulent life did not help her to gain a balanced perspective. She had been trained as a teacher, a now relatively respectable middle-class occupation for some women. She was the daughter of a battered woman and seems to have carried the effects of this in her insistence on the education of women toward personal moral agency. Wollstonecraft was in Paris at the height of the Revolutionary terror and it was here that she lost faith in Christianity. She carried with her the belief that women and men were created as equally human and constantly challenged the two-nature theory of sexual difference. She remained a professional writer, even under the most difficult circumstances. In Paris, pregnant with her first daughter and abandoned by her lover, Gilbert Imlay, she was yet able to produce a history of the first six months of the French Revolution. When in despair over her personal life and the dreadful scenes she had witnessed in Paris, she returned to England and attempted suicide by jumping into the Thames. Later, after her recovery, she trav-

elled extensively through Scandinavia, and published her obser-
vation on the working poor there as a book in 1795. 'The men
stand up for the dignity of man,' she asserted, 'by oppressing the
women'.[11] She went on to focus her attention on the plight of
poor women, who bear the burdens of all and are treated as the
'outlaws' of the world. This attention to the plight of the poor
was most unusual for her time and, as she pointed out the help-
lessness of women in the face of laws that always benefited men,
she was increasingly regarded with ridicule by her peers. Mary
was by now pregnant with her second daughter (the future
Mary Godwin Shelley, author of *Frankenstein*), and her lover,
William Godwin published some of her unfinished works, including her love letters to Imlay. It was these letters that tainted
her memory for generations. Her work for the poor and her radical feminist ideas of self-governance were forgotten in the face
of this testimony to her despairing love. Her death at the age of
thirty-seven seemed a very high price to pay for a search for
womanly independence.

Wollstonecraft had written *Thoughts on the Education of
Daughters* in 1786 urging that the 'main business of our lives is to
be virtuous'. After her loss of religious faith, however, she
turned her attention to reasoned reform, and the result was her
famous *Vindication of the Rights of Woman*, written in 1792. Here
she asserted the new principles on which she would base her
life: 'The first object of laudable ambition is to obtain a character
as a human being, regardless of the distinction of sex.'[12] From
this premise, she based all her conclusions about the equal access
to education that women should have, leading to careers as
physicians, farmers, or businesswomen, as their talents dictated.
She went on to become a political radical, rejecting all traditional
social hierarchies that confined women.

Mary Wollstonecraft tried in her life and writings to articulate what it meant for women to act as autonomous moral
agents, and to envisage the kind of social and political organis-
ations that would facilitate this goal. All her life she fought to integrate reason and emotion, and all her life she tended, because

of her own tumultuous life, to equate virtue with reason ruling the emotions. She recognises this tendency in herself, even that her newly developing self seemed often more masculine than feminine, or, as she would have wished, just human. She recognised that an emphasis on the 'natural' duties of women, arising from their roles in reproduction, would lead to women's subordination and privatisation. In her writing and in her own life she challenged the dominant eighteenth-century view that women's bodies are the main obstacles to women's moral agency. Her final conclusions were that women were either human or they were not. If they were, then everything else followed, and like all the women radicals of her age, she saw that the road to women's self-governance started from a good education.

One of the contemporaries of Wollstonecraft was Hannah More (1745-1797). Their early lives were quite similar in their religious faith, eagerness for education, and professional writing careers. More, like Wollstonecraft, was regarded as a bluestocking in her early life, but then, More's life took a definitive turn away from radical social politics, when she joined the evangelical sect known as the Clapham Saints.[13] More's subsequent life seemed, to her contemporaries, much more attractive and accessible as a role model for the women of her age than that of Wollstonecraft. The Clapham Saints were abolitionists, and More threw much of her energy into the work against slavery. This seemed to the group to be an obvious conclusion from Christian principles as did their other campaigns to make the Sabbath holier, to reform the manners of the rich and to revive the piety of the poor. The French Revolution convinced the group that traditional pious virtues needed even greater emphasis, and they despised the efforts of other women to push for greater freedom. Hannah More was gifted with boundless energy for the total reformation of English society along conservative Christian lines, and she assumed that women would play a leading role in this endeavour. The group, now led by More, founded many schools for the education of poor children from rural mining districts. Here they were taught, much to the disgust of the majority of male social reformers, reading, writing and above all, the scriptures. It was the thinking of the age that such an education would only encourage rebelliousness among the poor. To counteract this and prevent the English poor from revolting as the French had done, More wrote her *Cheap Repository Tracts* from 1795 on, and priced them at a level that all could afford. Two million copies were sold in the first three years, which made More a best seller and a pioneer in mass-market publishing. These tracts were by no means revolutionary in their content, however, as they advocated humility, piety, deference and obedience.

More gained enormous respect, not only for her inexhaustible energy, but also for the utter respectability of her life. No scandal ever tainted the reputation of this life-long virgin. She advocated all the traditional virtues for the poor and women. The poor should respect their 'betters' and women should return to the traditional virtues of chastity, modesty and piety. She had no doubts whatever that subordination suited women: 'To be unstable and capricious, I really think, is but too characteristic of our sex; and there is, perhaps, no animal so indebted to subordination for its good behaviour as women.' More was frequently referred to as Saint Hannah, but like many women reformers, the subordination she preached was not always apparent in her own behaviour. She was a formidable adversary to those who opposed her goals, but the general testimony of her life and work was much more acceptable to the age than that of women seeking freedom and equality. Despite all her good works, one would have to say that it was women like Hannah More, who revived all the ancient prejudices about women, bought into male desires for unchallenged superiority, and stalled any incipient movement for the real reform of women's lives.

The lives of More and Wollstonecraft left their society with another cliché about women – the contrast between cleverness and goodness in a woman, all the more so since Hannah More had abandoned the one for the other. More discovered the power in womanly virtue and respectability. Hannah More was also a novelist and her portrait of the ideal woman in her novel *Coelebs* was immensely popular, going into thirty editions by the year of her death. The model woman in the novel, Lucilla Stanley, rose at six, spent two hours studying Christian literature, consulted the household staff at eight, planned the meals, distributed the provisions, looked over the accounts, and made breakfast for her parents, 'as fresh as a rose, as gay as a lark'. After breakfast, she read with her father for an hour, and helped her mother to teach her younger sisters. The rest of the day was spent in making articles for distribution to the poor whom Lucilla visited a few times a week. So here was the model middle-class Christian woman, whose virtues are more familiar to women of the succeeding generations than Mary Wollstonecraft's passion for freedom.[14] Nevertheless, the day of the radical feminist politician was not far away, though society would never pay her as much esteem as it would to the Hannah Mores of the world.

So far in this chapter, we have been looking at the Enlightenment, together with some of the extraordinary women and men it produced. As Tarnas remarks, the Enlightenment was a compromise between the medieval Christian Creator God and the modern mechanistic cosmos. Tarnas goes on to chart the qualities of this new universe of thought, but before looking at these, it is appropriate to ask, what about the unenlightened?[15] For these, in both Catholic and Protestant communities, the traditional faith continued unchanged. Sometimes, as with the work of Hannah More, the tradition gained a new respectability. At other times, as with the revivalist groups in America, a new emotional element was added that reduced Christianity to a minimalist assertion about the saving power of faith. One of the most remarkable groups to challenge and survive the Enlightenment was the Society of Friends or Quakers. It is with the remarkable women in each of these groups that we will end the chapter. The contrast between the world changing effects of the Enlightenment and the intense religiosity of the other groups is well portrayed in the summary by Richard Tarnas.[16]

Tarnas lists eight characteristics of the Enlightenment that have gone into the creation of the modern mind. I list them here in very summary fashion.

1. The modern universe is an impersonal phenomenon, governed by regular natural laws that are understandable in exclusively physical and mathematical terms. Hence there is no need for a personal God.

2. The physical world has become the predominant focus of human activity, completely inverting the traditional Christian dualistic emphasis on the spiritual over the material. The drama of life takes place here.

3. Science has replaced religion as the pre-eminent intellectual authority. The transcendent is presumed to be beyond the competence of human knowledge.

4. The order of nature is derived not from a cosmic intelligence but from an order empirically derived from nature's material patterning. Only man (*sic*) possesses conscious intelligence.

5. Those who engage in sober, impersonal scientific investigation become the masters (*sic*) of the universe. The aesthetic, ethical and the emotional worlds lead only to a distortion of the truth.

6. The heavens and the earth are of the same substance, leaving to the realm of the superstitious all belief in a divine celestial sphere. The physical world is simply itself, not a visible sign of an invisible reality.

7. The theory of evolution teaches both the duration and the randomness of the universe. Man (*sic*) is simply another animal. The divine is no longer needed as a hypothesis and the revelation of Christ is simply implausible.

8. The independence of 'man' is radically affirmed, both in 'his' existential autonomy and individual self-expression. The goal of life is to attain the greatest possible freedom of 'man' from nature.[17]

The two periods of evangelical revival in the American colonies, called the First (1740-1750) and Second (1795-1835) Great Awakenings, have left their mark on every aspect of

American Protestant life. Prior to that, however, the English Puritans had brought their faith with them, together with all its beliefs, moral requirements and, of course, its prejudices. For our purposes in trying to trace the elements of the religious life of Protestant women, it is noteworthy that the Puritans initially carried the beliefs of the medieval church that women were evil, more prone to sin and heresy than men, and therefore needing to be carefully supervised and always in submission. For the early years of the seventeenth century, we have little access to women's own experience or evaluation of their religious lives, but eventually, a few women's voices begin to emerge. As is true for most religious traditions, these are not necessarily the voices that would have been chosen by the male religious leaders. The subjection of women was enforced in the colony churches for the first several decades. Gradually, however, a more positive image of the wife as the moral partner rather than the sinful accessory of her husband begins to appear. This is first heard in the sermons of preachers like Cotton Mather in Boston, who even appealed to the example of Mary as contrasted with Eve. Women began to be seen as the spiritual and moral equals of men, partly because women vastly outnumbered men in the congregations. By the early years of the eighteenth century, women outnumbered men by two to one.[18] Ministers' wives played a large part in this re-evaluation of women. They were educated in the scriptures and took their own burden of instruction, counselling, and providing exemplary role models for the women of the congregation. Such women began to write sermon notes, reflections on bible passages, and moral pep talks and were admired for so doing. One key element in such exemplary lives was the new model of marriage that such a religious partnership presented. Women were no longer just serving a reproductive purpose, but were seen as the loving supporters and collaborators of their husbands. Eventually, however, as the eighteenth century rolled on, limits were placed on the extent of such partnership. The question of sexual difference, which was one of the main Enlightenment conundrums, came to bear on female-male relationships in the colonies. The cluster of womanly qualities that was presented under the guise of 'femininity' began to alter the relationships once again. Women were seen to be more naturally gifted as followers, because of their gentle, submissive natures. Women were frail, emotional, nurturing, and these qualities placed women in their own sphere of the family and away from the public eye. Within a century, the role of women had come full circle.

The life of Anne Hutchinson illustrates well the uneasiness of the colonists with any significant changes in women's contribution to the life of the colony. Anne was the daughter of a clergyman, and gladly used the opportunities available to her for a fairly broad education in scripture and its interpretation. She listened eagerly and carefully to sermons, taking and comparing notes. After her marriage to William Hutchinson, however, she reverted to the more expected roles of wife and mother, as well as that of mid-wife. In 1634, the Hutchinson family followed their minister, John Cotton to Boston, where they lived directly opposite Governor John Winthrop. Anne began to invite other women to her home on Sundays to review the content of John Cotton's sermons. This was seen initially as expected and praiseworthy behaviour, but independent theological thinking was soon suspected in the women's circle.

The 'New England Way' had been regarded as slightly antinomian, that is the belief that salvation in Jesus Christ superseded the need to obey more terrestrial laws.

Orthodox ministers declared that obedience to all civil laws prepared one for the coming of salvation by grace, thereby evading the issue. Anne Hutchinson was accused of being more antinomian than the men, in advocating a freedom that was intrinsic to the experience of salvation. She claimed a fundamental belief in the Holy Spirit who would guide a person's faith and action. This eliminated the need for magistrates and clergymen and was judged to be extremely subversive. Several antinomian men were disciplined, but Anne Hutchinson's teachings seemed to enrage the leaders because she was a woman. She was accused of seducing gullible women and even weak men by her teachings, and of disrupting the social order of the community. She was the worst example of the freedom that had been granted to Protestant women. Anne was banned from conducting home meetings, and called to trial first in the civil arena, then in the church courts. Much of the case against her was based on what was 'not fitting in your sex'. She was accused of acting more like a husband than a wife and of neglecting her motherly and wifely duties.

Anne defended herself ably and was a formidable debater. In the end, tiring of her spirited defence of her beliefs and practice, Governor Winthrop, the chief prosecutor said: 'We are your judges, and not you ours, and we must compel you to it.' In 1638, Anne Hutchinson was excommunicated from the congregation and banished from the colony. The family moved to Rhode Island, where soon afterwards Anne gave birth to a badly deformed child. This was interpreted by the Boston judges as proof that she had been 'delivered up to Satan' as the excommunication decree said. Anne was murdered by a group of Indians in 1643, and this was taken as further proof that God had abandoned this 'American Jezebel'. It is consoling to learn that Anne was surrounded by her women followers in unstinting support during her trials, and that she was but one of a number of women who tried to reformulate Puritan doctrine in the colonies.

Despite the initial religious enthusiasm of the colonists, a sense of apathy prevailed in religious circles in the early decades of the eighteenth century. The First Great Awakening in the 1740s changed this scene irrevocably. People were called to be reborn in Christ through emotional sermons on repentance and salvation. The evangelist George Whitefield aroused enormous fervour and enthusiasm and this was spread far and wide by itinerant preachers. The churches began to swell in numbers and the public experience of conversion opened up another new avenue for women. For one of the key understandings of this experience included the duty to preach its benefits to all. If God 'warmed the heart' then none could interfere. Jonathan Edwards was one of the leaders of the New England revival and he encouraged female converts to join a Bible study group. Some women invited Sarah Osborne to lead such a group and wrote a set of rules for themselves. They also collected money, initially for firewood, but eventually, as the group flourished, for the African missions. Sarah Osborne became actively involved in the revival, and even though her life was constantly devastated by tragedy, she continued her work. One novel aspect of her work was that she invited a group of free black people to meet at her home one day a week, and a group of slaves on Sunday. She gained a reputation for compassion, and crowds of all kinds, women and men, white and black, began to flock to her home.

We know from her letters that this work was constantly beset by criticism. She was assuming too much leadership, going outside her proper sphere by teaching men as well as women, and she was threatening the social order by making black people proud and rebellious by opening to them the experience of equal grace. Osborne ably defended herself, saying that it was God's doing. Besides the men preferred her teaching to that of the male leaders. She was not teaching people to be proud but merely helping them to be obedient to the faith. Besides, she herself found a great purpose and satisfaction in these activities that had not been experienced by her in more 'feminine' pursuits.

Similar stories of lives empowered by grace to move outside of narrow 'feminine' confines can be told of other women. Sarah Edwards was freed by her conversion from the need to seek approval from others. Her experience was indeed extraordinary and reminds us of the medieval mystical tradition. In 1742, she was involved in an intense religious experience that lasted for nine days, during which she was 'swallowed up in the light and beauty of Christ'.[19] 'I seemed to be drawn upwards, soul and body, from the earth towards heaven; and it appeared to me that I must naturally and necessarily ascend thither ... At the same time, I felt a far greater love to the children of God, than ever before. I seemed to love them as my own soul; and when I saw them, my heart went out towards them, with an inexpressible endearedness and sweetness. I beheld them by faith in their risen and glorious state …'[20] This experience freed Sarah from the need of ever again meeting other peoples' standards, including the expectations of the clergymen, and even of her husband. As the wife of the powerful religious leader, Jonathan Edwards, Sarah enjoyed some protection from harassment not available to other women, but she never backtracked on the experience of liberation afforded by her ecstatic experience. She died in 1758.

The Society of Friends, more popularly known as Quakers, was founded by George Fox in 1646, after a profound religious experience. From the beginning, it proved attractive to women, primarily because it stood for the equal spiritual status of women and men, which was to be made concrete in religion, the home, and society. One of the distinctive features of the Society of Friends was the belief in the Inner Light that was the source of divine presence for all. Salvation came to those who co-operated with this light. Since the Inner Light was available to all without distinction, it followed that all social distinctions were irrelevant. This meant that acknowledgements of people by their titles, was unnecessary, and this held equally for magistrates, bishops, and even monarchs. Besides since Quakers celebrated no set ritual or sacrament, priests were not necessary, and this wholly new Christian vision began to seem as if early Christianity had returned. The place of the clergy seemed superfluous in light of the Quaker vision. The Quakers then were easily recognisable by their behaviour. They systematically followed through on the implications of their belief in the Inner Light. A new wedding service was organised that would express the full equality of women and men, and the traditional words 'love, honour and obey' were excised. Eventually, slavery was seen for the abomination that it was, and Quakers were always to the fore in working for its abolition. For our purposes, one of the most radical implications was in acknowledging the right of women to preach and teach alongside men. George Fox led the way in always seeking the counsel of women for his endeavours. This did not mean, however, that women and men were completely in-

termingled. From the beginning, women's groups were formed
that were entirely independent, and it is from these groups that
a whole series of remarkable women leaders emerge.

The fact that Quakers acknowledged the right of women to
preach did not necessarily mean that the rest of society looked
favourably on the practice. One of the first English Quakers we
meet is the Englishwoman, Dewens Morrey, who was accused
by her parish priest of breaking the law that 'a woman must not
speak in the church'. Her punishment was 'to be whipt until the
blood did come', and the sentence was carried out that evening.
Dewens recovered and continued her preaching. By the beginning of the eighteenth century the Quakers had grown phenom-
enally and spread throughout England, the American colonies
and the West Indies. Women played a large part in this expansion, especially women such as Margaret Fell (1614-1702), who,
in the midst of her very active life, wrote *Women Speaking
Justified* in 1666 in defence of the preaching of women.[21] She had
married George Fox and opened her home, Swarthmore Hall, as
a kind of refuge for Quakers who were being hounded by both
church and state. Margaret had been imprisoned for this activity,
but her Quaker loyalty and commitment were never shaken.
What the social and church institutions resisted was precisely
what the ordinary people loved.[22] Here was a new and spirited
approach to the Christian gospel that actually made concrete its
commitment to full membership and participation by all women
and men. The basic principles of such inclusivity are laid down
in Margaret's pamphlet about women preaching. Women and
men were created equal before the Fall, and the evil wrought by
the Fall was fully repaired by the coming of Christ. Besides, the
ban on women speaking by Paul in Corinthians was addressed
precisely to that audience and was not intended to be applied to
the whole church throughout time. Margaret Fell was able to
give examples of many women who had spoken out in defence
of the Christian gospel, starting with Mary Magdalene, who had
been the first to preach the Risen Lord, and also the Mother of
Jesus, who proclaimed her faith in the Magnificat. Both George

Fox and Margaret Fell appealed to the experience of the Inner
Light of the Spirit to justify the necessity of new interpretations
of scripture as needed by changing times. 'Mark this, you that
despise and oppose the Message of the Lord God that he sends
by Women; what had become of the redemption of the whole
Body of Man-kind, if they had not believed the Message that the
Lord Jesus sent by these Women, of and concerning the
Resurrection? … else how should his Disciples have known,
who were not there!'[23]

One of the first Quaker women to become a public preacher
was Elizabeth Hooten (1600-1646) who met George Fox when he
was in his twenties and she in her forties. She was already well
established as a preacher of the gospel, and her faith, stamina
and unwavering loyalty had enormous influence on the then
troubled young man. Elizabeth was a missionary, first around
the north of England, and eventually throughout the whole
country. She was imprisoned several times, and while she
served an eighteen-month sentence in York Castle, she wrote to
Oliver Cromwell to complain about the inequities of the prison
system. The rich escape through bribery, she says, and the poor
are treated worse than dogs. Elizabeth used her time by continuing her missionary work to the prisoners.[24] Loveday Hambly
was another Quaker woman who donated her home to the
movement. She refused to pay tithes, and to use the titles
considered appropriate for the local magistrates. She was arrested
almost annually and spent as much time in prison as at home.
Her cattle and farm stock were taken and, at the age of sixty, she
was accused of 'rebellion' and once more imprisoned. The conditions in prison were so bad that she became quite ill, but still
insisted on continuing her preaching and refusing to pay the
tithes. Another woman, Barbara Blaugdone, who was a school-
teacher in Bristol, so upset the authorities by her Quaker ministry, that she was imprisoned, beaten, and then sent out of town
with the gypsies. As soon as the officials had departed, she left
the gypsies and returned to Bristol. Other Quaker women decided to take on the academic establishment and the 'hireling

priesthood', so they journeyed to Oxford and Cambridge to face
them on their own ground. Mary Fisher and Elizabeth Williams
preached publicly to the young theologians in Cambridge. The
mayor was so incensed by their behaviour that he ordered that
the women be publicly scourged in the market place. Two other
women received similar treatment in Oxford, though they were
dragged to the public pump and had water forcibly pumped
down their throats. Other Quaker women travelled much further afield to Tuscany, Turkey, Norway, Barbados, Bermuda
and Newfoundland. In places such as Malta, Corinth, Smyrna
and the new colonies of Massachussets and Virginia, it was
Quaker women who led the way in missionary work.

Mary Fisher, after recovering from her Cambridge ordeal,
took ship to the West Indies. While there, she felt called to visit
the Turkish Sultan, and set out for the East. The English consul
in Smyrna refused to allow her to continue her travels and put
her on a ship for Venice. Mary, however, persuaded the captain
to put her ashore in Greece, and from there she set out over the
mountains and on foot through Macedonia and Thrace. She
finally reached the Sultan's camp and was granted an audience.
She so impressed her host that she was invited to remain for a
time in the camp. She finally returned to England 'without the
least hurt or scoff'.[25] Her travels were not over, however, as she
also visited Boston where Quaker women received very rough
treatment indeed. The rulers of the colonies considered religious
liberty and freedom of conscience, central Quaker teachings, to
be akin to treason, and they were determined not to allow such
teachings to take root in the colonies. Elizabeth Hooten, also a
Boston missionary, marvelled in a letter home to England that
men who had fled the corruption of bishops in England, were, in
the New World, acting worse than those they had fled. The
Boston magistrates even passed a law forbidding ships to deliver
Quakers to the port of Boston. The ship carrying Elizabeth Hooten
and her companion had to drop them off in Virginia, and the
two women, now in their sixties, set out walking for Boston
through what was then total wilderness. As soon as they reached

Boston, they were immediately delivered by soldiers back into the wilderness.

Elizabeth was not to be thwarted by mere earthly magistrates in her efforts to preach the gospel. She realised that a safe house was needed in Boston and returned to England to make the necessary arrangements. In her own inimitable fashion, she approached the king directly, got her permission to buy land and build a house, and sailed back to Boston. There she was again arrested, despite her royal pass, and sentenced to be whipped in the three towns of Cambridge, Watertown and Dedham, being forced to walk to each tied to a cart. Finally she was again dumped in the wilderness. She escaped bears, wolves and other hazards of the wilderness, including rivers, mountains and uncharted forests, and, as she wrote, was delivered from all by the Lord. Her next missionary journey was to Jamaica in the company of George Fox and, finally, she died in her own bed back in Nottinghamshire. Another Quaker woman, a native Bostonian was hanged for her missionary and sheltering work, but her execution so inflamed the public that the king rescinded the death penalty against Quakers.

The courage, perseverance and joy of the Quaker women is astonishing, but from their writing, it is evident that they felt as if they were participating in a Christian regime such as the earliest Christians enjoyed. What they believed, they acted upon fearlessly. Apart from the actual face-to-face missionary work, other women participated by publishing, book selling and writing. By 1700, over two thousand books had been printed and widely distributed. The Quakers also discovered that women had a gift for finance and many women were charged with the organisation of the community's money. As with so many movements, however, the participation of women became restricted as the Quakers became more established. The old patterns of so many religious renewals were repeated here. Margaret Fell, who is considered to be a co-founder of the Quakers, realised the direction that community organisation was taking. In her last letter, she castigated her brothers and sisters for their 'whimsical narrow imaginations', and warned that in turning their backs on the world and imposing conformity, they were beginning to follow a 'silly poor gospel'. Despite her warnings, the Quakers turned inward and women were pushed into the old familiar subordinate roles. Finally, the male ministers decided that the women ministers were taking up too much of their time and the women were disbanded. Women were actively discouraged from seeking leadership roles and the acts of bravery that had so characterised the early years were deemed to be inappropriate.[26] In the final analysis, the fifty odd years of equal Quaker participation by women, illustrate the power of the Christian gospel to call women to powerful social and church roles. Equally, this history illustrates the continuing unwillingness of men to allow such empowerment of women to become rooted in the church institutions as they settle into the surrounding culture. With this entrenchment, not only is the leadership and participation of women lost, but also the power of the gospel to inspire a counter-culture of care, compassion and courage is diminished and often obliterated.

The story of Jane Lead (1624-1704) fittingly ends this chapter. She was a mystic in an age when mysticism was increasingly discouraged, most especially in the Protestant community. She belongs to a tradition that actively opposed the rationalist tendencies of the Enlightenment, as did the Quakers and many others. Like them, Jane firmly believed in the necessity of personal transformation, but her pathway differed remarkably from that chosen by the Quaker women. Jane led an unremarkable life until she was widowed in 1670 at the age of forty-six. Then she began to experience mystical trances and from these she took her rules for living, as well as a language for communicating her new beliefs.[27] Some friends introduced her to the mystical thought of Jacob Boehme, the German philosopher, and she began to interpret her experiences from the perspective of his work, She became a principal founder of the Philadelphian society which was a fore-runner of the Theosophists. These traditions represented a stream of more or less underground thought that had been floating in and out of the Christian tradition since the days of Gnosticism. By the end of the seventeenth century, there were several new accretions to this tradition, including many versions of occult thought as well as Jewish and Christian mysticism. Among its beliefs was a strong confidence in the existence of an Inner Light similar to Quaker belief.

Jane Lead was an ecstatic who thought of herself as a prophet, needing therefore to communicate her views far and wide. What is unique in her writing is her ability to think in uniquely female rather than male terms. After wandering around in the mists of male thought, as she says, she eventually discovered within herself the 'inner Deep' which brought her to a sense of truth not available elsewhere. Here she meets Sophia, the figure of Wisdom who becomes her muse. Lead encourages women to follow her into this inner realm, which is 'one's own native country'. Lead describes Sophia as submerged within herself, but also submerged throughout the whole Christian tradition, starting from Eve. She then traces the female spirit as undercurrent throughout the history of Christianity, weaving in and out of the figure of Christ. Once united to her muse in a kind of marriage, Lead experiences herself as the Woman Clothed with the Sun, or Wonder-Woman.

It is an extraordinary vision, but this ordinary Englishwoman found within it a voice and a set of symbols with which she could communicate her experience. Her writing can be seen as a myth of evolving feminine consciousness, or just the dream fictions of an unbalanced woman, but her writing was as popular in her day as popular fiction is in ours. As Catherine F. Smith remarks, such writing cannot be simply categorised as mystical; it needs a new name. 'It is a special, integrative language built from occult thought by creative discontent in certain women.'[28] At any rate, it provided for Jane Lead a vehicle that was not available elsewhere. As far as she was concerned, previous male-centred traditions had outlasted their usefulness. This was an insight that was more familiar at the end of the eighteenth century than perhaps it was in Jane's day at the beginning of the century. It was the dramatic upheaval of the French Revolution that drew a line under all previous institutions and beliefs and heralded a new age. The effects of this world-shattering event were so dramatic that the twenty-first century is still attempting to deal with its aftermath.

CHAPTER SEVEN

The Marian Age

Historians commonly stretch the boundaries of the nineteenth century from the French Revolution to the middle of the twentieth century and this is the period that will be considered here. The French Revolution was the great dividing line in the political, and therefore the religious and cultural history of Europe and the fall-out from that convulsion was felt everywhere that had been touched by European influence. It signalled the end of the *ancien regime*, and the collapse of its systemic underpinnings. Though efforts were made at the Council of Vienna in 1815 to restore the old structures, the whole exercise was, by then, just wishful thinking. The French Revolution changed forever the face of the Catholic Church, most particularly in France and its dominions but, again, there was no region left untouched. The French Revolution inaugurated a period of instability and fluctuation in church-state relations that is still continuing. As with all such social upheavals, not much changed for women, despite some initial and very significant rumblings from the world of women in both religion and politics. The situation of women, both in the Revolution and in the post-revolutionary era, followed the pattern of every other politico-religious upheaval in the preceding centuries. Whether it was Reformation, Renaissance, Enlightenment or Revolution, the world and the church continued to refine and reinforce the dominance of males over the worlds of religion, politics and education, to the continuing and even increasing detriment of women. What is peculiar about the post-revolutionary nineteenth century is that the quite different worlds of Protestantism, Catholicism, and the now self-confident secular and industrial worlds were agreed on one thing: women were not full citizens, full church members or full human beings, and therefore could never fulfil a representative role in the world. All busied themselves about the task of finding new and more definitive reasons for excluding women from the mainstream of church and state, reasons that still govern, in large part, the conduct of women and men in today's world. The post-revolutionary capitalistic structures and the philosophical, theological and economic reasons that were proffered in their defence are still the structures and rationale that govern the world of the twenty-first century. I have called this the Marian Age because the Catholic Church offered the world the most complete pattern for women's lives in particular forms of the veneration of Mary that dominated the period, especially from 1850 until 1950.[1]

Prior to the French Revolution, the Roman Catholic Church presented to the world an aristocratic and majestic face, where the monarchical, imperial and aristocratic alliances, tortuous in their ever-altering arrangements, offered the church some assurance of protection and survival. In the Catholic states, the church held a monopoly of education and care of the sick, enjoyed exemption from many kinds of taxation, and wielded political influence that no ruler could ignore. In this aristocratic political structure the bishops were said to have 'administered more provinces than sacraments'. These structures continued to hold despite the growing anti-clerical mockery and the endless discussions about the 'rights of man' and the 'rights of the clergy', rather than the rights of God, and most certainly not the rights of women. Despite the philosophical discussions, it was a world known to all and the church leaders were regarded as lukewarm rather than utterly corrupt.

This was the world swept away by the French Revolution, though initially, no one had planned to sweep away the twin pillars of the *ancien regime*, the monarchy and the church. Just like the Reformation, what was wanted was the correction of abuses, not the total transfer of power. This is not the place to recount the chronological events of the period from 1789 onwards, but the storming of the Bastille unleashed forces that rolled across

France and the world in waves. Within a few short months, the
Catholic Church in France had been changed beyond recognition – diocesan and civil boundaries had become co-terminous,
fifty-seven dioceses had been suppressed, the pope's authority
had been reduced to a primacy of honour, and the method of ap-
pointing bishops had been altered. All clergy were required to
take an oath to honour the Civil Constitution, and eventually, as
every schoolchild used to know, the Goddess of Reason was en-
throned on the altar of Notre Dame Cathedral in Paris. The
Reign of Terror left marks on the French psyche that are still not
healed and the campaign of deChristianisation left the public
face of the Catholic Church changed forever. The Church, however, did not disappear, and when Napoleon transformed the
scene yet again, he realised the necessity of church-state relations, if only to capitalise on the social utility of religion.[2]

Several contemporaneous strands eventually shored up the
Catholic faith. One was the resistance of Pope Pius VII to
Napoleon after the latter had unilaterally altered the Concordat
of 1801. The pope was driven from Rome and imprisoned, and
the ensuing world sympathy initiated the journey towards
Catholic restoration. At the same time, a whole range of new
theological activity was taking place in Germany from centres
such as Tubingen, and the philosopher Immanuel Kant (1724-
1804) was beginning the vindication of religion by analysing
moral consciousness, thus opening the door for theologians to
explore the reality of religious consciousness.

Other countries, and eventually France itself, responded to
the Revolution, by stiffening their conservative muscles. This
was also the route taken by what might be called 'Old Europe'
and especially by the papacy. Any Catholic attempts to harness
the liberalising tendencies that had led to the Revolution were
soon quelled, and the end result was that France turned from its
Gallican tendencies to the opposite extreme of ultramontanism.
The ensuing brief revolts in 1830 and 1848 simply added fuel to
this conservative fire and then quenched for several decades the
hopes of those who sought to build a society on Catholic democ-

ratic principles. The two-year liberal honeymoon that accompanied the new papacy of Pius IX, soon gave way to one of the most conservative and reactionary papacies in the history of Christianity.

The French Revolution had contained every possible nightmare of every conservative and swept away the certainties of the Enlightenment. The innate reasonableness of humans now seemed not so obvious and both the established churches and established monarchies seemed to offer greater assurance. It had become blatantly obvious to everyone that the Fall of man was indeed a reality and that the old controls seemed to provide the safer option. Theologians began to preach the necessity of redemption and the inevitability of suffering. When such teaching trickled down to the pews it was directed mostly at women. The Revolution may have called a temporary halt to some elements of the Enlightenment, but the unenlightened had continued their believing ways with little interruption. It was from among the 'unenlightened' that both Protestant and Catholic churches were to receive the impulse that reinvigorated both traditions. In one case, the Second Great Awakening unleashed a new fervour among evangelical Protestants; in the other, a series of Marian apparitions in mostly poor and isolated areas summoned the Catholic Church to a new fervour. In a parallel movement that seemed to facilitate such a faith revival, the intelligentsia of the Catholic Church were silenced by the ever more repressive papacy of Pius IX.

The chief defect of the Enlightenment, from the Catholic religious perspective was that, as well as replacing faith in God with faith in 'man', it left no room at all for an appeal to the emotions. When, in 1802, Chateaubriand wrote *The Genius of Christianity*, describing Christianity as a living force responding to the needs of the human spirit, he pinpointed for many believers one of the deepest elements of the faith, and the element that had survived in the ongoing faith of the supposedly unenlightened. It is no surprise then, that the papacy turned toward the populace in search of support, and to that most religious dimension of the populace, the women. The papacy, then, which had been on its last legs in 1789, reached a peak of populist triumphalism during the nineteenth century. Many were now seeking what it had to offer. John Henry Newman in Oxford was looking for an authority that would determine when all argument must cease. He, and many of his Anglican friends, found that in the papacy. Rome seemed to save many from the pain of doubt and to offer a fortress within which all were safe. Rome also called into fresh usefulness an old threat for those who did not hasten to abide peacefully within this fortress – the fear of hell. Throughout the century, then, the papacy was increasingly taking on the dimensions of a popular force.[3] New forms of mass devotion flooded the Catholic world as more and more saints offered new models of holiness and new devotions flourished: devotion to the Virgin Mary, to the Immaculate Heart of Mary, to the Sacred Heart of Jesus, to the Eucharist, especially in the form of the Prisoner in the Tabernacle. This latter devotion received a huge boost as pope after pope was besieged within Rome as the 'Prisoner in the Vatican'. Reverence for the pope and his person now took on a central place in the Roman Catholic pantheon of sacred objects. The power of such internatuional reverence was not lost on the Vatican and it was no accident that the Dogma of Papal Infallibility was decreed as one of the main outcomes of the First Vatican Council in 1870. Most Catholics were increasingly prepared to accept, with little qualification, that the pope was Christ on earth.

A series of Vatican events turned the eyes and hearts of all believers towards Rome. In 1854 the Dogma of the Immaculate Conception was declared and we shall return to this. In 1862 and again in 1865, thousands of bishops, priests and laity converged on Rome for great triumphalist celebrations. In 1864, the great papal manifesto against the modern world, the *Syllabus of Errors*, was published. This was a document of eighty propositions that condemned almost every mark of progress in philosophy, science, literature and theology. Everything from pantheism to bible societies, from civil schools to ecumenism, from freedom

of speech to any other form of religion was condemned. It asserted that the occupant of the throne of Peter was by definition
holy, and that the pope had no obligation to keep pace with
progress. Astonishment and incredulity greeted the document
among Protestants and liberal Catholics, but among mainstream
clergy and believers, there was little resistance. Catholic intellectuals were silenced for decades. When the first Vatican Council
was finally summoned in 1869, there was no doubt as to the
pope's agenda. Such popular religious despotism was indeed an
extraordinary sight at the dawn of democracy. The great nineteenth-century debates about evolution, democracy, civil rights,
the abolition of slavery and the birth of feminism all left the
Catholic Church untouched for almost one hundred years. The
modern world came into being without Rome.

What of the lives and roles of women in these momentous
changes? It would be erroneous to say that nothing happened to
women, but certainly nothing happened that was really of lasting benefit to women. On the contrary, the old certainties about
the natural subordination of women in the overall scheme of
things were simply reinforced. One significant advance for the
benefit of women was the ending of the witch-craze. It was the
much-maligned enlightenment thinking of the secular philosophers that eventually brought to light the utter barbarity of this
crusade against women. A new debate was introduced about
the nature of women and their place in society, partly initiated
by women themselves as they began to take part in the intellectual ferments of the day. French women began to organise salons,
as we shall see, and even though men benefited from these hot-
houses of philosophical debate, the women themselves were
soon dispensed with when their usefulness was no longer essential. There was hardly a philosopher who did not tackle the
vexed question of women. Rousseau had suggested that women
needed as much education as men chose to give them. Kant suggested that women embody the 'beautiful' and men embody the
'exalted' and that engagement in learning would deprive
women of exercising the power over men given them by beauty

alone. The doctrine of the separate spheres of home and work was taking deeper and deeper root in the minds of all commentators, and many deplored the kind of self-education that women were undertaking through the new newspapers and magazines.

The mid-nineteenth-century Romantic Movement began to redefine the role of the sexes in the direction of mutual love, respect and happiness, seen as necessary for the well being of both women and men. This, however, remained at the level of theory, as the lives of most women and men of the lower classes grappled with the cruel and degrading conditions of industrialising society. The industrial revolution affected the lives of many women in a negative way, as henceforth the labour of women both inside and outside the home was understood by society as cheap labour, and the money earned by women as inessential to the economy. The industrialised world was a man's world and women were used and discarded for the benefit of the male. Nevertheless, since the French Revolution, the question of the role of women in civil society had become an active question. Since secular answers to secular question had begun to be sought, it seemed that everything that the church had decided about women had to be analysed all over again. It is important, then, to look at the revolutionary reflections on women. For about ten years, the possibility of a civic life for women was under active consideration but, in the end, the French Revolution failed women just as all other revolutions had done, and ended by reducing women even further in the order of nature in a universal reactionary response.

The Declaration of the Rights of Man in 1789 had given some consideration to the rights of women. It moved slightly toward abolishing the privileges of masculinity and establishing the equal parenting rights of both mother and father. A civil marriage contract was legalised in 1792, which also asserted that marriage was not an end in itself but a means toward mutual happiness. For the first time in the history of the West, the possibility of a civil independent status for women was envisaged. Howls of outrage greeted this 'filthy equity' and 'mingling of the sexes' from writers such as Edmund Burke, who went on to condemn the 'violation of the immutable laws of the sexual division of labour'.[4] A Pandora's box of women's rights had been opened, and when women began to act as if they indeed had freedom, even such miniscule moves were regretted. Initially men such as Condorcet and Talleyrand enjoyed the novelty of writing about the emancipation of women, and though Condorcet stood by his words, most others hastened to revoke such 'intolerable' freedoms. Talleyrand had stated clearly that it would be very difficult to explain why half the human race had been deprived of the rights of participation in government. Having toyed with such ideas for a few years, he eventually fell back on the 'order of ideas' which was said to transform this issue into a universal prohibition against women. He knew that he was on shaky ground and so he repeated the bribe that was to be re-offered to women on many subsequent occasions. If women returned to the 'pious care of her home', then the state would take care of her.

Condorcet was the writer who tried to produce an explicit formulation of the rights of women. 'Either no individual of the human species has genuine rights, or all have the same rights; and he who votes against the rights of another, whatever that person's religion, colour or sex, thereby forgoes his own rights.'[5] He realised that such injustice to half the human race could not be fixed in a day, because it represented a kind of delay in human consciousness, but he could envision no possible reasoning in the future that would again deprive women of such rights. Condorcet was executed for his continued commitment to such doctrines of equality, but he was among the first to include the issue of women's rights under a general heading of human rights and not in a special category of the 'order of nature'.

Mary Wollstonecraft had dedicated her *Vindication of the Rights of Women* to Talleyrand in 1792. Her concern was mostly the moral injustice of treating men as if they were the only true representatives of the human species, which had led to the total dehumanisation of women. She raged against the prescribed life led by women, always forced to follow male injunctions and not allowed to think for themselves. She was more fortunate than many of the French women who attempted to plead the cause of women, and who, like Condorcet, paid with their lives. One of the most remarkable of these women was Olympe de Gouges. She was the daughter of a butcher's wife, but claimed that her father was a local nobleman. For most of her life she had lived in a false world of extravagance and sham, but the coming of the Revolution gave fresh impetus to her attempts to be a play-wright.[6] Most of her dramas had been hissed off the stage, but her pamphlets began to draw attention to her formidable but undisciplined intelligence, especially her brief work, *The Rights of Women*. 'O man, are you capable of justice? ... By what sovereign right do you oppress my sex?' Thus she introduces her demands for equal rights before the law, in civic matters, in taxation and in the ownership of property. 'All female and male citizens ... must be admitted to all honours, positions and public employment according to their capacity and with no distinctions beyond those of their talents and virtues'.[7] She practically foretold and sealed her own fate when she wrote in favour of freedom of speech for women: 'Woman has the right to mount the scaffold; she has equally the right to mount the rostrum.' Olympe had no hesitation in criticising the women of the past for their preference for gaining their objectives through trickery rather than thought. Women's control of the nocturnal empire was over, she announced. Whatever about the writing skills of Olympe de Gouges, she was certainly not lacking in courage. She was one of the few who came forward to defend the king, Louis XVI, saying that whatever he was guilty of as king, as the citizen, Louis Capet, he should be treated justly. In defending him, and offering to fund his defence, Olympe had knowingly put her life at risk. The king was executed on 21 January, 1793, and another woman, Madame de la Tour du Pin, wrote, 'A great nation has just stained its history.' Throughout the following spring as the Girondins and the Jacobins raged against each other, Olympe de Gouges and other women begged for unity and reconciliation. The murder of Marat by Charlotte Corday brought on a wave of outrage against women. If this was what women were going to do with their rights, then no woman deserved such freedom.

Marie Antoinette was the focus of much of this outrage and the rage and fear of the public turned her into a monster. In the face of this, the former queen maintained her dignity and forgave all her enemies. She was executed on October 16, a white-haired old woman at the age of thirty-seven. Olympe de Gouges had refused to believe that the country she loved would execute her. She could have escaped her fate, but refused to flee. She was executed on 3 November for the crime of writing against the republic. 'I die the victim of my idolatry of my country,' she is reported to have said as she mounted the guillotine. Eight days later, Madame Roland, wife of the Minister of the Interior, who had publicly opposed the king's execution, and had stood by her husband through the twists and turns of his political career, was executed. A contemporary document even faulted her for her courageous bearing on the way to the scaffold: 'the firmness of her bearing on the journey from the Palais de Justice to the Place de la Revolution prove that no sorrowful feelings occupied her mind'.[8] The execution of these three women, Marie Antoinette, Olympe de Gouges and Madame Roland, was used to terrorise all women into silence, 'for justice, always impartial, offers instructions along with severity'. The lesson to be learned was that women, who tried to rise above their 'nature' and meddle in politics, were doomed to destruction. The brief summer of 'filthy equity' between women and men was well and truly over.

Meantime, in both the Protestant and Catholic communities, similar lessons were being taught in less violent ways, but with no less dramatic results. The Protestant communities were evolving and imposing a notion of 'true womanhood' that was to enforce the strict separation of the spheres for another hundred years, and the Catholic community was turning its attention to the usefulness of Marian imagery as an equally effective tool in the fight against the emancipation of women. It is to this latter development that we now turn.

The Catholic Church of the nineteenth century had very little sympathy with movements for the emancipation of women. Towards the end of the century, Leo XIII in 1885 had reminded the Catholic community that 'man is set over the woman' as he quoted Augustine of Hippo in his encyclical, *Immortale Dei*. In his more famous encyclical, *Rerum novarum*, he condemned heavy manual labour in factories for women, but mainly for the reason that they should be at home. No pope or politician had worried much about the heavy manual labour in the home, to which her 'natural disposition' confined her. It was not the teachings of encyclicals, however, which were most effective in maintaining the subordination of Catholic women, but the much less direct and brilliantly effective devotion to Mary, the mother of Jesus, which dominated the nineteenth and early twentieth centuries.

One of the main targets of the Protestant Reformation was the tendency of the Roman Catholic Church to add to the biblical revelation by an accumulation of devotions to the angels, the saints, and especially to Mary, the mother of Jesus. These devotions had increased in quantity and proportionately decreased in quality in the closing years of the middle ages. The symbolic figure of Mary was accruing to herself many of the doctrines that Protestants believed should be affirmed only of Jesus, the one mediator. Mary was regarded by many as the necessary avenue to the grace of Christ: *ad Jesum per Mariam* was the route of prayer chosen by many believers. Mary was reverenced as Co-Redemptrix in her capacity as mother of the Redeemer. The words addressed to her by the angel of the annunciation (Luke 1:28) 'Hail, full of grace' seemed to imply that, gifted with all grace, she was in a position to grant all grace. These and so many other forms of devotion had clustered around the figure of Mary, almost totally obscuring for many the biblical figure of the young Jewish woman, called Miriam. The exegesis of Luther and Erasmus had pointed out the errors of translation that were at the basis of many Marian devotions, and especially of the aforementioned angelic words. The Greek word *kecharitomene* signified only that Mary was highly favoured by God, as many others before her had been. Such observations, however, provoked outrage in the Catholic community and so the period following the Reformation saw an increase of Marian devotions, now with apologetic and triumphalist intent. Catholics set out to defend the honour of Mary against what was perceived as a Protestant onslaught, and this led eventually to the formation of several Marian sodalities, all with military names, such as the Blue Army, the Militia of the Immaculate Conception and the Legion of Mary.

The Council of Trent had mobilised the Catholic world in Mary's defence and this seemed amply justified by the victory over the Turks at the battle of Lepanto in 1571, for which the credit went to the recitation of the Rosary. A special feastday honouring the rosary followed and led to an inflationary round of festal additions in honour of Mary. The rosary became the weapon of choice against Protestant heretical aggression. One of the most regressive actions of the Council of Trent was the intentional acceptance of biblical mistranslations as providential errors designed by God for the glorification of Mary and as proof of other Catholic doctrines. Throughout the seventeenth and that most rationalistic of centuries, the eighteenth, the Catholic world increased its now feverish veneration of Mary. Marian devotion had become Marian religion. The Marian theologians were sufficiently aware of the proper ordering of the universe, however, to deny Mary the sacrament of Holy Orders, even as they affirmed that she had received in advance all the other sacraments. The basic principle of Tridentine devotion was *numquam satis*, meaning that one could never say enough about Mary.

The French mariologists Berulle, Olier and Eudes added their own additions, especially the suggestion that priests should have a marriage contract with Mary and that the Holy Heart of Mary be venerated equally with the Sacred Heart of Jesus. Secret societies were formed and many clergy dedicated themselves as slaves of Mary. One of the most prolific of the writers on Mary was Grignon de Montfort (1673-1716), canonised in 1947. His main work, *True Devotion to the Mother of God* was rediscovered to great acclaim in 1842, reminding people to concentrate all their energies on Mary, making her the central focus of their faith. In the middle of the eighteenth century Alphonsus de Ligouri published his equally influential book, *The Glories of Mary*, a collection of legends, teaching, miracles and traditional devotions as a handbook for preachers. One of his main emphases was on Mary, the mistress of the devils, and the assertion that 'all graces pass through her'. No one at the time questioned the theological foundations of such writings.[9]

The early part of the nineteenth century was relatively quiet with regard to Mary, but then in mid-century, almost coincident with the election of Pius IX in 1846, occurred a series of Marian apparitions that set their seal on aspects of Marian life, imagery and influence for a century and more. It is not necessary to enter into the detail of these apparitions, but three of them will be examined very briefly. The first of this series was that of the nun, Catherine Labouré, in Paris in 1830. Catherine had been longing for a vision, and to that end had swallowed a piece of linen, a relic of Vincent de Paul, the founder of her community. Around midnight, she felt called to go to the convent chapel and there she saw the Blessed Virgin surrounded by brilliant lights and the sounds of rustling silk. After several such meetings, Catherine received a vision of a medal that the 'lady' ordered to be struck. The lady was dressed in silk, covered by a white veil and at her feet lay curled a green and yellow snake. Brilliant rays of light flowed from the lady's fingers towards Catherine. Around the edge were inscribed the words, 'O Mary conceived without sin, pray for us who have recourse to you.' Throughout the following years, this medal became familiar to every Catholic in every part of the world and was worn by many as a guarantee of protection and grace.

The dogma of the Immaculate Conception of Mary was defined by Pope Pius IX in 1854, bringing to an end an extraordinary debate that had divided theologians for centuries. Both

Bernard of Clairvaux and Thomas Aquinas had denounced such devotion and the battle between the various religious orders had been so fierce that various popes had forbidden even a mention of the doctrine. Four years later, in 1858, the series of marian apparitions to the young French peasant, Bernadette, at Lourdes, set the seal of doctrinal integrity on the dogma when the lady of the vision identified herself as the 'Immaculate Conception'. In 1879, another series of visions happened in Knock in Ireland and the countryside was literally transformed by the arrival of thousands of pilgrims. An international airport now facilitates this pilgrimage, and similar developments have occurred at other Marian pilgrimage sites. The final series of apparitions to be mentioned here occurred in Fatima in Portugal in 1917 and this vision became famous for the secret that was supposedly communicated to the visionaries to be opened only by the pope. Speculation about this secret kept the Catholic world guessing for decades and added an aura of apocalyptic awe to the various convulsions of the twentieth century.

Despite occasional authoritative reminders of the peripheral nature of such devotion in the overall Catholic dogmatic structure, the Catholic people in general continued to hold these events and the pilgrimages, shrines, medals, literature and devotions that they generated, in loving awe as central to their life of faith. The apparent demotion of such devotions by the Second Vatican Council caused a hiatus and eventually turned the devotion of many in the direction of the liturgy. Nevertheless still for millions of Catholic believers, the forms of Marian devotion deriving from these – and the subsequent apparitions in Medjugorje – continue to be accepted as distinct elements in the Catholic form of Christianity. The obvious personal devotion of recent popes has served to add new vigour to these devotions, and pilgrimages to Marian sites continue unabated. Nevertheless, many see the proclamation of the dogma of the Assumption on 8 December, 1950 as a kind of bookmark closing the period of sustained Marian exaltation.

What has this to do with the history of women within

Christianity? Some, such as Carl Jung, saw the dogma of the Assumption as the apotheosis of the feminine. The figure of a woman now inhabited the heavens and the position of all women was thereby elevated. Whatever about the glorification of the feminine as a kind of psychological ideal, this was certainly not the case for the women of the Catholic world. It is probable that most believers saw Mary as an intercessor, one that made a distant male God more accessible. Many church leaders saw the Marian century as the triumph of a certain Catholic vision of women, and as the triumph of the dualistic division of humanity into two very different species, a dominant male and a uniquely glorified female. Mary, in her sexless, disembodied purity, presented a totally unattainable model for women. The cult of Mary served the interests of the nineteenth and twentieth (and twenty-first) century papacy very well in placing the question of women in orbit, so to speak, far away from the Enlightenment and revolutionary challenges of the secular world. The proclamation of the dogma of papal infallibility in 1870 only added to the apocalyptic finality of the Marian dogmas. Any questions about the rights or roles of women could now be solved – and are continually solved – by pointing to 'our tainted nature's solitary boast'. This woman is the greatest human who ever lived precisely because she is not quite human. That was the message of the Catholic Church to women in the face of the rationalism of the Enlightenment, the violence of the Revolution and the romanticism of the post-revolutionary period.

The theological conundrums arising out of this elevation of Mary continue to haunt ecumenical relations and Catholic theology. One intriguing sign of this is the ongoing theological question about Mary's death. As yet, the Catholic Church has taken no official position on this, leaving the question of Mary's quasi-humanity as an open question. This also, of course, affects the theological approach to the humanity of her son, and the increasingly convoluted papal teaching about the humanity of women adds another unfinished chapter to Catholic anthropological teaching.

The consequences of using Mary as a rearguard action against modernity still haunt the Catholic Church. Both clergy and people needed the image of Mary for different reasons. The clergy needed her as an image of the safe and perfectly pure woman, unlike all the other potentially seductive women they had to meet in the course of their ministry. The people needed a kind of female image of an approachable 'secondary divinity' who understood their plight and provided assured access to the unapproachable and fearsome male God. Mary then became the melting pot for the most divergent religious needs and desires.[10] The making of such an image of Mary is also the making of an image of women, and criticism of such an image of Mary is also a critique of a view of women. Mary was played off against women as the woman in the background, the lowly and virginal one, the intercessor, and the model for all women. Theoretically, of course, Mary was a model for all, but the detailed implications of this for the spiritual lives of men were never at any time worked out, apart, of course, from the lives of priests.

The dangers in such a mythologising of Mary is, as Roland Barthes points out, that all forget the fact that this image is a constructed one, made for a purpose, in this case the purpose of taming women as surely as the guillotine tamed French women. This kind of myth leads to the transformation of history into nature, and so much of the Enlightenment discussion of the 'nature' of women, is transferred effortlessly into the Roman Catholic imaging of Mary.[11]

Mary exists for many Catholics in a kind of history-free vacuum. The realities of her life are forgotten, and much less relevant than the details of the latest apparition. What Mary stands for has become a kind of enduring archetypal idea because all historical details have been removed from her image. There is no doubt whatever that some of this imagery is beautiful and has warmed the hearts of many women and men. There is no denying that Mary is the most frequently portrayed image in the traditional art of the west. Neither is there any doubt though that the image of the virginal Mary has placed the vast majority

of women in an impossible situation in the light of the Western
tradition about the superiority of virginity to motherhood, a
doctrine which became official teaching at the Council of Trent.
The image and myth of Mary contains assumptions about
women's lives that need to be challenged and she has become an
eternal resource for moral exhortations for women. The image of
the male Godhead has never been used in this way as the source
of specific moral exhortations for men. Such a Marian myth
promises much more than it can deliver. It operates in a kind of
circular fashion, promising the unattainable, deepening anxieties and then, in promising to heal such anxieties, merely deep-
ens them. Mary, then, is not the image of female nature, but the
Roman Catholic construction of what female nature ought to be.
Tragically, then, Mary becomes the instrument of the repression
of women. In the world of the early twenty-first century, such a
myth is being emptied of all moral significance, and is being
slowly replaced by a more biblically based testament to the role
of Mary in the lives of Christian disciples. In many parts of the
world, however, it is clear that neither clergy nor people are
willing to let go of the ancient and perpetually flexible Marian
imagery.[12]

Another use of Marian imagery is explored, controversially
but with much underlying truth, by Tom Inglis in a unique collaboration of English politicians and Catholic clergy in the construction of the Irish mother image of the nineteenth century.[13]
By the mid-eighteenth century, English politicians had come to
the realisation that they could not destroy Irish Catholicism
through persecution, and that an alliance with the Catholic bishops provided the best hope for the pacification of the Irish masses. A tentative power alliance was established between the
English state and the Catholic Church, which, among other
things, led to the founding of the Maynooth seminary in 1795.
This also served to keep the Irish clergy in Ireland, away from
the pernicious liberalising influence of continental seminary life,
especially in France.[14] Consequently, despite many divisions
among the clergy themselves, the landed gentry and Irish political

leaders, an alliance was forged between the Irish bishops and the emerging middle classes and the larger tenant farmers, who were the only ones with sufficient resources to send their sons to Maynooth. Throughout the nineteenth century the heart of the Irish Catholic Church shifted from the town to the country and a veritable explosion of building ensued, including churches, convents, colleges and hospitals. An astonishing one thousand eight hundred churches were built between 1800 and 1863, over two hundred convents, forty colleges and over forty hospitals. The new religious communities of women and men worked with the clergy in this venture, with the Daughters of Charity, who had been founded by Mother Mary Aikenhead, opening StVincent's hospital in 1834, and the Sisters of Mercy, founded by Catherine McAuley, opening Mater Misercordiae Hospital in 1861. These were the first two Catholic hospitals in Ireland, but they were open to patients of all denominations. The institutional power of the Catholic Church in Ireland was beginning to be obvious to all. The project of the alliance of the English state and the Irish church was to bring the benefits of western European civilisation to Ireland through the medium of Catholicity. A combination of personalities and ideologies in this scheme led to the introduction of intense rigorism into the Irish church, one of the effects of which was the puritanical sexualisation of the body. Much of the Irish Catholic civilising project of the nineteenth century, then, was directed to the control of the body, and women were the main targets of this venture. Within the home, it was the task of women to oversee the transformation of speech, manners, the arrangement of space, and sleeping and eating arrangements in such a way that shame and guilt were instilled, and a kind of vague indirect communication about sexuality replaced the previous direct, if rather bawdy, sexual culture.

Through the confessional, the priest became the civilising agent, entering into the most private and sacred dimensions of family life. The fear of hell – through what was called hell-fire preaching – and the refusal of the sacraments for any transgression were powerful punitive and control mechanisms. The church perceived that the main problem was the control of women's sexuality. Sex was preached as a disease lurking in the bodies of women. Once it was controlled, then the true delicate and refined nature of women would be revealed, on the model of the Virgin Mary, and the more immediate model of the nuns, brothers and priests who were now more visible everywhere.[15] The church set out to save women from themselves and to transform women into the kind of mothers who could bring up their daughters in true Catholicity. The Sunday sermon, with its hints about 'some among us', was another powerful means of social control, and the schools carried on the process from the earliest age. The results were that the Irish lower classes began to behave like minor sixteenth-century aristocracy. A parallel, though subtler, controlling process was exercised over the men in the bachelor drinking groups in local public houses. In this way, delayed marriage became much more common for both women and men, in an effort to control the size of families as well as the worth of the family farm.

The Irish mother was crucial to the project of the institutionalising of religious behaviour in the nineteenth century. The mother created the home and then served as the link between home and church, home and school. In this way, by devoting herself to family and church, the Irish mother became one of the great moral powers in Ireland, as a conduit for the influence of the clergy. As a consequence, without hardly knowing it, women gave up ambition, creativity, continued education, and adopted the prescribed behaviours that were being advanced by the post-revolutionary forces in Europe as well as by the Catholic purveyors of Marian devotional morality. The Irish famines of the mid-nineteenth century decimated the Irish poor, but many of the medium and large farm families were left relatively unscathed. It was indeed a watershed event of horrific proportion and has left its mark on the Irish psyche to this day. The civilising and religious project of the Irish church gained momentum after the Famine and, in many ways, produced the Irish political and religious culture of the twenty-first century.

Marian devotion acted in Ireland as elsewhere as a double-edged sword for women. In one sense, processions, pilgrimages, novenas, May and October devotions added colour, excitement, and devotional satisfaction to what was often a humdrum life. Such events were often the only real excuses offered to women for leaving the tasks of the family home. The apparitions at Knock in 1879 raised the intensity of these devotions and Knock pilgrimages brought thousands travelling to this small village. Convents often added their own fairly sentimental, often imported elements to such devotions, which also added excitement and joy to the life of young girls. On the other hand, such devotion to Mary was a deliberate church strategy for the creation and maintenance of a certain kind of woman, and especially a certain kind of mother. The mother came to be regarded as a desexualised creature, who accepted confinement to her home as her 'natural' habitat. The mother was also charged with the practices of home ritual, and in Ireland, this was the recitation of the rosary. The necessity of sex was promoted almost as a penitential practice for such mothers, a necessary but lesser part in her greater vocation as housewife, guardian, cook, and protector of her family. The French revolutionary strictures about the necessity of a neat and well-run home for the male politicians, who had to struggle in the politics of the day, had also come home to roost in Ireland. The work of the Irish mother was not seen as work – in fact going out to work was judged to be one of the greatest transgressions. What the mother and housewife did at home was seen as a natural consequence of her being, and therefore not deserving of praise, and remarkable only in the breach of this hidden universal contract.

'Irish motherhood as primarily involving the sentimental and moral education and care of children within the home, did not exist among the majority of the population at the beginning of the last (i.e. nineteenth) century.'[16] It was a confluence of several forces, most especially from a religious point of view, the influence of the priest and the imagery of the virgin Mary, which produced this delicate yet powerful new creature. Mothers acquired a new Catholic moral power in this arrangement at the expense of acknowledging the power of the priest as the arbiter of morality, and at the cost of totally negating her own gifts, ambitions and interests outside the home. It was the tragedy of the post-famine years right up to the late twentieth century that most of her children were raised for export, and it was often the tragic task of the mother to decide who would stay and who would go. The Irish mother was taught to play her part in the nineteenth-century project of depriving women not only of their rights as human beings, but also of their desire for such rights. It was not only a Catholic project. The same goals and ideologies influenced both the secular world of industry and economics, and a Protestant world increasingly fractured by the advent of modernity. Here again, it was a constructed model of womanhood that was the main weapon in keeping modernity at bay, and preventing the benefits of liberalisation from changing the lives of women.

'We now see woman in that sphere for which she was originally intended, and which she is so exactly fitted to adorn and bless, as the wife, the mistress of a home, the solace, the aid, and the counsellor of that ONE, for whose sake alone the world is of any consequence to her. ... She herself, if she were inspired by just sentiments and true affection, perceives that she has attained her true position. ... The good wife! How much of this world's happiness and prosperity is contained in the compass of these two short words!' And so it continues for sermon after sermon and tract after tract in the Protestant communities of the north-eastern American states.[17] The cult of domesticity, which permeated American Protestant culture throughout the nineteenth century, placed women in the home as her proper sphere, finally attained by her through the good graces of clergymen. Here, she was assured, was the main locus of her identity and her work. Here she was to be confined for the benefit of herself, her family and society. Without her in the home, her husband could not bear the toil that was required of him at work. Without her, the sons would not be able to take their place on the national scene. The successful rearing of sons and the daily consolation of the husband, these were the rewards for the good wife. No one mentioned the daughters, because it was assumed that they would be learning by osmosis in the home the tasks of good wifehood and good motherhood. This is the cult of domesticity. To console women for what one might regard as a vast international conspiracy to keep them from the marketplace, they were assured that as far as virtue was concerned, women were superior to men. This massive topsy-turvy jump in the evaluation of women, changing their identities from the Jezebels of history to the pure maidens and mothers of the mid-nineteenth century was, of course, based on economics and politics. Women were to leave the fields of politics, industry, and production, as well as literature, education and the arts, free for men. They were, at last, in their true place, at home in the service of the menfolk of their family. As a consolation, they were awarded the badge of superior virtue, but a virtue that was best kept hidden from the world.

Men, on the contrary, were now painted as violent beasts who could not control themselves at the sight of a woman, and who would not be responsible for their actions should they come across a paragon of womanly virtue outside her proper place. Women were now responsible as guardians of the social order. It was the task of women to tame the husbands and sons so that they might take their place as good citizens. A sexually uncontrollable male could be tamed by a woman through love and decency. A sexually uncontrolled female, however, would bring the world to a standstill. The world order would collapse, should the virtue of women be compromised. In a world where men saw less and less of their children, the role of the mother was magnified out of all proportion. In turn, it would then be the fault of the mother if the children did not develop properly. Women were again offered the ambiguous messages of praise and blame. In addition, it was asserted that women were 'peculiarly susceptible' to the Christian message, as the churches realised that men were becoming more casual about their religious observance. Women now were to practise their Christianity out of gratitude for their elevated status, and were to come to the realisation that women were indeed more Christlike than men. Women were the ideal imitators of Christ in their ability to bear suffering, their patience and their silent, invisible struggles. This argument, interestingly enough, is repeated in the twenty-first century by Pope John Paul II.

There is no doubt that many women heard, and still hear, such a message with joy. There were certain advantages to such a scenario. Some education was offered by the churches to women to train them for this exalted role. For almost the first time in history, women could win the appreciation of a grateful society where men were abandoning the churches and concentrating on political power and economic success. In the religious life recommended for them, women could experience the benefits of spiritual rewards. Women's groups met together to study scripture, discuss child-rearing, work for the missions and promote the general moral well being of society. Morality had now taken on a female face. The church had very little to say about the morality of the marketplace. Occasionally a woman's voice was raised to question the confinement of such virtuous women to the home. If so virtuous, why were they not running the world?

In fact, women began to move beyond the home in an almost natural extension of their motherly rules to the outside world.[18] They founded mothers' groups, missionary groups, benevolent societies and reform groups as they sought to spread their good influence to the godless cities and the lands of the barbarian. They collected money to care for the poor, orphans, widows and abandoned women. They worked for social change in the area of temperance, prison reform, child labour, and paid special attention to the prostitutes. For the first time, many women became aware of the double social standard of society with regard to prostitutes and their male clients. Many reforming women threatened to publish the names of the male clients, as they realised that the closing of a brothel meant that men took their business elsewhere. In this way women made themselves essential to the conduct of Christianity. They contributed large sums of money, and endless working hours to the Christian project, and in the process, gained the skills of administration, finance and leadership. Church and society responded by declaring that women had special gifts for charity that were lacking in men, and so the sexual differentiation of religion and spirituality continued, for despite all their work – Christianity would not have survived without them – women were almost totally deprived of power in the decisions that affected their lives. The Protestant women of North America mirrored in their life and work the clergy-women alliance that was contemporaneously recreating institutional Catholicity in Ireland.

Sooner or later, some women were bound to tire of their role as perpetual helper and invisible assistant. By mid-century, this had already begun to happen. As usual the breaking point was reached on the issue of women's public speech. One of the central tasks taken on by women was the abolition of slavery. It was a cause that needed to be promoted and women began to speak publicly on behalf of slaves. At the same time, and often in the same cause, women began to question the ban on the preaching of women in the churches, and also to challenge their own inability to use the vast sums of money collected by them. It was in the context of these and other issues that the Christian feminist movement was born, as women began to query the burden of virtue that had been laid on them, without any appropriate power to act on their own initiative. As Sarah Grimke wrote in 1837, 'I follow him through all his precepts, and find him giving the same directions to women as to men, never even referring to the distinction now so strenuously insisted upon between masculine and feminine virtues: this is one of the anti-Christian "traditions of men" which are taught instead of the "commandments of God". Men and women were *created equal*; they are both moral and accountable beings, and whatever is *right* for man to do, is *right* for women.'[19] In a language that got more challenging by the decade, Sarah Grimke and her associates had inaugurated what has come to be called the feminist movement.

It is interesting to note the agreement on the status of women that existed, not just between the Catholic and Protestant under-standings of women's role, but also in the now increasingly vocal secular field. Most European women were still believing Christians throughout the nineteenth century. Both the secular and religious worlds were in agreement on the essential details of a woman's role. For both, the female body was the incarnation of women's alienated existence and marked her out as a servant of the human species.[20] Both agreed that the heart was central to female existence, and that this constituted one of her main gifts to society, gifts of sensibility, refinement, love and patient ser-vice. The new Christian devotions to the Sacred Heart of Jesus and the Immaculate Heart of Mary, added the dimension of self-sacrificing and suffering love, and the understanding of this as a new kind of martyrdom. Since the body of woman had been somehow rehabilitated in its home confinement, there was a new emphasis on the proper care of this body in good hygiene. Christian moralists feared beauty and the unnecessary titillation of the body and so the necessary practices of hygiene were hedged around with warnings about keeping the eyes averted, and not touching the body unnecessarily. Nevertheless, even Christian moralists realised the value of female beauty as a weapon to be used against the unwillingness of men to take on the burdens of the family. There was even a positive Christian value to be seen in soft flesh, delicate hands, small feet and sweet-smelling flesh. The nineteenth century had the same fear of female orifices as the fourth, but were much more indirect in referring to the 'unmentionable' parts of the body. Even the underwear that covered these parts was now called under the general name of the 'unmentionables'.

Secular society rejoiced in the return of the corset, with its im-agery of the confinement and control of the body. Advertise-ments assured women that the corsets were like a tutor who trained undisciplined bodies. The natural function of childbirth was increasingly removed from the hands of women, and was treated by male physicians as an illness, a kind of supervised asceticism. Public sensitivity had to be guarded from the facts of pregnancy and childbirth and women now had 'interesting conditions' rather than pregnancies. Tales about cabbage leafs, storks and midwives finding babies now replaced the natural facts of reproduction, with the result that for the first time in the history of the human race, many women reached adulthood knowing little of the 'facts of life'. Playing with dolls became part of the life of the middle-class child, both as a means of awakening maternal instincts and also of maintaining ignorance. Even though the medicalisation of child-birth developed through the century, it was also asserted that women, the daughters of Eve, were intended to suffer the pains of childbirth, and so there was both medical and religious resistance to any easing of these pains. In the countryside, the traditional practices of pregnancy and childbirth continued for several decades, but with the advent of the mass media, the focus turned to the hospital rather than to the home.

Post revolutionary Europe fell in love with the feminine ideal of sweetness, delicacy, refinement and virtue. For the Catholic Church, the new feminine ideal presented a counterforce to the world of men, and as men abandoned the church the nineteenth century became feminised. The Protestant model woman was created from the same ingredients, but was provided with a larger range of options. For both Catholic and Protestant women, the burdens of their new superior virtue weighed heavily until, for one group, the feminist movement presented challenges that have never been adequately faced, and for others, the wars of the twentieth century changed the roles of women and men forever.[21] For all women, however, the Christian European inheritance which shaped the nineteenth century response to women, still continues to shape in subtle and mysterious ways the twenty-first century response. It is to the feminist challenge that we shall turn in the next chapter.

CHAPTER EIGHT

The Feminist Challenge

The nineteenth-century legal expert, Sir William Blackstone, called the 'greatest of all English jurists', decreed that 'husband and wife are one, and that one is the husband'.[1] Sir William, who added that the husband could keep his wife in more or less perpetual imprisonment and beat her at will, may have been speaking of the known historical past, but he was to be proved increasingly inaccurate in the future. The nineteenth century was to see one of the greatest revolutions in the understanding of women, their nature and their roles, in the history of the Western world, a revolution that was led by women for women and about women. This movement was and is described as feminist, a word also of nineteenth century coinage. It represented a change in women's consciousness that was unprecedented and still meets as much, if not more, resistance as it did at its origins. The feminist movement is so multi-faceted that it is difficult to pinpoint its origins, but the precise set of circumstances that facilitated the development of such a ferment of new ideas was apparent both in Europe and the United States from the early nineteenth century. Developing from both secular Enlightenment and explicitly Christian roots, the feminist movement touched every aspect of nineteenth century life, but it is particularly the religious strand and the religious consequences that will be of interest to us here.

As we have seen, Enlightenment philosophers, both male and female, had provided the Western world with a new arsenal of ideas that had been percolating through both secular and religious life for decades. These included notions of tolerance, reason, progress, natural rights, freedom, educational rights and personal fulfilment. Protestant social ideas had also been having an effect on the public consciousness, ideas such as religious individualism and the priesthood of the laity. Even though many of these concepts had not become concretised in actual law-making or life, they were in the air and were perceived as becoming more attainable. Such ideas had been declared anathema by the Roman Catholic tradition that was, effectively, to insulate itself from such movements through the dogma of papal infallibility for another one hundred years. Women were central to such debates and, throughout the nineteenth century, two distinct representations of women were becoming more or less normative. One of these entailed a reflection of the common humanity of all, leading to an egalitarian and humanist current of thought about the woman as citizen. The other strand was more rooted in images of the 'eternal feminine' and led to a more traditional and dualistic reflection on women as wives and mothers. From the beginning, this paradoxical approach had remained central to both secular and religious branches of the feminist movement: was the emphasis to be on women as human, or on women as female?[2]

This was, initially, a movement begun by white middle-class women who looked either to politics or religion as the engines of change for their agenda. Throughout the nineteenth and twentieth centuries, waves of feminist challenge and change rose and fell, with the religious and secular streams initially interacting, but eventually separating almost completely. Within each strand, dozens of variations presented themselves, so that it is never possible to speak simply of feminism, but of a multitude of feminisms. There were, nevertheless, several overlapping elements clustering around the notions of personhood, sexuality, political and religious rights, and education. These resulted in long legal battles centring on demands for changes in marital and inheritance laws that affected women, admission to education at all levels, self-determination of the female body in opposition to such edicts as those of Blackstone and centuries of his predecessors, and economic independence. The religious feminists focused on similar rights within the religious institutions and therefore set out to tackle the ancient strictures against full participation by women, especially the right to speak and teach, and the double standard in morality. Common to all strands of feminism was resistance to war and demands for peace. By the last third of the nineteenth century, an international 'sisterhood' had developed, that not only served to make feminism visible, but also diversified the goals and self-consciousness of the movement in significant ways.[3] Before long, an anti-feminist movement challenged most of these developments, especially those affecting the traditional principle of separate spheres for women and men.

There is no doubt, however, that it was the move for the abolition of slavery in England and the United States of America that galvanised the feminist movement and gave it its first international leaders. For decades it had been dawning on religious leaders in America that there was a painful incongruity about the fact that the self-proclaimed greatest democracy in the world was also the greatest slave-owner. This had also become a political question in the context of the campaign about extending the vote. For voting purposes, a black male slave was considered to constitute three-fifths of a white male. The initial debate did not consider women at all since they were not part of the public polity, but more and more women were beginning to think they should be and to act as if they were. Women in the American States had been hearing the language of democracy, which from the beginning was couched in religious imagery, and they were drawing their own conclusions. The correspondence between John Adams, one of the founders of the American Constitution, and his wife, Abigail, is well known. She wrote to remind him to 'remember the ladies' in the drawing up of the Constitution, and he responded, 'I cannot but laugh,' calling her saucy and the 'real ruler.' 'Depend upon it,' he added, 'we know better than to repeal our masculine systems.'[4]

The literature on the early days of feminism is so extensive that I have chosen to focus only on the lives of the Grimke sisters,

Sarah and Angelina, for the issues involving the Quaker origins of the feminist movement, and on Elizabeth Cady Stanton for feminist attitudes toward the Christian scriptures. It was absolutely inevitable, as both male religious and political leaders and the women of the new feminist movements relied on traditional religious teaching and scripture, that vast divergences would occur in their interpretation of this religious heritage. One of the first women to give voice to such divergences in the context of the abolition of slavery in the American southern states was Sarah Grimke.[5] Sarah and Angelina were born fourteen years apart (1792 and 1805) in an affluent slave-owning family in Charleston, South Carolina. Sarah relates that, as a child, she once saw a slave being whipped and this caused her to have a life-long revulsion to slavery. The sisters grew up in an unusually independent atmosphere, but their father constantly obstructed their efforts at an education beyond the minimum. It was a highly religious household and the sisters were aware of the incongruence between the daily reading of the Bible and the obvious cruelty to the slaves. The Grimkes were part of the Episcopal Church and there it was a tradition for the women of the household to instruct the slaves in the teaching of the gospel. It was absolutely forbidden, however, for slaves to be allowed to read the scriptures on their own. The endless contradictions ate away at Sarah's religious commitment to the church of her upbringing, and in 1823 she was accepted as a Quaker, to the intense displeasure of her family. Angelina had joined the Presbyterians in 1826 with a longing to do God's will on earth and break through the 'crippling bonds' of her sex.[6] Both sisters had experienced the conversion that was part of the religious revivalism of the time, and for Angelina, this meant that the one God replaced every earthly authority and every earthly institution. Eventually Angelina also joined the Quakers in 1831, and both sisters were henceforth disowned by their families. Both admired the simplicity, intense spirituality and religious freedom for all that was so evident in Quaker practice of the time. The Quakers had adopted as a policy that one of the chief ways to follow the will of God was to work for the abolition of slavery, with the Pauline text to the Galatians (3:28) as their main biblical mandate: 'There is no longer Jew or Greek, there is no longer slave or free, there is no longer male and female: for all of you are one in Christ Jesus.'

Sarah became a powerful spokeswoman for the abolitionist movement, emphasising the totally destructive aspects of slavery for all. It corrupted the owners, the slaves and the whole society and was utterly inconsistent with the moral responsibility of Christians. Throughout the years 1836 to 1847 both Sarah and Angelina travelled the length and breadth of New England preaching against slavery, and were recognised as excellent speakers. Angelina's opposition to slavery was rooted in her sense of the moral responsibility of Christians, and soon led her to a realisation of the necessity of women's rights. 'My idea is that whatever is right for a man to do is morally right for a woman to do. I recognise no rights but human rights. ... the rights of the slave and the woman blend like the colours of the rainbow.'[7] Those who defended slavery on Christian grounds used scriptural texts and arguments that were quite familiar to women. We are all called to God's servitude and all we need to serve God is inner freedom. The obedience and hardships suffered cheerfully by slaves would aid their eternal salvation. Both Sarah and Angelina despised such arguments, and replied that moral responsibilities entailed moral rights. Jesus, they argued, made no such distinctions. As their knowledge of the scriptures grew they could point out that there was not even a word for slave in Hebrew and that the core of the message of Jesus was the announcement of liberty for captives.

As the abolitionist movement intensified, questions were raised about the presence of women on public platforms, and their speaking to what was called 'promiscuous' groups, that is groups composed of women and men together. Like her sister, Angelina, Sarah had been realising the connections between the slavery of slaves and the slavery of women, and in 1837 she began to publish her ideas on the subject of the 'Equality of the Sexes'. The work for abolition had taught them the strategies needed to end women's oppression also. Two other famous women abolitionists, Lucretia Mott and Elizabeth Cady Stanton, had come to the same realisation in the same context. At the great abolitionist rally in London, they had been refused permission to speak or even to sit with the men. Their response was to call the first Women's Rights Convention at Seneca Falls, New York in 1848, where their litany of the injustices visited on women by men were similar to the platform of the Grimkes.

Sarah Grimke's letters on the Equality of the Sexes caused uproar. They were published as a series in the *New England Spectator* and evoked an immediate response from the Congregational Ministerial Association of Massachusetts in the form of a pastoral letter, denouncing the sisters. Sarah immediately responded to 'this extraordinary document' that endeavours to prove that a woman has no right to 'open her mouth for the dumb'. She professes herself willing to abide by the decrees of the New Testament, which have been invoked by her accusers, but with a proviso. Sarah says that she must enter a protest 'against the false translation of some passages by the *men* who did that work, and against the perverted interpretation by the *men* who undertook to write commentaries thereon. 'I am inclined to think, when we are admitted to the honour of studying Greek and Hebrew, we shall produce some various readings of the Bible a little different from those we now have.' This was the basic position of the Grimke sisters – the scriptures had been mistranslated and misinterpreted through the ages, but in themselves all the scriptures supported the cause of women's full participation. As we shall see, the critique of Elizabeth Cady Stanton went far beyond this position. Sarah quotes the Sermon on the Mount, one of her favourite texts, and says she finds no discrimination there – women and men are equally invited to follow its precepts. The ministers, calling themselves the 'lords of creation', had repeated the ancient censures against any public role for women. Sarah insists that her light and the 'rays of her candle' are included among those not to be hidden under a bushel. Her opponents tell her that her influence should be hidden, and if it is it will become a 'mighty power'. 'This,' says Sarah, 'has ever been the flattering language of man since he laid aside the whip as a means to keep woman in subjection.' Perhaps he is now sparing her body, but he has chosen to wage war against her mind. 'How monstrous and how anti-Christian, is the doctrine that woman is to be dependent on man!' Sarah quotes an old dictum: 'Rule by obedience and by submission sway', and interprets this to mean that women should 'study to be a hypocrite, pretend to submit, but gain your point', and she points out that this has been the essence of the household morality which women have been expected to follow. When the ministers suggest that the role of women is to encourage people to go to their pastors, Sarah responds, 'The business of men and women, who are *ordained of God* to preach the unsearchable riches of Christ to a lost and perishing world, is to lead souls to Christ, and not to *pastors* for instruction.'[8] This assured and clear voice is one of the first feminist voices to lay out the claims of moral equivalence for women and men. It is a new voice, without equivocation, and without any hesitation in claiming its legitimate place in the Christian community. Sarah was convinced that her claim was rooted in the demand of equal moral rights and accountability for both women and men in the Christian dispensation. It is also the first genuine example of feminist exegesis, as Gerda Lerner points out, demonstrating an 'awareness of what we would today call sex-role indoctrination and of its pernicious influence on the self-confidence and self-respect of women. She also repeatedly and vigorously stressed the need for female autonomy and self-definition.' One wonders how far Sarah might have gone had she been allowed to follow her 'passion' for education.[9]

In 1838, Angelina married the well-known abolitionist, Theodore Weld, and Sarah became part of their household. Angelina and Theodore designed their own wedding ceremony and removed from it all reference to the wife's obedience or submission to her husband. Theodore Weld renounced all 'unrighteous power vested in a husband' and both promised that the only influence they would use would be rooted in love. This was to be a marriage of fully equal Christian believers. Nevertheless, for both sisters, their public life was virtually concluded. With just a few exceptions, the sisters confined their lives to domestic responsibilities, though they continued to maintain interest in both the abolitionist and feminist movements. From now on they concentrated also on founding educational establishments to further opportunities for women to receive the kind of education they desired but did not receive. In some ways, Angelina was the more radical of the two. She called her ideas about her willingness to obey only God, 'ultraism'. She had a deep suspicion about all forms of human domination, and saw the desire to dominate another human being as sinful. Why, she wondered, would God expect us to submit ourselves totally to another fallible human being? Such oppressive power is always based on inequality and is therefore against the will of God. Angelina judged that all war, oppression, injustice and violence were rooted in just such a lust for power. She condemned the 'sickening adulation' and 'silly foolery' of those who suggest that men need such power, since it is clearly forbidden in the gospel. Both Grimke sisters were also pacifists in their acknowledgement of no power except that of moral suasion. They would not admit of any reason for taking up arms, again on biblical grounds, and condemned all institutions based on violence. It is no wonder that their contemporaries saw them as anarchists, but both sisters professed themselves willing to die for their beliefs. After the marriage of Angelina to a non-Quaker, both sisters were expelled from that community, and their writings become even more radical. Now Christian institutions are included in their critique: 'Our slavery to ecclesiastical institutions is tottering to its fall,' says Sarah and adds that the institutional dimension of the churches cannot bear the light of day any more than the institution of slavery.

By the end of 1837, they had given up worship in any Christian denomination, describing them as 'places of spiritual famine'. The Grimke sisters were challenging centuries of

Christian understanding about the interaction of church and state and, in particular, the two-kingdom doctrine of Augustine and Luther. They had no patience with the unfolding of history. Angelina wrote passionately that the '*time* to assert a right is *the* time when *that* right is denied'. In a moral argument that pre-dates by a century and a half the American Catholic Episcopal argument of the late twentieth century, she speaks of the 'seamless robe' of moral values. All moral reforms, she claims, are 'bound together in a circle like the sciences; they blend with each other like the colours of the rainbow; they are the parts only of our glorious whole and that whole is Christianity, pure *practical* Christianity.'[10] When Sarah died in 1873 and Angelina in 1879, they left behind, on the brink of the twentieth century, a radical feminist heritage that foresaw many of the issues concerning the role of women in church and society for the following century. Their life and vision was necessarily radical because in their day, slavery was an all too present reality, and the possibility of liberation for either women or slaves was, as yet, only the substance of dreams. These dreams of spiritual and political freedom made it impossible for them to live easily in the institutions of their time, but neither sister ever departed from her convictions.

In 1995, feminists celebrated the centenary of the publication of the first part of *The Women's Bible*, published by Elizabeth Cady Stanton in 1895. In the intervening one hundred years Christian feminism had advanced along many different routes. The celebration included the publication of a new series of feminist exegesis, edited by Elisabeth Schüssler Fiorenza, and dedicated not only to Elizabeth Cady Stanton, but also to the African American exegetes who were Stanton's contemporaries, Anna Julia Cooper and Sojourner Truth. These four women, each a pioneer in so many exegetical ways, are now accompanied by hundreds of women exegetes, some of whom might not describe themselves as feminist, but all bringing the new translations, interpretations and understandings of scripture that Sarah Grimke had so desired. This work also continues in Asia, Africa, and South and Central America in ways undreamt of by even the most inspired nineteenth-century feminist. Here there is space to explore only a small portion of this vast exegetical and hermeneutical richness, but the task must begin with Elizabeth Cady Stanton.

When Cady Stanton began her work on the Bible, it is more than likely that she was quite unaware that she followed a long line of women exegetes. Most Christian women throughout history had been forbidden access to the Christian scriptures, whether through almost universal illiteracy as a result of deliberate exclusion from education, or because of the intentional barring of women from study of the sacred texts. There is a cluster of texts that were favourites of women through the centuries. They include the first chapters of Genesis, the women of the gospels, especially Mary Magdalene, some Pauline quotations, particularly the baptismal formula from Galatians, and the last book of the New Testament, Revelations. During the Middle Ages, the most favoured text of nearly all exegetes was the Song of Songs. Hildegard of Bingen, the women of Helfta and Christine de Pisan all read and studied the Bible, though they had to engage in the rhetoric of self-diminishment in order to forestall clerical disapproval. Because of the nature of women's history and the loss of the achievements of each generation, there was no ongoing tradition. The women could not build on each other's insights because, for the most part, they were not available to them. Nevertheless, there is an amazing unanimity among women over hundreds of years about two particular biblical insights. One is the emphasis on the *imago dei* for women: that women are created in the image of God. Secondly, Eve is God's masterpiece, created from better material than Adam. Adam was created from the dust of the earth, Eve from human flesh. The rehabilitation of Eve is a common thread in most of the texts available to us, but this insight had to be discovered anew by the women of each generation.[11] With the women of the Reformation, as we have seen, the women of the Resurrection scenes, again Mary Magdalene in particular, offered biblical justification for preaching and teaching by women. Sarah and

Angelina Grimke share with all these women the basic belief that the Bible was wholly on the side of women. The jarring notes, they believed, were the result of mistranslations and male dominated, usually hostile, interpretation. With Elizabeth Cady Stanton, we enter a new world of biblical criticism that takes into account the historical and cultural contexts of the biblical texts, and challenges head on the traditional understanding of both the literal and allegorical understandings of the texts. Cady Stanton saw clearly that the scriptures were quite ambivalent about women, and this insight was gained in the rough and tumble of textual exchange as the early Christian feminists and their opponents defended their position. It was obvious that the same text could be used to uphold entirely different positions. Whereas women of previous generations had been left with little choice but to submit to the clerical interpretation, this was not the only choice available to the women of the late nineteenth century. Cady Stanton set out to discover what exactly the Bible said about the subjection of women beyond the readily accepted belief that all anti-women texts were the results of male intransigence. She discovered that the Bible itself was androcentric, written wholly from a male perspective and, having been officially interpreted for centuries only by men, it had now become a political tool in the hands of male churchmen to impose their will. In a word, she discovered that the Bible was a man-made book, and could not be blamed on God. For the first time in Christian history, Elizabeth Cady Stanton then raised the question of the kind of authority the Bible could have in women's lives. For the first time, the Bible became a problem for women, and this feminist insight became a major problem for mainstream biblical interpretation.[12]

This is the context from which *The Women's Bible* sprang. It was extremely controversial from the very beginning. Cady Stanton sought but failed to find a team of collaborators to help her in this monumental task. She had been struggling for women's rights for over fifty years when she took on this final task, and her goal was to break the hold of institutional

Christianity on women's lives. She directed all her attention to the texts about women in an effort to prove that, contrary to commonly accepted beliefs, Christianity had not elevated the position of women, but had 'plunged women into absolute slavery'. She pointed out that the entire eighteen hundred year Christian tradition of women's inferiority and natural subjection was firmly rooted in the Bible and that the radical equality promised by Jesus had never been realised. In her own turn, she was to be shocked that most women refused to accept her vision, and, as she saw it, refused to become self-conscious agents of their own liberation.

When *The Women's Bible* was finally published in 1895 and 1898, most women's groups disclaimed any connection with it. Even her closest friends, such as Susan B. Anthony, thought that attacking the Bible only served to alienate the clergy. Cady Stanton was not about to give in and responded with challenges about the right to comment freely and the integral freedom of Christianity. When she died in 1902, she was still longing for dialogue among women about the Bible and its implications for women's faith and lives. Today it is possible to see the narrow lens through which Elizabeth Cady Stanton was looking at the Bible. The series, which commemorates her achievement, *Searching the Scriptures*, and a multitude of annual feminist biblical studies, carries on the task, which she took on single-handedly. It is impossible, however, not to be moved by the intrepidity with which this woman in her seventies, after a lifetime of work for women's Christian liberation, challenged the Bible itself in her efforts to uphold the dignity and self-development of women. She refused to accept any authority that tried to preach the inferiority of women.[13]

Anna Julia Cooper was an educated middle class black woman from North Carolina who managed to bypass all the taboos of her age and gain a doctorate from the Sorbonne in Paris in 1925. She was literate in Latin, Greek and French and when she died in 1964, she had reached the remarkable age of one hundred and five. In 1886, Anna entered the campaign for women's rights with the firm belief that black women were created equal in intelligence and every other human capacity to women and men of all other races. She challenged the churches to demonstrate their Christian principles by espousing the principles of equality and dignity for all women, beyond the indignity and oppression of both racism and sexism. Christ gave us ideals, she wrote, not laws or formulas, and these ideals need to be constantly reinterpreted, according to the different circumstances of time and place. In her reading of the scriptures, she was always conscious of her black heritage and this is supremely evident in her re-writing of the parable of the Good Samaritan as the story of a black man beaten by white robbers. Despite this, the middle class and privileged status of Anna Julia Cooper is evident in her writing. She subscribed to the nineteenth century myth of 'true womanhood', and believed that women were a universal caste with a special nature and essence. Her reading of the scriptures was not a feminist reading but she was one of the first exegetes to point out the dual oppression of women by race and sex.[14]

Sojourner Truth lived to be one hundred and four and spent her first thirty years as a slave. She never learned to read or write, but when she died in 1883, she had left an indelible mark on the history of women as a highly intelligent, self-possessed and irrepressible social reformer. Together with Harriet Tubman, she had organised the Underground Railway as an escape route for slaves from the United States to Canada. In 1851 she spoke at the Women's Rights Convention in Akron, Ohio and continued to work for the dignity of women throughout her life. Sojourner Truth intentionally stood for a different tradition of women's wisdom. As a slave, she was forbidden to learn to read, but she did not need reading as her brilliant mind was imbued with the tradition of oral learning. Simply by hearing it read, she had memorised most of the scriptures, and often remarked to her more 'learned' sisters, 'You read books, I talk to God.' It is said that she preferred to have children read the Bible to her, because they did not feel the need to comment. From her mother she had learned a mystical model of learning and prayer and her visionary wisdom, while utterly part of her African tradition, is akin to the visionary lives of medieval women.

This visionary literacy gave Sojourner Truth intuitive religious insights, and with these tools she critically interpreted the scriptures from the 'witness' within herself. She compared the testimony of scripture with the testimony within herself and concluded that men had inserted many of their own opinions into the Bible. 'And how came Jesus into the world? Through God who created him and a woman who bore him. Man, where is your part?' Therefore, she concluded women were quite capable of governing the world. Sojourner Truth tells us that she herself experienced the 'unbearable light' of God and could not have borne it had not Jesus come between her and the light. Her exegesis of the creation story shows brilliantly how her understanding of the great mystery of God governed her understanding of scripture. She is commenting on God's need for a rest on the seventh day and his need to wait for the 'cool of the evening' to walk in the garden and concludes that these details are added by men. 'Why then it seems that God cannot do as much as I can; for I can bear the sun at noon, and work several days and nights in succession without being much tired. ... No, God does not stop to rest, for he is a spirit, and cannot tire; he cannot want for light, for he hath all light in himself.'[15]

That same extraordinary sense of self-possession and self-knowledge is evident in the speech of Sojourner Truth at the 1851 Convention:

That man over there says women need to be helped into carriages and lifted over ditches, and to have the best place everywhere. Nobody ever helps me into carriages or over puddles, or gives me the best place – and ain't I a woman?

Look at this arm! I have ploughed and planted and gathered into barns, and no man could head me – and ain't I a woman?

I could work as much and eat as much as a man – when I could get it – and bear the lash as well. And ain't I a woman?

I have borne thirteen children, and seen most of 'em sold

off to slavery, and when I cried out with my mother's grief, none but Jesus heard me – *and ain't I a woman*?[16]

It is from the tradition of such women that a distinctive black feminist exegesis began. When they went to the scriptures for insight on the conditions of their enslavement and its brutality, they found comfort, courage and the tools of a challenging analysis there. Such insights were to be needed when the granting of the vote to black men and its refusal to white women, threatened to tear the feminist movement apart, and served to reveal the racist underside of much white middle-class essentialist feminist rhetoric.

Nevertheless, eventually the vote was won for women throughout Europe and in North America. It was an ambiguous victory, and the true result of the gaining of women's suffrage was postponed by the dreadful carnage and social disruption of two world wars, and dozens of less global conflicts. The fight for women's suffrage had been directed almost entirely by and for the land-owning white middle-class Protestant population. The Catholic population of North America was growing by leaps and bounds but it consisted mostly of the immigrant poor, whose efforts were bent on survival rather than on suffrage. Besides, following the pattern of the Protestant clergy, the Catholic hierarchy was opposed to suffrage for women. Cardinal Gibbons declared in an interview in the *New York Globe* in June 1911: 'Women's suffrage … I am surprised that one should ask the question. I have but one answer to such a question, and that is that I am unutterably opposed to such a question, always have been and always will be. … Why should a woman lower herself to sordid politics? Why should a woman leave her home and go into the streets to play the game of politics? Why should she long to come into contact with men at the polling places? Why should she long to rub elbows with men who are her inferiors intellectually and morally? … When a woman enters the political arena, she goes outside the sphere for which she was intended.'[17] Here we see the full nineteenth century portrayal of the 'ideal woman' confined to her home, providing a haven for her husband and children, and assured, when she remains there, of her moral superiority. It is also evident in this short quotation, and hundreds like it, that the Catholic Church had few plans to tackle the world of 'sordid' politics inhabited by men, except to harness the talent and energies of their women members to deal with it on the home front. To this end the Catholic world was flooded with images of saintly models, such as Thérèse of Lisieux, whose practice of the 'Little Way' made her one of the most popular saints of the twentieth century, at the end of which she was declared a Doctor of the Church. This was a spirituality of hiddenness, and devotion to the small ordinary tasks of everyday life and was perfectly suited to the church's agenda. When the dimension of missionary sacrifice was added to this, a global dimension was added. At the same time, in even the smallest towns all over the world, the Catholic population had access to a Catholic school and a Catholic hospital.

The proliferation of Religious Communities of sisters throughout the nineteenth and early twentieth century is nothing short of astonishing. In many places, such as Ireland, this development had started much earlier, as, for example, with the life and work of Nano Nagle (1718-1784), the founder of the Irish Presentation Sisters, Sophie Barat, whose life spanned the whole of the nineteenth century and who founded the Society of the Sacred Heart, and Catherine McAuley (1778-1841) whose Sisters of Mercy also spread to almost every town in Ireland. Many of these burgeoning communities were French in origin, but grew to have an international membership and apostolate. Such were the three largest communities in England in the last quarter of the nineteenth century, the Sisters of Charity, the Little Sisters of the Poor, and the Faithful Companions of Jesus. Marie Madeleine d'Houet (1781-1858), the founder of the Faithful Companions of Jesus, was similar to Mary Ward in her desire to imitate the active life of the Jesuits. The members of both communities had been called 'Jesuitesses' in an effort to trivialise their public ministry of teaching. Like many of the French communities, the sisters were soon scattered to many parts of the globe. Germany also provided many communities of sisters to the New World. Among these were the School Sisters of Notre Dame, founded by the remarkable Theresa Gerhardinger. Almost without exception these women founders had to exert every ounce of energy in order to get their communities off the ground, struggling by ingenuity, prayer, and often subterfuge to by-pass the ecclesiastical and canonical obstacles placed in their path. The international character of many communities helped to expand the sisters' vision and to lessen the burden of local episcopal interference. The founding stories of all these communities should be better known, as the 'ice age' of the twentieth century has served to conceal their initial vigour and enthusiasm.[18]

The total revision of Canon Law in 1917 for the first time in six hundred years placed the active communities of sisters in a paradoxical situation. Through their work in education, health care and social service – by now absolutely indispensable to the life of the church – they represented for many people the public face of the church. Nevertheless, Canon Law attempted to control even the most minute facet of their daily lives and to treat them as if they were cloistered in medieval fashion. New regulations forbade nuns to care for babies, nurse maternity cases or teach in co-educational schools. There were extremely stern strictures about 'particular friendships' which tried, and often succeeded, in removing the most necessary intimate human contact from the lives of the sisters. Even the most essential cooperation with men was often thwarted in this way. Throughout the twentieth century, there was an increasing emphasis on the mechanics of the spiritual life and the details of external appearance.[19] This does not mean that many sisters did not live extremely spiritual lives, but that a whole series of unnecessary obstacles were placed in their path, and consumed untold amounts of energy. The Second Vatican Council (1962-1965) put an end to this particular strain of Religious Life for women, and inaugurated new developments, whose consequences are still unfolding at the beginning of the twenty-first century.

The history of Catholic women in the nineteenth and early twentieth century has yet to be written. Many women were active, of necessity, in the labour movement, in work for women's rights, and in missionary work of all kinds.[20] The nineteenth century feminist movement had been forgotten even though women enjoyed the initial fruits of its efforts in their right to vote and acquire an education. The stern condemnation of the so-called Modernist movement of the early twentieth century had caused a great silence to descend on the Catholic Church. It is doubtful if any Christian women would have considered themselves to be feminist. Most would not have been aware that such a movement even existed, except for biased media tales about the outrageous behaviour of the 'suffragettes'. Maude Petre (1863-1942) was one woman who could not restrain herself from speaking throughout the modernist crisis.[21] 'Modernism' was the name given by Roman Catholic leaders to attempts by some few Catholic scholars to bring the tools of modern scholarship to bear on scripture and Catholic doctrine. There never was a united modernist conspiracy, but even the least hint of modernity brought the wrath of the church to bear on such men as Alfred Loisy and George Tyrell. Maude Petre is to be numbered in this group, as she was a friend of many of the men usually named as modernist participants. She came from an old English Catholic family, which had remained faithful during the harrowing days of the penal laws. Maude had an education that she described later as 'superficial and amateurish', but similar to the education provided at the time to most 'sisters of educated men'. Nevertheless, her confessor, weary of her endless questions, suggested that she study in Rome. There, none of her doubts were removed, but she did receive a sufficient theological basis to develop her thought. In 1900, Maude Petre and the Jesuit, George Tyrell, met at a retreat centre and in him she found a soul mate. She was placed immediately in the centre of the modernist crisis and wrote: 'the so-called "orthodox" are bent on driving the new thinkers out of the church! God help us all.' Eventually, Tyrell was dismissed from the Jesuits, and she

provided him with a home and an annuity. As a result of his criticism of Pius X's encyclical *Pascendi*, which condemned modernism as the 'synthesis of all heresies', he was refused the sacraments of the Catholic Church. As he lay dying in 1909, Maude
sent for a priest to minister to him on his deathbed. He refused
to retract any of his teachings and was buried in the Anglican
churchyard in Storrington.

What had been Tyrrell's supposed wrongdoing? Together
with the scripture scholars, Alfred Loisy and Albert Lagrange,
the historian, Louis Duchesne, and many others, Tyrell was attempting to alert the Catholic community to the growing body
of scholarly and scientific information that raised questions
about long-held Catholic beliefs. Tyrell taught that it was the right
of each age to adjust the expression of Christianity to contemporary knowledge, and so to 'put an end to this utterly needless
conflict between faith and science which is a mere theological
bogey'.[22] Petre committed herself to the continuation of Tyrell's
work and published a series of volumes from his unfinished
writings. She was refused communion in her own diocese, but
she simply cycled to the adjoining one. She was determined not
to be driven from the church. She served as a nurse in the two
world wars and worked ceaselessly for ecumenical concerns.

Despite her strong sense of her own dignity and abilities, it
would be difficult to call Maude Petre a feminist. She wrote
against the 'suffragettes' and accused them of trying to be men.
She wrote about 'real feminism' which had more to do with the
acceptance of femininity as the defining characteristic of all
women. She saw her role as belonging to the private sphere, and
repeated much of the rhetoric of 'ideal womanhood' despite the
fact that she exercised a public teaching and writing role that
was quite discordant with her professed beliefs about women.
She looked on women as having a 'humanising' influence on
men and thought that, if women had to work outside the home,
they should bring these feminine gifts to humanise the work-
place. There is no doubt whatever that Maude Petre was a
strong and independent woman and she wanted all women to

be 'true to themselves, choosing work which corresponded to the needs and capacities of their own nature'. Maude Petre was a woman caught between two worlds. Because of her background and relative financial independence, she could work in politics, have a publishing career and engage in correspondence with some of the most important thinkers of the day. On the other hand, she maintained a fairly judgemental attitude towards those women who, as feminists, had to fight for similar privileges. Nevertheless, one cannot fail to appreciate the blurred vision available to her, living as she did between two worlds. Her determination to remain within the Catholic fold meant that she had to maintain a certain censorship over her life and words. Her writings offer us a unique glimpse of a woman dealing with the suffocating atmosphere of the early twentieth-century Catholic Church in as creative a way as possible.

The modernist agenda was finally recognised as part of the mainstream Catholic agenda at the Second Vatican Council, announced by Pope John XXIII in 1959, and finally gathering from 1962-1965. It was the watershed event of the twentieth-century Catholic Church, both in its revealing of the global diversity of the church, and in its adoption of precisely the biblical, historical and theological challenges that had been at the core of the modernist crisis. The council has provided Catholics with a completely new religious vocabulary, and a whole series of catch phrases, which sum up worlds of conciliar meaning. Among the most popular of these phrases is the 'signs of the times', a phrase which captures the challenge to two thousand years of Christian tradition presented by the world of the twentieth century. One of the most significant of these signs was the place of women, half of the church's membership, and more than half of its active membership, in the world and the church. In one of the great coincidences of recent Christian history, the second wave of the feminist movement took shape in the sixties just as the council was gathering strength. The meeting of these two forces has left the church reeling, and presented it with its greatest challenge for centuries. It would be impossible to chart the growth and significance of forty years of Christian feminist thought and action, but one particular issue has focused the entire debate. This is the issue of the priestly ordination of women. The word 'priestly' is of utmost importance. Since the early years of the twentieth century, women had been ordained in a variety of Protestant traditions. In the traditions, Protestant, Catholic and Orthodox, however, where ministry is focused on the persona of the priest, the ordination of women seems to have presented insurmountable obstacles. This still remains the case for the Roman Catholic and Orthodox traditions, but in 1992, the Church of England, after an agonising debate finally voted to accept women priests. It is, then, to the story of that journey toward the ordination of women that we now turn our attention.

The theological issues involved in the discussion of the priestly ordination of women are among the most basic in Christianity, and touch every dimension of Christian life and sense of Christian identity. Along with this theological complexity, the issue is also one of the most emotion-driven – together with the issues of abortion and clerical celibacy – in the whole spectrum of contemporary Christianity. One of the most fascinating dimensions of the whole debate is the constant *frisson* of dread and horror that accompanies the issue, illustrated most piercingly by the comment of the male Anglican priest reported widely in the media in November 1992 in the wake of the approval of the ordination of women by his tradition: 'We burned them before, we can burn them again.' The level of fear, rage and violence in this comment is truly astonishing, not to mention the sense of identification with the medieval and subsequent inquisitors. While acknowledging this pervasive sense of impending doom in the opponents of women's ordination, it is to the development of the theological issues that we will turn our attention, together with the historical and cultural contexts.[23] The public theological and ecclesiastical debate on the ordination of women has taken place mostly in the Anglican/Episcopal tradition, so that is the first strand that we will follow, however briefly. There has been very little official public debate in the

Roman Catholic Church, though theological and historical explorations have been ongoing. Briefly, in 1984, there was a public exchange of letters between Archbishop Runcie of Canterbury and Pope John Paul II, setting out their respective positions on the subject. This is an illuminating document and we will return to it shortly. Since the mid-nineties, the topic of the ordination of women has been considered to be officially and dogmatically closed in the Roman Catholic Church, but the debate has, if anything, intensified on an unofficial level. To that, we shall also return.

One section of the debate on the legitimacy of the ordination of women has centred on the exact nature of the historical evidence concerning the ordination of women as deacons in the early church in documentary and archaeological evidence. The shaky nature of church response to the historical evidence is apparent in the fact that, in 1920, the Church of England asserted that the ordination of women as deaconesses was in fact a true ordination. This decision was reversed in 1930, raising the question of the quality of the ordination of the women who had been ordained in the intervening ten years. This kind of admission and retraction has dogged this topic from the beginning and added untold and unnecessary canonical and theological difficulties. At this time Protestant women missionaries outnumbered men by two to one and there was increasing agitation about their lack of recognition and status. Throughout the first half of the twentieth century, the numbers of Protestant churches ordaining women increased. In 1956 the Presbyterian Church in the United States ordained Margaret E. Towner with full ecclesiastical privileges. Other churches followed suit and the Harvard and Episcopal Divinity schools opened their full theological programmes to women. In the mid-seventies, Ruth Patterson, a Presbyterian, became the first ordained woman in Ireland. By the end of the seventies, the ordination debate was over in many mainstream Protestant churches.[24] All the churches, however, were challenged by the huge change in public consciousness brought on by the civil rights movements. In 1963 both Betty

Friedan and Pope John XXIII published writings that were credited with putting their finger on the thirst for full human dignity by women and all those deprived of their rights through long-standing institutional and political injustice.[25] Both documents pointed to a growing hunger for full participation by many groups in church and society, but since women outnumbered all other groups suffering discrimination, their voices began to predominate. It is the growing articulation of these women that gave rise to what has been called the Second Wave of the feminist movement. All discovered a 'profound bias' against women in social and ecclesiastical organisation, teaching, and policy. In 1974, this ferment was publicly recognised by the World Council of Churches' conference on sexism. By now women had been coming together in consciousness-raising groups and Bible-study groups and were finding a new language for the articulation of their awareness of their social and ecclesiastical positions. Theological and exegetical studies were multiplying and the first assaults on the exclusionary language of church worship and customary ecclesiastical language were being made.

Without the larger Christian world being aware of it, the major event had already taken place in Hong Kong in 1944, when Florence Tim Oi Li had been ordained as the first Anglican woman priest for a community deprived of priestly ministry. After the war, when the news broke on the ecclesiastical world, the official reaction was negative. The Archbishop of Canterbury, Geoffrey Fisher, demanded of Bishop Hall, the ordaining bishop, that Florence Li be suspended. Hall replied in September 1945: 'I write with intense personal regret to say that I am unable to accept your advice,'[26] A larger rift was prevented by the willingness of Florence Li to resign voluntarily. Despite fifty more years of tortuous, meticulous and often heart-breaking discussion, the basic point had been made. A woman could function admirably in the priesthood and be accepted by an appreciative congregation.

The emotional responses gave rise to genuine biblical, theological, historical and ecumenical study of the issues. Many of these are listed below (note 23), and the issues were gradually leading to consensus. It was soon realised that the scriptures did not offer conclusive evidence for or against the ordination of women. The supposed masculinity of God and the maleness of Jesus were central to the discussions, as were the anthropological questions about the nature of women and their sexuality. The long-lasting Christian traditions about the damaged nature of women and their links with evil were invoked endlessly. The standard arguments about male headship over women, the status of women as daughters of Eve, the decrees in Corinthians and Timothy about the silence of women in the churches, and the supposedly continuous tradition against the ordination of women were endlessly invoked, proved inconclusive or downright wrong and re-invoked by opponents with new arguments. As the twentieth century rolled to its end, there were some arguments that had to be automatically allowed to die. Traditional beliefs about the inferiority of women were no longer acceptable. Ancient fears about the return of the goddess and the unreliability of women's emotions, though constantly fuelling the emotional debate, were now barely capable of articulation, and were accounted more pagan than Christian.

Finally women themselves took the initiative. On 29 July, 1974, the feast of Martha of Bethany, eleven women were ordained in Philadelphia by two retired Episcopal bishops. The following September, four more women were ordained in Washington. In 1976, the American Episcopal Church agreed that the ordination of women would henceforth be a reality. It was in the mid-seventies as we shall see that Roman Catholic support and opposition to the ordination was at its height. In England, the debates continued centring on three main issues, the nature of church, sacrament and vocation. Much debate also took place about the tone of the discussions, and its increasingly unChristian dimensions. Throughout the seventies the now wearying and 'sterile' discussion continued. In 1978, a motion to remove legal barriers to the ordination of women was defeated and, as a result, the Movement to Ordain Women was founded.

In 1984, the motion was finally passed, and legislation to enable the ordination of women was drafted. By 1990, the Church of Ireland decided that no further delay was needed. At Christ Church Cathedral, Dublin, Virginia Kennerley was ordained to the Anglican priesthood, surrounded by clergy and friends from many Irish churches. The Church of England task was completed by the Synod of 11 November, 1992, and the historic debate was finally concluded amid great joy and equally great fears that a schism in the Church of England would ensue. A conscience clause was included for those who could not accept the teaching, and for several years fear and unrest prevailed. Margaret Webster, one of the founders of the Movement to Ordain Women, wrote in 1994: 'So what does it all amount to? What is going to happen after all these years of slog and prayer, tears and laughter and fizz? This ordained Christian priesthood – what difference will incomers make?' She responds by naming the realities of the situation: 'the women are there now, ordained, in post, actual women, presiding at the Eucharist, being with other human beings, discovering how to work in new ways with their colleagues. If there is to be some fresh understanding, a new covenant, the burden must not be placed all on the women. We must work at this together as Christ's body.'[27]

In 1984, as we have seen, an exchange of letters was initiated between Archbishop Runcie of Canterbury and Pope John Paul II in Rome on the subject of the ordination of women. It is, perhaps, the only dialogue on the subject in which the Vatican has been engaged, as internal official discussion within the boundaries of the Roman Catholic Church has been discouraged and finally forbidden. The series of four letters was published in 1986.[28] In 1984, as we have seen, the Church of England had just accepted the possibility of the ordination of women and was proceeding to put legislation in place to facilitate actual ordinations. The first letter from John Paul II was sent in December 1984 and addressed the Archbishop of Canterbury with affection, respect and 'brotherly frankness'. The main point of the letter, however, is to point out that over the past few years there has been an 'increase in the number of Anglican churches which admit or are preparing to admit women to priestly ordination'. The pope spoke of the 'progress in communion' between the two churches and commented that 'in the eyes of the Roman Catholic Church' such ordination places 'an increasingly serious obstacle to that progress'. Before replying, Archbishop Runcie held a year-long consultation with all bishops of the Anglican communion so as to gain information on the exact *status quaestionis*. Runcie, after acknowledging their mutual love and respect, admits that differences persist on this issue, but that the Anglican churches which have chosen to ordain women have done so for 'serious doctrinal reasons'. Archbishop Runcie included a much more detailed letter to Cardinal Willebrands, outlining these reasons. Six months later, Cardinal Willebrands responded with the Roman Catholic doctrine on the ordination of women. From this correspondence, the doctrine of the two churches on the issue can clearly be seen, in perhaps its most distinct format, since the beginning of the debate.

The Church of England statement contains seven points, starting with the growing conviction that there exist 'in scripture and tradition no fundamental objections to the ordination of women'. The New Testament by itself alone does not permit a clear settlement of the issue. Those Anglican churches who have chosen to ordain women continue to be convinced that there is nothing in 'divine law' to forbid their action. Runcie now proceeds to the positive reasons for the ordination of women, especially the 'most substantial doctrinal reason which ... actually requires ordination: the fundamental principle of the Christian economy of salvation – upon which there is no question of disagreement between Anglicans and Roman Catholics – is that the eternal Word assumed our human flesh in order that through the passion, resurrection and ascension of Our Lord Jesus Christ this same humanity might be redeemed and taken up into the life of the triune Godhead.' Another reason, and another piece of common ground comes next: 'that the humanity taken by the Word, and now the risen and ascended humanity of the Lord of all creation, must be a humanity inclusive of women, if half the human race is to share in the redemption he won for us on the cross'. As we shall see, Runcie is here pushing the Roman Catholic Church into the kind of formulation that it would not easily make. The Archbishop of Canterbury is obviously referring here, inter alia, to the ancient Christian formula about the inclusivity of salvation, *aprolepton atherapeuton*, dating back at least to Gregory of Nyssa in the fourth century, 'what is not assumed is not redeemed'.

The next point deals with one of the doctrinal sticking points for the Roman Catholic tradition, namely the representative nature of the ordained priesthood. Anglicans would argue that 'the priestly character lies precisely in the fact that the priest is commissioned by the church in ordination to represent the priestly nature of the whole body and also – especially in the presidency of the Eucharist – to stand in a special sacramental relationship with Christ as high priest in whom complete humanity is redeemed'. This complete humanity of Christ is all the more perfectly expressed in a priesthood open to both women and men. The archbishop now moves to a more cultural argument, one that has always been discounted by the Roman Catholic tradition, which claims that cultural advances are irrelevant to the argument. Runcie says that most human societies have surrendered an exclusively male leadership and, as a result, 'the representative nature of the ministerial priesthood is actually weakened by a solely male priesthood'. Finally Runcie points out that those churches which have taken the step of ordaining women have found that it is 'generally beneficial', and that, despite 'deep divisions', there are no compelling arguments which might lead to a decision to discontinue the practice. While the archbishop is obviously not experiencing a real enthusiasm for ordination, it is to be remembered that the Church of England was at this time still facing the actual implementation of the decision to ordain women. On a personal note, Runcie says that he would have preferred to wait for an ecumenical consensus; nevertheless he fervently hopes that ecumenical dialogue will continue between the churches.

Cardinal Willebrands concedes that ecumenical dialogue will continue before beginning to enumerate the Roman Catholic doctrinal reasons why women should not be ordained. They repeat the substance of the Declaration, *Inter Insigniores*, of 1976, and foreshadow the Apostolic Letter, *Ordinatio Sacerdotalis* of 1994. Roman Catholics see the issue of an ecumenical consensus as having a 'profound theological dimension', thus moving the ecumenical discussion to a much more serious plane. The main argument is then explained, and it is the argument from tradition: 'The practice of the church to ordain only men embodies her fidelity under the guidance of the Holy Spirit to what was given by Christ.' As expected, Willebrands completely discounts any sociological or cultural argument. The place of women in 'secular' society has no bearing whatever on the solution of a theological and sacramental issue. The specific theological objection of the Roman Catholic Church is then outlined and it is the argument about representation. The priesthood is representative, but only in the sense that it represents Christ, the head of the body, and, quoting from *Inter Insigniores*, 'we can never forget that Christ is a man', and his male identity is an inherent feature of the economy of salvation. What of the inclusion of women in the humanity of Christ? Willebrands goes on to articulate the bridal imagery of the Hebrew and Christian scriptures and refers also to the role of Mary as model of the church. Willebrands concludes with the clinching Roman Catholic argument: the 'priest does not primarily represent the priesthood of the whole people of God. However unworthy, the priest stands *in persona Christi*.' When stated in this way, the theological issues can be reduced to two, namely the ecumenical consensus and the representative nature of the Christian priesthood.

This, then, is an outline of the discussion at the official level. Whatever about the theology of the Anglican communion, there is one obvious missing ingredient in the Roman Catholic discussion, and that is the voice and experience of women. At no stage in the debate were Roman Catholic women consulted, at no stage was it even a matter of consideration that their experience might be integrated. The debate was conducted as though women were entirely irrelevant to the arguments. When women consult not only their own experience as Christians, but also when they begin to consult the Christian tradition as exegetes, theologians, historians, liturgists and canon lawyers, the parameters of the debate change dramatically. Such women refuse to accept the peripheral role they have been assigned, on the presupposition that there is something inherently more divine about maleness than about femaleness. It now remains to sketch all too briefly a small part of the riches provided by such women Christians, both within and without the scholarly world of academic life, in the hope of sketching the outline of the massive theological gap that exists between the official theology of the Roman Catholic Church and the vast agenda of feminist Christian theology. There is no suggestion whatever here that the women mentioned are focusing on the issue of ordination as their main, or even peripheral concern, but their work points to the development of a theology rooted in women's experience that deals with the main underlying issues of the debate. Unfortunately, more women are omitted than included here; all that is attempted is a flavour of the often brilliant work on offer.[29]

A huge work of biblical reclamation has been done by hundreds of women scholars since the sixties, but the work has focused, in particular, on the task of hermeneutics, or interpretation. Moving on from the joy of conquering the blindness that prevented women from seeing what was actually before their eyes in the scriptures, feminist hermeneutics of today is a highly sophisticated and rewarding work. Here I quote only from the work of Elisabeth Schüssler Fiorenza and her task of 'searching the scriptures' in the double vision of feminist hermeneutics. A *hermeneutics of suspicion* invites readers to investigate the biblical text as they would the 'scene of a crime', looking for clues and signs that point to a new future for women beyond violence and exclusion. A *hermeneutics of re-vision* seeks texts for 'values and visions' that will lead to transformation and liberation. This double-vision task seeks to 'dislodge' texts from their patriarchal frame, in order to 'produce a different cultural and religious imagination'. It is in the context of such work that questions about women's Christian identity are faced.[30] After decades of work in feminist theology, Rosemary Radford Ruether produced one of the very first volumes of feminist systematic theology.[31] Here she points out that the 'uniqueness of feminist theology' lies in its use of the criterion of women's experience as an explosive critical force, 'exposing classical theology, including its codified traditions, as based on male experience rather than on universal human experience'. With this essential insight, Ruether reconstructs theology in a feminist mode, tackling areas of methodology, God-language, the much-debated 'nature' of women, Christian anthropology, christology, mariology, evil, ministry, ecology and eschatology. She has returned to these topics again and again, leaving an invaluable corpus of theological work that will be basic to feminist thought for generations.

Elizabeth Johnson has tackled one of the most powerful of all theological topics: the mystery of God.[32] Johnson describes her task as one of liberating transformation. Respectful of their own equal human dignity, conscious of the harm being done by the manifold forms of sexism, and attentive to their own experiences of suffering, power and agency, these women are engaged in creative 'naming towards God', as Mary Daly so carefully calls it. From the 'matrix of women's own experience' she seeks the 'right way to speak about God' and queries whether the reality of women and their lives can provide suitable metaphor for speech about God. Johnson explores the nature of women's experience, the formation of language, the history of language about God, and the traditions of Sophia and the Trinity. She concludes her work with an exploration of the 'suffering God' and has left believer and non-believer alike an indispensable tool for charting their own God-experiences. One of the constants in traditional male theological reflection about women has been the notion of the 'nature' of women as something apart from God, and in no way capable of representing the divine for the rest of the Christian community. Several feminist scholars have tackled this issue, from the European theologians, Kari Elisabeth Borresen[33] and Catharina Halkes[34] to the women whose work is included in the volume edited by Ann O'Hara Graff about feminist approaches to theological anthropology.[35] All these works are informed by the searchings of women in conversation with each other, in an effort to unmask the restrictions on the being of women by generations of negative anthropology, and to discover a new language to express the identity, value and meaning of being a female human being. Other collections of scholarly feminist essays range over the whole scope of Christian reality from a feminist perspective. One of the first of these was aptly named *Freeing Theology* and explores issues of revelation, the Godhead, christology and anthropolgy, church and sacraments, as well as moral theology and spirituality.[36]

This is but the tip of the iceberg in the now vast field of feminist theology and it is growing daily. Women have been joined by many men in this search for a theology that is fully inclusive of the whole human race. The last two chapters will explore only two of the many dimensions of this enormous work of feminist Christian insight. It is largely conducted in an ecumenical setting, and has global contributions and implications. In a very real sense, as far as the Catholic Church is concerned, the work of feminist theologians is irrelevant to the essential work of the church. Nevertheless this scholarly corpus has begun to permeate many levels of the Christian reality, and has changed forever the faith life of many who may not even be aware that feminist theology exists.

CHAPTER NINE

Seeking a Spirituality for Women

Throughout the history of Christianity, women had to learn how to integrate their lives into a tradition that was sometimes unsure about their right to be there in the first place, and often quite hostile to their presence. Women were trivialised, ridiculed, scorned, and often hounded to their deaths after accusations of witchcraft or heresy. At the very least, one might say that official Christianity did not make the concrete living of Christianity by women a priority, except in the sense of the restriction and curtailment of the Christian lives of women to the private sphere. On the other hand, as we have seen, many women found the Christian tradition to be a source of inspiration, sustenance and encouragement. There is an unbroken tradition of women attempting to seek the 'more' that Christianity professed to offer its members. Despite a tradition of unbroken resistance to their aspirations, women, from one generation to the next, overcame extraordinary obstacles to their perceived call to full ecclesial participation, and managed to repeat in their lives the profession of faith of the third century martyr Perpetua: 'I live by the authority of my name,' that is, the name of Christian. It is true that most Christian women of subsequent centuries had never heard of Perpetua, nor did they know about the existence of her prison diary, yet the same spirit of discipleship was at the centre of their lives. For a variety of reasons, the lived experience of the Christian faith by women, that is the spirituality of women, has become a vibrant question in the churches since the mid-point of the twentieth century. It is to the spirituality of women that we now turn our attention, because it crystallises the situation of women in Christianity for the past fifty years.

Our concentration will be especially on feminist spirituality, because women, who are both feminist and Christian, have delved
with precision, historical awareness and theological sophistication into the issues that seem to swarm from the examination of
a spirituality for women in a still overwhelmingly patriarchal,
androcentric and hierarchical church. It will first be necessary to
look very briefly at the succession of events that made the twentieth century the most violent century in history. Not only were
the theatres of war expanded to circumscribe the globe, but also
the death-dealing power of weaponry seemed to expand proportionately. The early years of the twenty-first century do not
promise a more peaceful scenario for the immediate future.

As Paul Johnson points out, the twentieth century was
launched by Einstein's principle of relativity, which opened a
window on a new universe where space and time were now
seen to be relative, and where the absolute notions of philosophy and science were no longer tenable.[1] Mistakenly but inevitably, relativity was confused with relativism, and to the dis-
may of Einstein, the twentieth century proceeded to make moral
relativism one of its hallmarks. To the further despair of this
greatest mind of the century, the theory that he had elaborated
was detoured into the invention of nuclear warfare. For this, and
multiple other reasons, society was more and more cut adrift
from the moral universe created by the Judaeo-Christian tradition. The coincidence of the other 'great minds' of the twentieth
century in the fields of psychology (Freud and Jung), politics
(Marx, Lenin, Stalin, Hitler, and Mussolini), literature (Proust,
Joyce and Yeats), and the practitioners of warfare thrown up in
the two World Wars, served to provide a total re-evaluation of
world culture. 'The mighty educated States', all traditionally
Christian, denied themselves no horror, as Christians murdered
other Christians in the millions.[2]

As a result of the wars, and the ensuing devastation, the
twentieth century experienced the largest movement of peoples
imaginable, leading to enlarged populations in the United States
of America, Canada and Australia, as well as in many European

countries. Post-war affluence, resulting from the advent of electricity, the automobile, and subsequently the many forms of technological advancement, led to the creation of a huge and relatively materialistic middle class. In the midst of the Second World War, the 'greatest single crime in history' occurred, namely the extermination of the European Jews. Theologians call this event the *mysterium tremendum* of evil, and the horror was so great that it removed forever the easy recourse to glib theological responses about the ability of a good God to bring good out of even the greatest evil. The previous announcement of Nietzsche about the death of God seemed to be fully realised in actuality.

The intervening years of the twentieth century saw peoples and their leaders, philosophers, saints and poets attempt to fill the vacuum that had been created by such a magnitude of evil. The 'free market' of capitalism became more ruthless, while at the same time providing previously unimaginable levels of affluence for the few, and the necessities of the good life for perhaps more people than ever before in the history of the human race. Though the picture is almost lurid in its horror, when one looks back over the whole century, it seems that the world was just recovering from one horror, when it was visited by another. The closing decades of the century were marked by both a thirst for independence in countries previously bound either by colonial or communist restriction, and a thirst for a union of mutual support in places such as Europe and the Americas, and in institutions such as the United Nations. The opening years of the twenty-first century seem prepared to topple such co-operative and supportive attempts in the apparently fruitless search for an assured security against new forms of terrorism.

The twentieth century has furnished the vocabularies of its peoples with a new range of language which sums up the history of the century: genocide, holocaust, apartheid, terrorism, famine, gulags and concentration camps from Auschwitz to Guantanamo Bay in the opening years of this century. A very few extraordinary people bestride the century with lives that have inspired hope in millions, people such as Nelson Mandela, Jean Vanier, Mother Teresa of Calcutta, Mahatma Gandhi and Martin Luther King, all of whom gave their lives for the betterment of those who had not benefited from the most affluent of centuries. All were intensely religious people, and found in their various faiths motivation and inspiration to continue their apparently insuperable tasks. Since this volume explores the history of Christianity, most of those mentioned are Christian, so it is appropriate now to turn to the vicissitudes of Christianity throughout the twentieth century, in a very general way.

Not surprisingly, the utter failure of the Christian Churches to deal with the enormous suffering and injustice of the two world wars led to a deep sense of disillusionment, which made itself felt through the decades of the sixties and seventies. Numbers dropped at astonishing rates in all the churches, and the departure of priests and nuns from the Catholic Church was nothing short of a devastation of these traditional modalities. In the Catholic Church, this was partly a result of the stern and wilfully blind resistance to modernity for the first half of the century. Every new form of government, scholarship, literature, theology or spirituality was condemned, including democracy, science, modern biblical exegesis, new forms of thought such as existentialism and liberalism, and even historical studies. All came under the heading of the supposed heresy of modernism. On the other hand, the Catholic Church felt able to make concordats with Hitler and Mussolini, as for example, in 1933, Catholics were advised to accept the new Nazi regime in full.[3] Pius XII became pope in 1939 and was the last pope to regard the church with the old Augustinian vision of universal and absolute spiritual power.[4] He was also to be the last Tridentine pope.

All Christians regarded his successor, John XXIII, as one of the most lovable and innovative religious leaders ever encountered, and this is certainly true in conventional Christian history. Nevertheless, though his ecclesiastical vision was to change the church forever, John XXIII still laboured under many of the old clerical anti-woman prejudices, and declared in his diary that the best advice he had ever received was the stay away from women. The summoning of the Second Vatican Council, however, will forever mark Pope John XXIII as one of the foremost creators of the twentieth-century Catholic Church. His favourite word, an explosive one in mid-century Catholicism, was *aggiornamento*. This referred to the updating of the church and the acceptance of the reality of the 'signs of the times', among which he included the new advances in the secular lives of women. In two dynamic encyclicals, John XXIII effectively rejected the negative condemnations of previous popes in both the nineteenth-century *Syllabus of Errors* and the twentieth century condemnation of modernism.[5] He freely accepted the reality and necessity of democracy, human rights, the welfare state, the separation of the powers of church and state, and freedom of conscience. He stretched out the hand of dialogue to the other Christian churches, as well as to communists and other political groupings. He was the first to express a preferential option for the poor and to condemn racism. In internal ecclesiastical affairs, he envisaged some transfer of power from clergy to people and, in his relationship to the council, completely revised conciliar theory. Neither John XXIII, nor his successor Paul VI, provided any ecclesiastical machinery for the furtherance of these aims, and so their full effect was never realised. Indeed, after a few dynamic decades, a dreadful inertia seems to have overcome the church in its ability to accept the reality of the People of God proclaimed as the central reality of the church by the council.

Paul VI, unlike his predecessor, did not hesitate to interfere in the proceedings of the council. In retrospect, the Catholic Church has been floundering in a sea of confusion ever since, in great part because of the act of Paul VI in reserving the topics of priestly celibacy and artificial contraception to himself, and away from the deliberation of the assembled bishops. The subject of sex is central to these two issues, and therefore the women of the church were clearly presented as one of the greatest problems then facing the Catholic Church. Celibacy, of course, clearly affects the clergy, but the point of celibacy is to present women as somehow inimical to the priesthood, and therefore inimical to the ecclesiastical notion of the divine. It can be said that every day of the last half of the twentieth century has been marked by the fall-out from this decision of Pope Paul VI. Thousands of men left the priesthood and the empty seminaries have never been refilled. Millions of married couples decided, in good conscience, to ignore the teaching of the subsequent encyclical on contraception, *Humanae Vitae*, in 1968, and they were joined by hundreds of priests who could not continue as priests with the obligation of teaching the content of the encyclical. The erosion of papal and episcopal authority has never been healed, despite the enormous respect many believers show toward Pope John Paul II. Almost in inverse proportion to the stern imposition of the teaching of this encyclical, and the repeated reinforcement of the discipline of clerical celibacy has been the growth of an independent Catholic press, the growth of a dissenting theological tradition, and the spread of public debate on ecclesiastical issues in the secular media. Situated right at the heart of these developments is the Christian feminist movement, seen by many as tantamount to a new Reformation. Before turning to the global feminist input to Christian debate in the latter half of the century, it is important to recognise two related and innovative developments, the ecumenical movement and the explosion of interest in spirituality.

The closing years of the nineteenth century had witnessed several ecumenical stirrings in several different Christian contexts. Among the most organised of these groups were the Student Christian Movement and other movements for young people such as the YMCA and the YWCA. These groups were supra-national and supra-denominational and there was therefore an effort to find a formula of faith to which all could adhere, and which would include or exclude potential members. Formulas such as 'all those who accept Jesus Christ as Lord and Saviour in accordance with the scriptures' were found useful toward this end. It was from such groups that later ecumenical leaders emerged. At the World Mission conference in Edinburgh in 1910, it was realised that the credibility of Christianity depended on at least the desire for unity among the churches. In the following decades there was a distinct push toward an examination of the central teachings of Christianity, and several world conferences tackled these issues with courage and openness. Proceedings were interrupted by the world wars and in 1948 the ecumenical movement was anchored in the World Council of Churches, as the community of churches that acknowledges Jesus Christ, and that searches for the meaning of Christian faith in the world of today. At the inaugural meeting in Amsterdam, there were one hundred and forty seven churches representing over forty countries. The Roman Catholic Church was not officially represented at this meeting, and was not to play a full part for another three decades. The Orthodox Churches were represented by envoys from the Patriarch of Constantinople. Over the next decades, the political contexts of many churches added an enormous challenge to the ecumenical deliberations. The opening of the Secretariat for Christian Unity in Rome by Pope John XXIII in 1960 gave greater visibility to ecumenism in the Catholic Church.

Meantime, around the world, the ecumenical movement was actually functioning in many parishes and congregations. Barriers were being broken as members of different believing groups came together. For the first time, Roman Catholics met ordained women in other traditions. Friendships were made and several interchurch co-operative ventures were initiated. In many instances, these projects were largely carried forward by women. The Second Vatican Council encouraged such *rapprochement*, and from the seventies on, many bilateral and multilateral discussions have taken place. The almost universal agreement that ecumenism no longer meant a return to Rome had eased anxieties in the mainstream churches. At the same time, it created even greater anxieties among those of a more fundamentalist turn of mind. It was the Vatican that named the ordination of women by the Anglican Church in England as a 'monstrous obstacle' to ecumenism in 1992, and such it has remained. Even though the ongoing debates over the priestly ministry, the position of the pope and inter-communion have somehow slowed the official ecumenical dialogue, nevertheless, there is a growing coming together of worshipping communities at the local level in every country of the world. Students for ministry study together in theologates and create life-long friendships. Above all else, the search for a spirituality to sustain believers through the turmoil of the late twentieth and early twenty-first centuries still draws women and men together in a shared Christian endeavour. The Christian feminist movement, in particular, has always insisted on an ecumenical dimension, and it is to that we now turn.

The ingredients for a spirituality in the twentieth century were much more diverse than ever before. As well as the traditional mainstream (or malestream) Eurocentric traditions, both Catholic and Protestant, there was the newer but very powerful Liberation Theology from Latin America, Africa and Asia, and the strong movement for religious freedom associated with the United States of America. Added to this was the growing feminist theological tradition, which was becoming evident all over the Christian world by the seventies. In a way that had not happened before, all these traditions were intertwined and in dialogue, or argument, with one another. From all these ingredients a twentieth-century spirituality was taking shape that was at one and the same time biblical, traditional, liberating and critical. By the end of the century, bookstores were full of volumes on spirituality for people in all walks of life and every shade of faith commitment. Since there was no longer a commonly understood theological language, partly as a result of the Second Vatican Council, people turned inward, away from the apparent cacophony of voices claiming their allegiance. This followed the major paradigm shift of the century, the turn to the personal as an authentic source of divine revelation, which resulted in the articulation of a huge diversity of spiritual experience and expression.

Many definitions of spirituality were offered to try to encapsulate this new experience. All agreed that the word 'spirituality' originated in the life of the Spirit, as described in the Pauline tradition, indicating a life lived in the Spirit, rather than in the world. All further agreed that along the way the life of the Spirit was placed in dualistic opposition to the life of the body, and that this dualism was further specified as male-spirit and fe-male-body. In later monastic circles the life of the spirit was ac-quired at the expense of, and in denial of the life of the body. Within this complex of meanings it seemed virtually impossible, by definition, for women to have spirituality, since their very existence was understood to be naturally carnal. During the Middle Ages, as we have seen in Volume Two of this series, many spiritual claims by women were feared as demonic. For women, there was a prescriptive spirituality that included the obliteration of all that was female and sexual in order to remove what was seen as the essential obstacle to the coming of the Spirit. From the nineteenth century on, as we have seen above, the image of 'ideal womanhood' provided the ingredients of a spirituality of 'femininity' that emphasised what the culture of the time demanded from women, namely silence, obedience, service, beauty, invisibility and devoted motherhood. One could say that the creation of a feminist spirituality was an almost in-evitable progression from these prescriptive models, but there still exist today many examples of 'female', 'feminine' and 'fem-inist' spirituality for women, and it will be important to distin-guish among these before proceeding with a description of the many feminist spiritualities that are now experienced every-where.[6] In direct opposition to such a development is the paral-lel and 'startling' development of what have come to be called fundamentalist tendencies in all the main religious traditions of both east and west. These new religious experiments, while claiming to be 'going back to basics', including the literal inter-pretation of scriptures and the re-emphasis on core doctrines, are essentially modern and innovative experiments to meet the challenges of the twentieth century. A key perspective of such fundamentalism is to divide the world into realms of light and darkness, good and evil, and to institutionalise a conflictual mentality as central to the religious response.[7]

Three documents in particular from the Second Vatican Council can be credited with (or later blamed for) the creation of a new sense of church membership among Catholics. These are the Constitution on the Sacred Liturgy (*Sacrosanctum concilium*), which opened the way for a fuller participation by all in the celebration of the liturgy; the Dogmatic Constitution on the Church (*Lumen Gentium*), which recalled the original definition of church as the whole People of God rather than exclusively the clergy and opened the way to holiness for all; and finally the Pastoral Constitution on the Church in the Modern World (*Gaudium et spes*), which portrayed the church as a learning church, ready to discern and attend to the hopes and joys of all.[8] The initial response to these innovative church commitments to a new ecclesial identity was often electrifying for women, who will be our main concern here. Untold numbers of women flocked to theological studies and from there to a huge variety of ministerial involvements. Congregations of sisters with a now depleted membership opened their buildings to provide retreats, workshops, and spiritual renewal of all kinds to an audience of women that had been hungering for such nourishment. Women scholars in a variety of institutions delved into the history of Christian women, and nuns began to share their spiritual insights on prayer and other forms of the spiritual life. As attempts were made to bridge the divide between sisters (who had joyfully discovered their lay status) and other women, the traditional models and definitions of spirituality became inadequate, and it was obvious that new models were needed. Five years after the ending of the Council, however, the limits of spiritual innovation were delineated in the appearance in 1968 of both *Humanae Vitae*, which repeated the ban on artificial contraception, and Mary Daly's *The Church and the Second Sex*.[9] On the one hand, Catholic women were to be deprived of the ability of making mature choices about the most intimate details of their married and sexual lives, and on the other, the Catholic

Church and its academic institutions showed themselves incapable of absorbing and unwilling to recognise the long Christian history of deprivation suffered by women. Despite her impressive scholarship, Mary Daly was promptly fired, and an internal ecclesiastical war was begun on all who disagreed with the encyclical. The consequences of both events continue to this day. A new generation of scholars took up where Mary Daly left off, and Catholic women began to look elsewhere than to an apparently unsympathetic Catholic Church for their spiritual nourishment. The end of the prescribed spirituality of 'femininity' was at hand.

Before proceeding to an examination of feminist spirituality, it will be helpful to look at the spirituality of femininity and femaleness. Femininity, though named as such in the nineteenth century, had a long ancestry in the Christian tradition. It has antecedents in the fourth-century development of Marian models for the growing numbers of virgins in the city churches of the Roman Empire. In these models, following on the development of Marian symbols of virginal life, the renunciation of sexuality was seen as essential, and a two-tier model of Christian existence emerged for the few who followed the counsels of perfection and lived a monastic existence, and the vast majority of others who 'fell' into marriage, thus taking a vast downward detour on the way to holiness. The latter group were effectively ignored by spiritual teachers until the nineteenth century. The virgins, however, were interpreted by the 'Fathers' as living lives of reparation for their status as daughters of Eve. As we have learned, this was not always how the women saw themselves, but the imposition of the spirituality of repentance and atonement for their very existence, laid the foundation for the spirituality of femininity. Women were to be secluded from all public life, and silence, obedience, and suffering were to characterise their lives. These requirements were re-interpreted as sacrificial love in later centuries and in the twentieth as receptivity. Women were not to lead, take the initiative, or have authority over men. They could not represent humanity before God, nor teach and preach publicly. Their 'spirituality' was not necessary to the official church, nor was their reflection on how the biblical revelation affected their lives. Preaching was forbidden to them, implying that the church had no desire for, nor any need of their reflective biblical input. In the context of the declaration of the infallibility of the decree against their priestly ordination, women were declared incapable of communicating Christ to the Christian community, but only of receiving Christ from ordained men. Women, however, were still burdened with their very ancient task of repairing the ravages of patriarchy, and bearing joyfully the excesses of the abuse of male power. Such are some of the ingredients of the spirituality of femininity, and all women will necessarily admit that they have internalised large portions of this spirituality, since it has been inserted in the bedrock of Western culture, wherever European influence has spread.[10]

The spirituality of femaleness is rooted in a recovery of the sense of the goodness of the body, and therefore necessarily of nature, since women had been associated with nature in opposition to the identification of men with culture. Perhaps this is the greatest task facing women today – the reclamation of the goodness of the female body after centuries of degradation and manipulation, coupled with sexual fear and fascination. It is in this tradition that can be found the *frisson* of horror at the thought of female priests. The bodies of women were seen as antithetical to the notion of the divine. In a direct continuation of this tradition, some Roman Catholic authors go to extraordinary lengths to demonstrate the suitability of the male body for the celebration of the Eucharist. Hans Urs von Balthasar writes in this vein in an astonishing use of male bodily symbolism: 'The priestly ministry and the sacrament are means of passing on seed. They are a male preserve. They aim at inducing in the Bride her function as a woman.' He later adds: 'What else is the Eucharist but, at a higher level, an endless act of fruitful outpouring of his whole flesh, such as a man can only achieve for a moment with a limited organ of his body.'[11] To this, the feminist theologian, Tina Beattie responds: 'This is the Eucharist understood not primarily as Christ's identification with the universal human tragedy of death, but rather as the identification of Christ's death with the uniquely male experience of male ejaculation. ... Ultimately this means that women have become bystanders in the metaphysical consummation of homosexual love.'[12]

Many have named the issue of human sexuality as the largest piece of unfinished business in the Christian tradition. In view of such interpretations of the Eucharist, it is obvious that we are a long way from the completion of that task, at least at the official level. Women cannot wait for the official church to face this challenge, and they have come to the conclusion that, without the input of women on their own bodily identity, the official church is utterly and, by definition, incapable of even tackling the issue. Women have proceeded to the exploration and affirmation of their own bodily goodness in light of their identity with the *imago dei* in the first Creation story. This does not mean that women are perfect in their humanity, but that their human dignity as embodied females must be respected as an essential minimum before any other assertions are made. With a whole advertising industry harvesting billions of dollars and euros from the sexual manipulation of women's bodies, one can see that this will be an ongoing task.[13]

The scandal remains that in the whole two thousand year tradition of Christianity, there is no single reflection on the marvellous beauty of the woman's experience of giving birth, nor on the experience of carrying a child in the womb for nine months, and especially not on the ecstasy of the sexual encounter from a woman's perspective. This most creative of human acts was instead imputed as sin in women, and there are endless anecdotes, even down to our own day, of women being required to go through the experience of 'churching' in order to purify them after the experience of childbirth. The whole process of reproduction was seen as sinful and unworthy of admittance within the confines of the church building. It is in the same vein that, as we have seen, nuns engaged in the practice of nursing were forbidden to participate in the care of maternity cases. Feminists

have pointed repeatedly to the anomaly of the Christian tradition, whose central mystery is rooted in the incarnation, but
whose central fear seems to be associated with the bodies of
women. Writers such as Susan Ross have illustrated well how
the sacramental tradition has, in a sense, hijacked the activities
of women, removed them to a supposedly 'higher' plane, and
then made them into 'sacred actions', visible signs of invisible
grace. Meanwhile, the very actions of women that are the
human bedrock of these actions have been trivialised and removed from the circle of what is to be considered holy.[14] Thus
baptism, one's birth into the Christian community, is made the
main channel of grace, while birth is made sinful and the principal source of the 'original sin'. The endless work of women in
feeding families is ignored, while the sacred meal, the Eucharist,
becomes the main point of exclusion for women. The church
never hesitates to point to the 'natural' gifts of women in healing
and caring for others, but this work must never come under the
heading of ministry. The revelatory power of women's lives has
been denied, short-circuited and made invisible. It is this power
that women began to reclaim in the twentieth century, and one
can almost understand the fear of the church before the powerful reality of women's everyday lives. In women's own self-
knowledge, the traditional alignment of women and evil is coming to an end. What makes the task more difficult is that this
traditional Christian perspective has been so woven into the fabric
of Christianity that its ramifications are everywhere. Its roots lie
deep in ancient taboos about the ritual impurity of women's
bodies, in the ancient – and contemporary – fear of the Goddess,
in the centuries-long fear of witches, and in the secret knowledge of women about their own bodies. Acknowledging the full
dignity of the female body as the image of God strikes perhaps
the most profound challenge to traditional images of the deity.

Christian feminist spirituality picks up many of these
themes, but there is a specific intentionality about feminist
spirituality that is not necessarily present in the other expressions. Feminist spirituality begins in the effort to unmask the

false consciousness of their own reality experienced by women who live in the 'feminine' culture described above.[15] From the outset it is important to observe that there are multiple approaches to this false consciousness, and multiple resulting spiritualities. Here I am using the phrase 'feminist spirituality' not because there is only one, but because there is a kind of joint starting point in the diversity of feminist actualisations of whatever faith tradition is concerned. Gradually, the false consciousness that implies that humanity can be understood by referring only to male reality is replaced by a feminist consciousness that exhibits two characteristics. The first is an awareness of the systems, doctrines, institutions and cultures that created the false consciousness in the first place. This entails a study of the oppression of women and an adherence to one or a combination of the many resulting forms of feminist analysis. All of these approaches are agreed in rooting the oppression of women in the fact of her biological sex. One is oppressed simply because one is a woman, and women as a whole are part of an oppressed group. This prevents women from blaming themselves for something that is beyond their control and names patriarchy, the almost universal domination of men, as the key cause of this oppression. Within Christianity, this patriarchal arrangement is compounded by the religious arrangement of hierarchy and by the religious belief that such an arrangement is part of the divine plan for human beings. The approach any individual feminist takes to patriarchy is determined by her allegiance to any of the following feminist groupings.[16]

Liberal feminism aims especially at the achievement of human and legal rights for women within the prevailing socio-political system. *Cultural feminism* is concerned with the specific contributions brought by women to the making of a better world, such as peace-making, relationships, nurturing and the like. It implies that women have a certain moral superiority and that elements of the gospel vision are more congruent with the human qualities of women than with those of men. *Socialist feminism* is defined by the set of social relations among men, along race and class lines, which is supported and maintained by their control over women. This is the source of the division of labour, which was intensified by the industrial revolution and its accompanying ideal of true womanhood, and which confined women to the private and unpaid sphere of reproduction. Even when women were forced by necessity to work in the public sphere, or when they chose work as their natural right, this work was devalued in proportion to the work of men. The ramifications of these decisions still haunt every political platform.

Radical feminism, finally, provides a critique of society as a whole also, but regards patriarchy as the key organising principle, especially in its claim by some males to power, and by its aligning of femaleness with powerlessness. From this varied analysis, feminists have come to understand somewhat better the forms of sexual, class and racist oppression, that continue to dominate our world. The key question asked by feminists in all of this is why is the world organised along these lines? Whose interests are being served? Whose interests are being ignored? Whose voice is not being heard? This brings us to the second dimension of all feminist analysis, which, besides the necessity of an awareness of the cause of oppression, also demands a commitment to the flourishing of all life, especially of the lives of women.

It is obvious then, that since patriarchy is seen as the root cause of oppression, the alternative vision of the world of feminist spirituality will be characterised by the choice of non-patriarchal and non-hierarchical ways of acting. The change from one world to the other entails a genuine conversion of morals and perspectives that can take a lifetime of conscious effort. Even though the world of feminist spirituality is not peopled just by those from the Christian tradition, the vision of a world of true equal regard for all persons and for all of creation seems rooted in the first biblical creation story. The forms of human community to be adopted must not entail any form of subordination of one group to another. It is the opinion of Sandra Schneiders and other Christian feminist commentators that feminist spirituality finds its most natural home within the radical form of feminism.[17]

There are three main issues which take Christian feminists into profound critique of the their tradition. The first has to do with the notion of patriarchy. It is obvious that the church is organised along patriarchal lines, and that because of this, not only are women excluded from any leadership or decision-making roles, but that also and inevitably the whole doctrinal structures of the tradition, as well as the interpretation and preaching of the scriptures, and the public representation of the divine in the context of worship, is completely male-dominated. The voice, intelligence, faith and gifts of women are considered superfluous to the core presentation of Christianity to the believing community. The question to be faced by feminists is whether or not this flows from the will of God, or from male design. If the former were the case, then it would seem that the presence of women within the Christian tradition is unnecessary. Many thousands of women have come to this conclusion and have abandoned their spiritual home. Many thousands more remain in a state of suspended animation that is well described in the research carried out by Miriam Therese Winter and her colleagues. After interviewing hundreds of Christian women, the researchers concluded that they had 'defected in place', that is that the women were still visibly part of their tradition, but their hearts and spirits were elsewhere.[18] Thousands of other women have responded by what Elisabeth Schüssler Fiorenza calls 're-claiming the centre', that is, by refusing their imposed marginalisation, and by re-imagining themselves firmly at the centre of the tradition. It is from this choice by women that the movement known as 'Womanchurch' has arisen. This is an assembly of women who work intentionally at providing a woman-centred zone where women can worship freely, without the incessant need for a mental re-interpretation of language and symbol.

The second major question to be tackled by feminist spirituality is the question of the relentless use of male language and symbol in the description of and prayer to the Christian God. It is the realisation in everyday Christian life of the now famous dictum of Mary Daly: 'When God is male, the male is God.'[19] This is one of the most fundamental challenges to traditional Christianity and has been taken up by every feminist theologian. Scripture scholars claim that a God who asserts only the normativity of maleness cannot be a God for women.[20] Others enlarge this to include a male saviour, and assert that a male saviour, viewed as primarily male rather than human, cannot offer salvation to women.[21] What is crucial about these observations is that they are not just made in the field of theological and philosophical speculation, but arise from the lived experience of the Christian faith by many women.

Finally, the question of how the human nature of women is to be described is seen as crucial. Is there one human nature in which both women and men share, or is human nature a dual reality, as is implied by the greater part of Christian writing about women, to this day. This question is addressed in the context of Christian anthropology and raises the most wide-ranging issues about the possibility of women to claim full humanity without qualification. The issues arising from this consideration seem almost endless, because they include the most basic assertions of the Christian faith with regard to humanity, issues of sin and salvation, of grace and creation, of pain and pleasure, of violence and tenderness, of vocation and ministry and of the very identity of each individual in her or his embodied reality.[22] As will readily be seen, the notion of the experience of women in many differing contexts and times underlies all these issues and serves to prevent them from being consigned to the traditionally rarified atmosphere of theological speculation. As women attest constantly, their very survival depends on their testimony in these areas being attended to and heard. In their own consciousness-raising groups women have learned to 'hear one another into speech' on these issues, to begin the journey into spiritual self-awareness, and to celebrate their insights in ritual, art, song and dance.

Feminist spirituality, then, is the 'reclaiming by women of the reality and power designated by the term "spirit" and the effort to reintegrate spirit and body, heaven and earth, culture and nature, eternity and time, public and private, political and personal, in short, all those hierarchised dichotomous dualisms whose root is the split between spirit and body and whose primary incarnation is the split between male and female.'[23] It remains to chart some of the main themes and features of feminist spirituality and to look very briefly at the work of feminist theologians in reclaiming the name of God for women.

For obvious reasons, Catholic feminist spirituality, after 1977 and the publication of *Inter Insigniores*, on the inability of the church to consider the ordination of women, and even more after the series of statements in 1994-1995, which made this teaching part of infallible dogma, has developed primarily on the margins of the Catholic Church, and certainly outside its official structures. Despite their different circumstances, this is also true of other Christian traditions. Feminist spirituality is recognised on special 'women's days', but in no tradition, even where women are ordained, has it been fully integrated into the normative life of any Christian tradition. This gives women the freedom to experiment and improvise as they search for language, symbol and ritual that will express their own relationship with the divine. What has been accomplished so far is the work of centuries, crammed into a few short decades. At the same time, this continued marginalisation makes the promise of ultimate recognition and integration even more difficult as the tradition of feminist spirituality and the often increasingly retrenched 'official' tradition move farther apart. Within this marginal space there is often tumultuous activity, generating creative excitement and spiritual healing and renewal. Much of this is ephemeral, rarely recorded and very much confined to seasonal celebrations, such as commemorations of remembered saintly women, ritual celebration of the stages of women's lives, and celebrations of the seasons of the year that recall ancient cultural festivals of pre-Christian origin. One of the central tasks of feminist spirituality is the ritual healing of the pain of women, from the pain of continued exclusion, to the actual pain of the violence of assault and rape.

A significant feature of feminist spirituality is story telling, the claiming aloud of the significance of each individual life, the recognition of patterns of joy and grief, of struggle and liberation, and above all of connectedness with all creation. All feminists share a profound connection with non-human nature, its revelatory power and its cyclical beauty. There is also a deeply felt recognition of the links that exist between the rape of the earth and the rape of women. Feminist spirituality is committed to the relationship between personal growth and transformation and the politics of social justice. Several commentators divide feminist spirituality into two strands, the aesthetic or romantic strand and the ethical strand. The aesthetic strand deals mainly with what might be called nature mysticism, the connectedness between women and the earth, and looks *inter alia* to ancient goddess and witchcraft traditions for some resources and inspiration. It focuses on the goodness of creation and all created things, especially on the goodness of women's bodies and sexuality. The ethical strand looks to the demands of social justice. It focuses on the unmasking of the abuse of power and has recognisable links with traditions of liberation theology in the developing countries of Latin America, Africa and Asia. The prophetic dimension of the gospel vision is important in this tradition and the theological principle articulated by Rosemary Radford Ruether well sums up its concerns: 'whatever denies, diminishes, or distorts the full humanity of women is, therefore, appraised as non-redemptive'. It must be presumed that such denial does not 'reflect the divine'. On the other hand, 'what does promote the full humanity of women is of the Holy' and 'does reflect the true relation to the divine'.[24]

While the diversity among all feminists, Christian and otherwise, is now an established fact of the twentieth century feminist movement, this diversity is connected with the starting points and goals of any particular group. Several commentators have elaborated on the diversity of feminists with connections to the

Christian tradition, and have described their varied stances.[25] Among these is the distinction between Feminist Christians and Christian Feminists. The former, with the word 'feminist' acting as adjective to the noun 'Christian' would include women whose primary commitment is to the Christian tradition, to which they have a deep attachment. Nevertheless their feminist stance comes from the often angry realisation that their presence is a problem for the institution. Often the more committed they are, the more they are perceived as a problem. Their ability to worship is forever altered by the overwhelming maleness of the language and symbolism, and they seem to find themselves in a continued state of anger and rejection. Much of their energy goes into negotiating their anger and learning how to live in the conflictual surroundings of the institution. Many ordained women experience something like this when, despite their ordination, they feel that real power to act effectively has been taken from their hands. Nevertheless, the visibility provided by such women is of enormous benefit to other churchwomen, who often have no appreciation of the dilemmas involved in such public ministry for women. In fact, much of the work of the twentieth-century church at the parish and congregational level is performed by such women, and without them, the churches would not survive.

Christian Feminists reverse the two words and point to the group of women whose primary commitment is to feminism, though within the Christian context. Such women may make flying visits to their local parish or congregation, but their main spiritual sustenance does not come from their former locations. They have discovered a need for an alternative community, and find this in groups specially founded for the purpose of providing for such women. Such groups have multiplied in every country, the largest group being WomenChurch in North America. In these groups, there is no longer an effort to negotiate with a patriarchal tradition and its masculine symbol system. Such women are creating new language and new ritual and pouring their energies into direct political involvement and action for the flourishing of women and all creation. A huge network has been created among such groups and there is, therefore, an intermingling of insights, traditions, and experiences. These groups are intentionally ecumenical and often inter-faith as well, and may well represent the cutting edge of ecumenical activity. There is no attempt to imitate the rituals of the institutions, but new ritual grows from the needs of the group. The main criterion has to do with what is life-giving for women, following on the theological principle outlined above. These women are no longer, like their sisters in the first group, working for the reform of the church, but they are busy being church in their own context.

A third group might be called post-Christian Feminists. These are women who have found the Christian tradition to be so steeped in patriarchy as to be beyond redemption. The reasons are multiple and the responses likewise. There is room for only two names to represent a multitude of women, Mary Daly and Daphne Hampson, though neither woman might now be happy with the description of post-Christian feminist. Daly describes her departure thus: 'My graduation from the Catholic church was formalised by a self-conferred diploma, my second feminist book, *Beyond God the Father: Toward a Philosophy of Women's Liberation*, which appeared in 1973.' She goes on to say that the journey between her two feminist books, that is, between 1968 and 1973 was like 'leap-frogging galaxies in a mind voyage to further and further stars'. She says that she sometimes has trouble recalling herself as author of the former book.[26]

Daphne Hampson, after doctorates in Oxford and Harvard, played a leading role in the campaign to allow women to be ordained in the Anglican church in Britain. Subsequently she left the church, because she believed that Christianity and feminism are incompatible, and that the Christian myth is untrue. Nevertheless, she has continued to work as a theologian and was the first President of the European Society of Women for Theology Research. She has continued to enter into dialogue with women from the Christian tradition, and states her position as believing 'that God is equally available to people in all times and all places'. She denies 'there could be a particular revelation of God in any one age, which thenceforth becomes normative for all others'.[27]

This gives a mere glimpse into the variety of expression taken by feminism within the Christian tradition, at the turning point of the twenty-first century. All such traditions necessarily deal with similar themes, even though the method of approach and the experience may be quite different. Here are some of those themes, the first being that of *Naming the Self* and starting from this experience. Women have learned, and taught one another to become aware of and trust their own inner wisdom. The search for identity is an ongoing process, but once on the road, there is no returning to a prescribed self-understanding. When a woman asks: Who am I?, her question is shaped by a number of different contexts, from family to heritage to nationality to faith tradition. With the realisation that patriarchal traditions have socialised women to be other-identified, and that many traditions, including the Catholic Church, continue to do so, women realise that they have to make a transition from this state, or fail to reach their true potential. On this journey, voice has become one of the strongest metaphors for women's development, and is intrinsically linked with a Christian woman's faith journey today.

A second major theme is *Embodiment*, as one might expect. For most women, one of the longest journeys is the journey to the unity of body and spirit. It is a multi-faceted experience where childhood learnings have to be unlearned, and society's assumptions have to be challenged. Likewise the ongoing Christian beliefs about women's bodies have to be understood and unmasked in order to face their enslaving potential. Exploring embodiment also brings a woman face to face with the fact of violence against women, historical and contemporary, the violence of war, rape, pornography, and of the self-inflicted violence of anorexia and drugs.

Women have often been told that they are better at *relation-*

ships than men as part of the popular wisdom of coming of age. This 'wisdom' has also been used to place the burdens of relationships on women, as well as the blame for their failure. Nevertheless, what most women have found to be essential to their development is friendship and connectedness. They are prepared for the intimacy and accountability of freely chosen friendships, and also for the pain of betrayal. Women, then, have engaged in the task of creating self-defined women's communities where truth can be spoken and joint commitments worked out. Women have intentionally designed such communities in non-patriarchal ways, with shared leadership and consensus decision-making. One of the essential tasks of such groups is to learn to deal with anger and to face it directly.[28]

Women are *healers*, as both history and experience testify. They have learned that all healing is circular, not only bringing a balance of body, mind and spirit, but also involving the giving and receiving of care. Exploring healing also brings up the societal issue of women's health, which is an issue well beyond the scope of this book in its complexity. One dimension of the work of healing, which women have had to learn, is the art of receiving, an often difficult task in a society and church that has seen women's task as primarily that of 'self-sacrificing love'. Healing also raises questions about God and the kind of God that can offer healing to women. Women would answer without hesitation that such a God must be characterised by vulnerability and compassion.

Finally, feminist spirituality always circles around themes of *play, humour, beauty, wisdom* and *vision*. It involves the creative use of imagination in the invention of a world free from patriarchy, sexism, violence, racism and oppression. Women are learning to live in anticipatory fidelity to such a vision and learning the art of breaking out of old moulds. Women have also learned that, as Gandhi taught, 'the way to peace is peace' and in agreement with Nelle Morton, that the 'journey is home'. Feminist spirituality is about starting on this journey and discovering that one is at home on this journey.

Perhaps the most challenging of all the ingredients of feminist spirituality is the naming of God, a naming that points to the mystery of divinity beyond any name. This is a huge topic that may well be the major focus of theology for the twenty-first century. It has ramifications beyond feminism, but feminist exploration of God will shake the foundations. Feminists from the beginning have challenged the stranglehold on the language of God/he and point out that the ruling male metaphor for God has expanded to fill a whole metaphysical universe. Within the Roman Catholic tradition and its official language of worship and teaching, the exclusive use of the pronoun 'he' and the supposed inclusion of women in the collective 'man', without ever naming women, has caused not only confusion, but also grief and anger to many women. When the liturgy is celebrated, or a Catechism is written for a world composed, apparently, of men only, many women no longer even make the effort to include themselves. Others, apparently, do not seem even to notice the anomaly in religious settings, whereas the use of language in most other settings today has been altered to indicate the audience addressed. This has often met with howls of outrage about political correctness, but the necessity of such language restructuring seems blindingly obvious to many of those excluded.

Religious settings are, however, more emotionally laden with traditional overtones of revelation and theology. Initial attempts at addressing the problem fall under the heading of 'inclusive language'. Most church documents – but by no means all – now speak of women and men, or use plural forms, whenever the whole congregation is being addressed. Even though all agree that God is spirit, it is still argued that the only appropriate pronoun is 'he'. When choir directors, preachers, or readers try to avoid the use of 'he' by repeating the divine name, the text becomes cumbersome and artificial. Language tinkering, then, does not solve the problem. Several feminist theologians have tried to address the more substantive issues in works of outstanding quality. Here we will give a brief summary of some of these works.[29]

All commentators point out that there are two main emphases in the Christian tradition about God: for the first one thousand years, God was generally spoken of in a relational sense, and from the scholastic period on, the Being of God was primarily emphasised. In this latter context of God as Supreme Being, there seems no possible convergence for women and God. Some possibilities exist when God is spoken of in a relational sense. Here to summarise a vast amount of material, we shall look at four options chosen by Christian feminists, who see themselves as totally committed to their respective Christian traditions.

First of all, there are a number of feminists who have re-dedicated themselves to the belief that God is Father, Son and Spirit. These are the revealed names of God and there is no possible alternative. Jesus called God Father. Father, then, is understood to be the ontological name of God. God is always, everywhere and essentially Father. This is understood as having nothing to do with maleness or femaleness or the cultural understanding of this name. These male names do not have a sexual connotation, because the tradition says they do not. Since the Father, Son and Spirit are revealed names, history, culture, and above all, feminist analysis, are totally irrelevant. Besides being a rather skewed understanding of how language functions, this position, however sincerely held by its proponents, does an injustice to the feminist position. Feminists do not object to the use of Father, but to its exclusive use.

The next group of feminists take a hermeneutic or interpretative stance, which can lead in several different directions. First of all there are feminists who emphasise both masculine and feminine *traits* in God, as the Bible reveals. God is mother hen, a woman in labour, a baker-woman, and a homemaker searching for a lost coin. All these are biblical images revealing a feminine side to God the Father, alongside his strength, mighty power and roles as judge and lawgiver. These images are seen to relativise the ubiquity of male language and imagery. God thus becomes a different kind of man, with some womanly traits. It is abundantly clear, though, that there is a whole range of womanly traits that can never be affirmed of God, the traits, that is, that are associated with femaleness.

Other feminists in this group emphasise the feminine *dimensions* of God, especially two biblical dimensions indicated by the words *Sophia*, and *Ruah*. Sophia, Wisdom, is seen as a female personification of the divine as seen in such texts as Proverbs 8. In the New Testament, these Wisdom texts are used to express the saving power of Jesus: he is the 'image of the invisible God', the 'radiant light of God's glory', 'the firstborn of all creation'. This is often seen as the most usable of all feminine biblical images of the divine. The figure of Sophia is common in the scriptures, but the image disappears almost completely in the patristic period, and this feminine dimension of God was never fully integrated into mainstream theology.[30] Ruah, in biblical tradition, is the Spirit of God, the Shekinah hovering over the waters of creation. Ruah is a feminine term, but it has become fully masculinised in Latin (*Spiritus Sanctus*) and in English. Feminists wish to reclaim this image, with all its biblical possibilities.

Following on these two usages of dual biblical traits and dimensions for God, there is an attempt to speak of God in equivalent images. God is Father and Mother, God and Goddess. Such usages would release the mind for other more imaginative divine names, according to some feminists. The obstacles are insuperable, it would seem, as such usages open the way for endless debates about God in the context of sexuality and gender. Besides, there are many feminists who wish to move beyond the parental images of God, which can leave the believer permanently in the state of childhood. Feminist Christians seek a God to whom adults can relate.

Another group of images available to the feminist Christian are those associated with the gospel images of Jesus the Prophet. Nothing in the life and words of Jesus would indicate that he saw women and other marginal people excluded from his mission. His words and deeds do not offer an endorsement of patriarchy. The frequent use of Abba as his normative name for God is a definite non-patriarchal usage, because this Abba often seems to be struggling to get people's attention. Abba is not a God of control but of invitation. The community of female and male disciples that is illustrated in the gospel accounts is an egalitarian community – despite the demands of the male disciples – and though such a community has never been actualised anywhere in subsequent Christian history, it remains as a built-in critique of all patriarchal models.

Some few feminists have attempted to harvest a usable image of God from the bridal imagery of both testaments, that is the God/Spouse/Husband and believer/church/wife parallelism. This, however, is one of the least helpful God images, because the wife is always portrayed as an unfaithful and blame-worthy partner to her ever-faithful and totally sinless spouse. Again, the relationship is inherently unequal, and implies that such continued infidelity from the wife will attract a deserving punishment.

A third group of feminists engage in a theological, philosophical and symbolic reconstruction of God-language and imagery. One of the most comprehensive of these is that undertaken by Catherine Mowry LaCugna in her work on the Trinity. She points out that the community of persons in trinitarian relationship has been exploited by patriarchal Christianity to illustrate the necessity of the headship of the male over the female following the pattern of the headship of the Father over the Son. She points out that the 'point of trinitarian theology is to convey that it is the essence or heart of God to be in relationship to other persons, that there is no room for division or inequality or hierarchy in God; that the personal reality of God is the highest possible expression of love and freedom; that the mystery of divine life is characterised by self-giving and self-receiving; that divine life is dynamic and fecund, not static or barren'.[31] Others have tried to rename the Trinity for liturgical usage in phrases such as Creator, Redeemer, Sustainer, or similar formulas. Other feminists have followed, in part, the apophatic tradition of the

SEEKING A SPIRITUALITY FOR WOMEN 265

medieval mystics in recognising the utter incomprehensibility of God. They point out that the common and often thoughtless usage of the name of God has trivialised the divine and given the impression that we actually know the reality behind the name. They attempt to restore a sense of awe and follow the dictum of Augustine: *si comprehendis non est deus*, that is, if you think you understand, what you understand is not God. Feminists also discover the incomprehensible God in hitherto unexpected places, as in the lives of women and other 'ungodlike' creatures. A sense of mystery is, hopefully, thus restored to God.

The study of language, its symbol and metaphor in the late twentieth century has challenged God-language in many ways. Since God is unknowable, the biblical language for God is replete with metaphor. Apart from the personal names for God, metaphors from nature – rock, light, water – are used frequently. The problem is that many of the personal names have been literalised and used as actual names for God, such as Lord, King, Father. People expand on the metaphor by using it literally: God is a king and we are his obedient but often rebellious subjects. The confusion is often illustrated, even at the highest levels of theology, by the insistence that God is Spirit, but must always be addressed by the male pronoun. The glorious diversity of mystical language, especially the language of the medieval women mystics, provides many new approaches to God, usually intimate, affective and claiming the experience of direct access. When this work is better known and understood, the language and approaches to God-language will be vastly enriched.

A final group of feminists uses a heuristic, experimental approach to God-language, on the understanding that the personal experience of God is shaped by the experience of the self. When our self-understanding changes, our God-understanding changes. Heuristic theology, then, is experimental, playful and imaginative. It adopts a 'what if...' approach. It does not intend final statements about God. Sallie McFague is the best example of this stream of feminist theology, when she experiments with new

God-names such as mother, lover, and friend. She speaks of the
world as God's body, and then proceeds to ask how our attitudes to both God and the world would change if such were the
case. She responds that we would reverence and care for the
world and that we would have the experience of living within
the body of God.[32]

One of the most dramatic and radical approaches to God is to
enter the debate from the standpoint of suffering, depression,
and oppression. What kind of God is then encountered? ask
theologians from many different perspectives. The suffering of
women had always been interpreted as a punishment for the sin
of being female. What if such suffering is, on the contrary, god-
like? What does the labour and suffering of giving birth, the outrage at injustice and the grief at loss and violence say about
God? Is God present in the degradation of women and how
would one name such a God? Women had been taught to see
this suffering as just punishment. Feminists name it as part of
the evil of patriarchal and unjust structures, including ecclesiastical structures, and raise new questions about the God who was
affirmed as the author of such a system.[33] This is not an attempt
to glorify suffering but to relocate the image of God in women,
children and others who suffered 'in God's name' and ask about
the presence of God in such events. The feminist intuition is that
if God were not suffering with the women and children and
other victims of injustice, then there is no point to faith in God.
One might add to the list the millions of women who lived their
Christian lives branded as sinful 'daughters of Eve'. What God
was the centre of their journey of faith? Unfortunately the potential riches to be gained from a response to such questions are
forever obliterated from the story of Christianity.

Elizabeth Johnson points out that the symbols, imagery and
language we use for God have a profound influence on the life
of the church. As she says: 'The symbol of God functions.'[34] She
considers the practical effects of God language on the everyday
life of the church and of believers. 'The way a faith community
speaks about God indicates what it considers the highest good,

the profoundest truth, the most appealing beauty. This language, in turn, molds the community's corporate identity and behaviour as well as the individual self-understanding of its members.' When she further comments that 'exclusive use of male God language is both religiously idolatrous and socially oppressive', we can add that the history of women's journey through Christianity has provided abundant illustration of this statement.[35] This, of course, presents serious ethical questions to the Christian community and it is to this dimension of the history of women in the late twentieth- and early twenty-first-century expressions of Christianity that we will turn next.

CHAPTER TEN

Towards an Inclusive Global Ethic

In the past week, in March 2003, there has been much commentary about the portrayal of the first war on television. People all over the world, should they choose to be ringside observers of the obscenity of war, can watch each censored detail unfold before their eyes. It is more than likely being beamed also to the space station as it circles the globe in outer space. The globe has been reduced in imagination to the size of the slightly less than circular object that graces many a classroom. All this 'global awareness', however, does not mean that people are more aware of or sympathetic with the other peoples who inhabit our earth. Indeed, one of the reasons for the current war is fear, the kind of fear that comes from knowing too much about our global neighbours. Even in Ireland, once insulated from immigration by its poverty and by its position on the outer edge of Europe, a new global presence is apparent. A recent comment by a well-known broadcaster remembers his schooldays in Dublin in the fifties when there was but one nationality in his school. Now there are over one hundred. The churches too, long professing to have a worldwide mission, have persisted with a Eurocentric self-identity until very recently. The variety of nations now gathered under the name of Roman Catholic can be judged by the growing number of languages in which the papal blessing, *urbi et orbi*, is recited. Christianity now has a global face and the problems of the globe have become the church's problems. The traditions of Western Christianity, once passed on unquestioningly by Western missionaries, are now facing the challenges of enculturation and indigenisation. It is also becoming increasingly obvious that perhaps the greatest challenge to a one-dimensional Christianity is being offered the world over by Christian women, for it is the women in every age who have been given the burden and gift of translating the Christian message into the living of everyday life. This chapter will try to give some thumbnail sketches of the worldwide challenge to traditional Christianity that has been mounted in the past few decades by women from almost every country in the world. Since it is feminist Christians, primarily, who are tackling these issues in their attempts to translate the Christian message in the context of women's lives, it is to the feminist critique and reconstruction that we will turn. First it will be important to get a brief glimpse of the worldwide situation of Christianity at the beginning of the twenty-first century.

Today, for the first time since the seventh century, the majority of Christians are not of European origin. The centre of gravity of Christianity has been moving south and east for decades.[1] Nevertheless, the influence of the West remains dominant and intentionally so. This also means that for the women of all newly evangelised countries over the past century, the negative Western paradigms of women's human and Christian identity have been communicated to the different cultures. In all areas, the older churches still hold the predominance of leaders, and in the Roman Catholic tradition, this means that all the institutional leaders in every country are male. The World Council of Churches has tried to mirror more accurately in its leadership the variety of nations and races composing its membership. There are still huge gaps of understanding, as so few texts are translated and transmitted from church to church. This is partly because the churches that comprise what might be called Old Christendom feel themselves to be the guardians of orthodoxy.

Despite its openness, there was not a great deal in the documents of the Second Vatican Council about the church of the poor. Now the situation of the poor, and the political, economic and social causes of their poverty, are no longer just abstractions but daily observable realities. The very presence of so many new peoples in a small country like Ireland is testimony to the fact of global economic inequality. As these peoples begin to find their voice in their new homes, they also raise our consciousness about the racist and sexist dimensions of both their past and present lives. On the world scene, the most Catholic continental block is Latin America, where over ninety per cent profess to be nominally Catholic, and where the new evangelical churches, often originating in the United States, are growing by leaps and bounds. This is an extremely volatile region that has not always benefited from the 'special interest' taken in its affairs by its northern neighbour, the United States. There is unprecedented urban poverty and whole countries are crippled by the burden of international debt. It is from such contexts that the phenomenon known as 'Liberation Theology' has grown. This is a theology arising from the analysis of their situation by the poor and dispossessed in which the gospel call to liberation is seen as the central core of Christian teaching.

The nations of Africa are engaged in disentangling themselves from their colonial past and are slowly moving toward a common African identity. Christianity is a recent phenomenon in most of Africa and the continent is almost evenly divided between Christians and Muslims. The Africanisation of Christianity is taking place everywhere, and the earlier apologetic mood of trying to prove their orthodoxy along Western lines is giving way to a new self-confidence. The indigenous culture of the local community is affecting the Christian reality in its worship, organisation, theology and discipline. Most communities see a married Roman Catholic priesthood as essential.

The history of Christianity in Asia goes back to the very beginning of the tradition, but it has remained a small minority religion in all Asian countries with the exception of the Philippines. Nevertheless because of the vastness of the population in what we call Asia, the Christians there number ten per cent of the world's total. Christianity is learning to become an Asian religion, and has entered its own period of analysis of its colonial past. The most dominant fact of religious life in Asia is pluralism, and this will dominate the religious debates of the twenty-first century. As we shall see, the brilliant voices of

Asian feminist Christians have taken on this challenge with intelligence, courage and panache.

Meanwhile the churches of Old Christendom in Europe and North America are still struggling with the aftermath of the Enlightenment, industrialisation and more recent technological developments. Statistics continue to show a huge decline in those who profess to be Christian, and in many places a casual and contemptuous attitude toward all religion prevails. At the same time, especially in the United States, there is a continuing growth in Pentecostal and evangelical churches that are fundamentalist in their self-understanding. Even though religion has been privatised in the United States, it still wields a huge influence over public policy. Here the Christian groupings are working against each other, with the mainline churches attempting to side with the poor, while the fundamentalist churches are pushing for more defence spending and less taxation of the wealthy. Nevertheless many of these churches show great vitality and diversity. In every country where there is an opportunity for decentralisation and diversity, religious communities seem to be growing; where there is inflexibility and further centralisation, the decline seems most obvious.

This very brief and necessarily spotty overview of Christianity at the beginning of the twenty-first century seems to herald the dawn of a new kind of Christian faith and Christian organisation. The resources for religious enthusiasm are abundant on special occasions such as papal visitations or more local traditional festivities. Nevertheless the cohesion of European Christianity seems to be loosening in every conceivable way. This is especially evident where Christianity has been under siege or where the majority of Christian believers have been consigned to a life of poverty, dispossession and indignity. In general, despite the essential numerical inaccuracy of the description, this world has been called the Third World. The phrase will be used here also because it has been chosen deliberately by many feminist theologians from these regions as the best self-description of their situation. Feminist theology from the Third World shows an extraordinary vitality, and even though its origins can be traced to contact with First World feminism in the seventies and eighties, Third World Christian feminism has deepened its roots in its native soils, and each region has developed in its own unique way. The astonishing newness of the feminist Christian critique may be a result of being marginal as far as official mainstream theology is concerned in all the churches, but for the women engaged in such theologising, there is nothing marginal about it.

Even though the diversity is remarkable, and growing yearly, there are common characteristics shared by all Third World feminists, as well as by their First World sisters.[2] Among these characteristics are an essential rooting of all theology in the experience of women, and a methodology of *praxis*, which departs from and returns to this experience in cycles of analysis, reflection and celebration. The emphasis on doing theology from the centre of such experience is, if anything, even more crucial in the Third World. This is an advocacy theology, oriented to the flourishing of women's lives and directed to attaining the full humanity of all women. It is a theology of liberation arising quite specifically from the experience of oppression, sometimes centuries of oppression in a Christian context. Of necessity, such theology is dynamic, pluralistic and local and never aims at universal statements that will stand true for all women in other circumstances. The emphasis is on 'doing theology' in very specific contexts with very specific groups of people, each of whose voices is of equal importance. Third World feminist theology likewise shares the negative and positive dimensions of earlier feminist theology. The negative dimension is a critique of and struggle against all forms of oppression, including patriarchy, racism and sexism, both in the secular contexts of the politico-economic structures of society and in the ecclesial context of the Christian churches. The positive dimension aims at reform, reconstruction, and a reinterpretation of the Christian tradition, especially the scriptures, the central doctrinal structure, and the core symbols, in the light of women's experience and in new social and cultural contexts. There is a new global awareness that gender, race and class are closely intertwined, and as a result, feminist theology has become much more complex and multi-dimensional. All Christian feminism has to deal with the double dynamic of Christianity as at once oppressive and liberating, and this double lens itself takes on a variety of perspectives in the many contexts of global reflection.

One of the most important institutions in raising feminist consciousness worldwide has been the World Council of Churches, with a series of international conferences throughout the seventies and eighties. In 1975, the United Nations initiated the Decade for Women, and this persuaded the Council to declare a Church Decade for Women starting in 1988. This led to a host of grass roots and international activities for women, including several international conferences. A whole generation of international Christian feminists was thus enabled to exchange ideas and, in consequence, situate their own feminist analysis more firmly in their own contexts.[3] From such works there arose a new perspective on feminist theology, with huge regional differences in terms of approaches and contexts, but several common themes. Among these themes, emphasis was placed even more firmly on the *doing* of theology, and therefore the demand that the feminist theologian (and liberation theologians generally) be immersed in the world from which the theology emerged. A feminist theology that did not share the world of experience and struggle and that did not arise from solidarity with poor and marginalized women could not be considered valid. This emphasis has persisted in all Christian feminist theology and has displaced the traditional understanding of a detached, value-free and emotion-free theology, uninfluenced by time, place and culture. It is not difficult to discern the difference between the Roman Catholic theology of women's ordination, which specifically excludes the voices of women and denies any cultural conditioning, and the global feminist theology, which demands such a rooted context.

We turn now briefly to the three main arenas of Christian

feminist theology from the Third World, namely Africa, Latin America and Asia. What is immediately striking here – even more so than in First World feminist theology – is the ethical nature of the task. All feminist theology begins with a critique of the conditions that oppress women, and therefore all such theology is aimed at change that is structural, communal and personal. Feminist theology is both a personal and communal discipline that entails a new way of seeing, and a new commitment to the flourishing of all women. It is never simply an armchair discipline, but presumes a changed consciousness and an altered praxis. This is abundantly evident in every Third World feminist theology and specifically in the theology of Mercy Amba Oduyoye, one of the best known voices of African feminist theology. 'I am first and foremost an Akan, a member of a matrilineal society that speaks the language of Akan, found in Ghana and the Ivory Coast.'[4] Mercy Amba Oduyoye was secretary of the World Council of Churches from 1974 to 1986, and has had teaching experience in both Africa and the United States. Her feminist theology is rooted in Africa but is also deeply conscious of the global church and the world scene, and the place of Africa within these structures. She states among her aims the calling attention to 'African women's potential for contributing to the theological enterprise'. She points out that no one can assume that African men and African women will say the same thing about African reality. Women, she says, always have to announce their presence on the scene, otherwise, even in the presence of women, the old theological conversation continues on unchanged. Among the main biblical bases for an African feminist theology are the dynamism and diversity in unity of the Pentecost scene, and the absolute refusal to accept the traditional patriarchal, or any other, shortcut to this unity. The themes of Exodus and the reversal of values represented in Mary's Magnificat are also central, as well as the Lukan sermon of Jesus based on Isaiah, about good news for the poor, liberty for captives, sight for the blind and freedom for the oppressed (Luke 4: 18-19). She speaks of the 'irruption' of women into the con-

sciousness of church and society and the disruption of the peace
of principalities and powers.

African feminist theologians deny that issues of sexism 'belong to a minority of disgruntled, leisure saturated, middle-class
women of the capitalist West', as many patriarchal commentators assert. 'The fact is that sexism is part of an intricate web of
oppression in which most of us live.' African women also explore the specific limitations on women placed there by African
society itself, beyond the limitations of Christianity and Islam.
Women are supposed to keep to their place, and accept their
submissive role and to avoid all confrontation with men. The irruption of African women, however, has brought to light the
empowering spirit of religious traditions and the extraordinary
vulnerability of women to spirituality. This is why the healing
aspect of African churches is so powerful in the lives of women,
always the closest to catastrophe. In post-colonial and post-
apartheid Africa there are generally two strands of African theology. One is aimed at the indigenisation and enculturation of
African traditions; the other is more concerned with the devastation of racism through such inhuman structures as apartheid.
Women, as always, have to 'present themselves' and claim their
own space in these traditions, and claim for themselves the traditions that will be empowering for women. They remember and
re-integrate the powerful stories of their women ancestors, their
healing powers and prophetic gifts, and they celebrate the
ingenuity and creativity of African women through the ages in
providing for their families and communities against all obstacles.
African women, however, are far from romanticising these
traditions and are committed to pointing out to all who want
reconciliation without justice that there can be no reconciliation
between Satan and God. The major challenge still awaiting
African feminist theologians is the enculturation of the Good
News into a culture that is still patriarchal, racist and sexist. In
this aim they are joined to all other feminist theologians around
the globe.[5]

In 1996, the continent we call Asia contained over half the

world's population. As Rosemary Radford Ruether points out, if
we include the Middle East under the heading of Asia (all the
nomenclature is a Western construct in any case), we can say
that this region is the cradle of all the world's major religions.
While Christianity everywhere remains a minority of about
three per cent, numerically Asian Christians represent about one
tenth of the world's total. It is no surprise then that the major
concern of feminist, as well as all other Asian Christian theologians, is the reality of religious pluralism. Asian feminist theologians have been organising since the eighties, with the added
difficulties of more than usually large regional contrasts of
wealth and poverty as well as forms of government. Almost one
half of Asia is still under communist regimes.

The Asian feminist theologians have divided themselves into
the three regions of the Philippines, India and Korea, and from
these areas they assemble to discuss hermeneutic possibilities.[6]
Asian feminist theology definitely arises out of struggle,
whether the struggle for mere survival in the face of hunger, oppression and military dictatorship, or, as in the Philippines, the
struggles against the regime of President Marcos. Everywhere
that Christianity exists in Asia, it has been inculturated in the
Hindu, Buddhist and other overarching cultures, and so themes
of survival as a minority play a large part. In Asia, as elsewhere,
women had to 'present themselves' in order to be recognised, as
the male liberation theologians did not see gender as a significant theological issue. Each group of Asian feminist theologians
also seeks in its own cultural and religious heritage for positive
religio-cultural themes to use as a resource for developing an indigenous feminist theology. From a huge range of theological
reflection, there is room to identify only two: the seven-fold task
that feminist theologians from the Philippines have set themselves, and the Korean Minjung feminist theology of Chung
Hyun Kyung. The seven tasks of a Filipina feminist theology are
enumerated as follows: (1) an Asian cosmology that is holistic,
integrating spirit and body; (2) an anthropology of mutuality of
men and women, overcoming splits of mind and body, individ-

ual and society; (3) a christology that emphasises Jesus' humanness, not his maleness, and puts the cross in the context of the cost of discipleship to bring in God's reign (not the exaltation of passive suffering); (4) a mariology that lifts up Mary as disciple rather than emphasising her virginal motherhood; (5) a moral theology that focuses on the struggle against social and environmental sin rather than a sex-obsessed individualism; (6) a spirituality that integrates historical liberation and ecological wholeness; and (7) a gender-inclusive renewal of liturgy and language that draws on life-giving symbols and stories from indigenous traditions, as well as from Christianity.[7] The Christian story of Jesus is a particular problem in Asia and the fact of his crucifixion is seen as repugnant, and proof that he was not divine. Besides the Christian claim to the absolute uniqueness of Jesus is impossible for many Asians. Asian feminist theologians, in their identification with the oppressed, are developing a christology of one who suffered for siding with the marginalised. For oppressed Asian women, Jesus is one who took their side and who reveals a God who opposes injustice.

It is in this perspective that the Korean feminist theologian Chung Hyun Kyung is developing her theology, by introducing to Westerners the concepts of Minjung and Han. Minjung means all those in Korean society who are oppressed politically, exploited economically, despised socially, and kept uneducated. Korean feminists speak of women as the 'Minjung of the Minjung'. Han is central to the concept of Minjung theology, and stands for the frustrated sorrow and anger at unjust suffering, which accumulates because it is denied an outlet. Han is a collective experience and is transmitted from generation to generation. It can be expressed explosively in revolution, and creatively in ritual, dance, music and art. Again, for Korean feminist theologians, women's Han is the deepest form of Han. Chung uses these cultural images to enormous effect in her theology and demonstrates a threefold path for the creative and healing release of Han, which includes speaking, naming and action.[8] All those who were present at the World Council of Churches

Assembly in Canberra, Australia, in February 1991, speak of the electrifying effect of the ritual led by Chung, where, from the 'land of the Spirit', she invited the participants to empty themselves and 'listen to the cries of creation and the cries of the spirit within it'. Then she invoked the wandering Han-ridden spirits of the tradition, so that having named them, all could be open to the voice of the Holy Spirit. Among the spirits invoked were the spirit of Hagar, the spirit of male babies killed by the soldiers of King Herod, the spirit of Joan of Arc and her many sisters burnt at the stake, the spirit of people killed during the Crusades, and so on through the Holocaust, the devastation of Hiroshima and Nagasaki, and the other twentieth-century brutalities and tragedies, down to the spirit of the Amazon rainforest and the 'spirit of earth, air and water, raped, tortured and exploited by human greed for money'. The invocations concluded with the 'spirit of soldiers, civilians, and sea creatures now dying in the bloody war in the Gulf' and finally the 'spirit of the Liberator, our brother Jesus, tortured and killed on the cross'. She concluded with the image of the Korean goddess Kwan Yin, goddess of compassion and, for Chung Hyun Kyung, image of the Holy Spirit.[9] Some were outraged at such non-traditional imagery, but most were moved to storms of applause. The enculturation of Christianity, in global feminist guise, can be disturbing, disorienting, creative, and extremely challenging, but for Third World feminist theologians, it is only the first necessary step toward the full participation of women from all races and nations in the Christian reality.

The phenomenon of Liberation Theology in the Latin American context is, perhaps, better known to most Westerners. It may also seem to have more immediate relevance since the Western involvement in the massive inequalities and oppression in Latin America is more widely known and experienced. Besides, the processes of Liberation Theology have become well known in the universities of Europe and North America. Nevertheless, Latin American feminist theologians had to travel the road of all feminist theologians in announcing their presence to an initially hostile male theological community. They discovered that the gender of the theologian mattered enormously in the analysis of the concrete conditions that were the theological context, and that this fact had been ignored until the arrival of feminist theology. Throughout the eighties Latin American feminist theologians were organising and in 1994 the first world consultation was held in Costa Rica. The year 1992, the five hundredth anniversary of the European invasion of Latin America, provided a new impetus to all forms of theological work. From another huge palette of feminist theologians, there is space to choose only two, Elsa Tamez from Mexico and Ivone Gebara from Brazil.[10]

Feminist theology in Latin America is a communal task where the concrete present experience of oppression is seen as normative. The context of a great deal of this theology is the Basic Ecclesial Community which is a gathering of the poor for the discussion of their own lives in light of the gospel. In these communities, old forms of ministry are challenged as well as the traditional exercise of authority. The concreteness of such theological work is seen in the life of Rigoberta Menchu from Guatemala, who was awarded the Nobel Peace Prize in 1992. For her and her community, the Bible was the main weapon in the struggle for justice, which included the basic demand that 'every one of our Indian race has the right to eat'. Like Sojourner Truth before her, she challenged the ideology that 'Indians are poor because they are lazy' by pointing out that 'we're outside ready for work at three in the morning'. For her the lessons of the Bible pointed in only one direction: 'the only road open to me is our struggle, the just war. The Bible taught me that'.[11]

Elsa Tamez is a Mexican Methodist theologian, now active in Costa Rica, where she is President of the Seminary. Like Rigoberta Menchu, her theology is rooted in the Bible, which she knows is now seen as a dangerous book by many sections of society because of its teaching on the preferential option for the poor. Tamez points out, however, that there are differences between reading the Bible as a woman and reading the Bible from the point of view of the poor. Women find clear and explicit cases of their own marginalisation in the Bible. Besides, the Bible is used to prove that the segregation of women in society is sacred and willed by God, and this segregation has found its way almost naturally into family and church organisation. Women are called upon then to deny the authority of the texts that harm them and this attitude to the Bible creates great problems for Protestants. Therefore, Tamez suggests that women should make themselves strangers to the Bible, that is treat it as a new book, as if they were coming upon it for the first time, just with their own concrete life experience. She recommends, then, a double process of gaining distance from the Bible and of coming closer to daily life and finding there the necessary liberating keys that will give meaning to life in today's world. Part of the oppressive world that surrounds women in Latin America is the culture of *machismo* that, says Tamez, has influenced the traditional reading of the texts. Women must 'come closer' to their own lives and bring this new womanly understanding to the reading of the text. This is a new approach and needs discipline and perseverance.

Elsa Tamez is also concerned with the conflict between the Gods of the indigenous peoples and the God of Christianity. The peoples' Gods have been seen as idols, whereas the 'true' God has become a tool of the rich and powerful and has also been reduced to the status of an idol. She challenges liberation theology and feminist theology to choose their God carefully. The Christianity of the sixteenth century conquerors, she points out, is just as much a perversion as the 'pagan' religions of the conquered people. The Christianity of the conquerors was 'bad news' for the Indians generally, but gave glimpses of the God of Life. Tamez works with many of the legendary figures of Mexican culture and recognises that the 'struggle of the gods' will continue for a long time in Latin America.

Ivone Gebara is a Roman Catholic sister from Brazil who has been involved in feminist theology for almost thirty years. She brings to her theology, then, long years of reflection both on her cultural context and on the texts of Christianity. For her the written texts are always a source of suspicion because of what has been omitted about women and other marginalised figures. The Good News to be good must include women and men equally. From her political and cultural stance of a complete rejection of capitalist oppression, she reads the Bible to learn about justice, and to open up a space for women's experience. She brings to her reading anthropological, theological, feminist and pastoral assumptions, which place women at the centre of her analysis. She recognises that after twenty years of liberation theology, the poor are still poor, and blacks, Amerindians and women are still oppressed. Her feminist theology is born of a desire not to allow the next twenty years to have the same result.

Mary, especially in her Magnificat, plays a significant role in Ivone Gebara's theology. She asserts that Mary is much bigger than the biblical portrayal of her, and that there is much that has not been told but must be imagined. Mary is the travelling companion of the poor. Together with her co-author, Maria Clara Bingemer, she is central to the new feminist theology that is coming out of Brazil. For many years, Indians in Latin America were deprived of full participation in the Eucharist because of the European understanding of their less than human status. Now feminist theologians are reinterpreting the Eucharist as being symbolised and celebrated by the female body. In this celebration, the subversive memory of the death and resurrection of Jesus is made present. Women in their bodies are the ones who possess the Eucharistic ability to use their bodies as food. 'In the whole process of gestation, childbirth, protection and nourishing of a new life, the sacrament of the Eucharist, the divine act, happens anew'.[12] This same Eucharistic body of women is the body that is being exploited in fields, factories, homes, churches and on marches. It is the body of women, eucharistically given, which is key to the struggle for liberation.

All over the capitalist West, as we know, the pockets of poverty are getting larger, more pronounced and seemingly more intransigent to any solution. Here again women of colour

and poor women are coming together to voice their own struggle and to begin a journey toward liberation. Among these
groups, it is widely recognised that the cultural and religious
analysis of white Christian feminists is not adequate to describe
the reality of their condition and can even contribute to a further
oppression. From these groups, it is appropriate to look briefly
at one or two representatives of black *womanist* theology and
mujerist theology from the Hispanic communities, both living in
the midst of the First World.[13]

Delores Williams tells us that womanist theology is rooted in
the recovery of the survival and resistance history of black
women in the United States, in the context of the black family
and community.[14] bell hooks says that no other group in
America has been socialised out of existence as much as the
black female. Black females were asked to deny a part of themselves, their femaleness, in the interests of the fight against
racism, and then praised for being strong women. In America,
hooks says, the word 'woman' came to mean 'white woman',
and she critiques white feminists for reinforcing this situation in
their own struggle for the freedom of elite white women. She
comments that being strong in the face of oppression cannot be
equated with fighting oppression.[15] The experience of the black
female slave is at the core of the struggle for freedom for women
and at the core of a womanist theology. The voice of the black
woman has to be brought into theology, and there it challenges
both the sexism of black men and the racism of white women
and men. Womanist theology uses the experience of Hagar, the
exploited outsider, as a starting point for womanist biblical reflection (Gen 16:1-16, 21:9-21 and Gal 4:21-51). The Genesis texts
are read from the perspective of the slave Hagar rather than
from that of the slave-owner, Sarah the wife of Abraham. This
brings the revelation that liberation for the slave-woman came
not from God but from human initiative. Slave-women have to
evolve strategies for survival from no resources but their own
strength, and a wholesome shrewdness. Encounter, resistance
and endurance are the hallmarks of their lives.[16] Delores S.

Williams has coined the word 'demonarchy' to encompass all the forms of violence (including domestic violence), debasement and denial of dignity that have converged in the personal lives and historical experience of black women. This multi-layered experience, then, becomes the hermeneutical norm for black women in judging the appropriateness of biblical interpretation, theology and ethics. Whatever promotes the dignity of black women is seen as salvific. The Bible, then, is seen as an ambivalent document, often promoting the further enslavement of black women. God the liberator is not always on their side and black women are left to 'make a way out of no way'. For this reason, and also stemming from the paradigmatic experience of Hagar in the desert, the image of the wilderness is key to womanist theology. Because of the history of suffering that is intrinsic to 'demonarchy', the vicarious suffering of Jesus is not seen as redemptive by womanist theology. The cross appears as a symbol of the evil perpetrated by the dominant culture in its rejection of the Good News. It is the life of Jesus rather than the death of Jesus that is found to be redemptive from the black woman's experience.[17]

Emilie Townes seeks to recover hope from this story of oppression: 'It became a necessity, in my eyes, that womanist thought go on record about the hope, salvation, and transformation we have in our lives ...'. One then has to give reasons for one's hope, and the main reason is to be found in the 'subversive love' that is modelled in the life of Jesus. This subversive love is learning to build coalitions across racial, ethnic and gender barriers, and is thus enabled to move beyond the despair engendered by the daily experience of oppression. Womanist theology is also dependent on the creative power of honest story telling, and it is here that healing is found. The creative traditions of black women are wonderfully illustrated in the work of Alice Walker, Zora Neale Hurston, and many others, and these works also represent key hermeneutical resources for womanist theology.[18] The fact that so many black women 'don't never get used to it' is a catalyst for action, encouragement and hope.[19]

From the perspective of the experience of Hispanic women in the United States, women such as Ada Maria Isasi-Diaz, who fled from Cuba with her family as a young woman, have created a critical theology, called *mujerist*, which has grown from the experience of anti-Hispanic ethnic prejudice in the United States. This theology bears many of the marks of womanist theology, though it derives from a totally different set of experiences of oppression. It is a theology that is communal, and rooted in story-telling and ritual celebration. The experience of liturgy is particularly important for Hispanic women who have often felt the official Roman Catholic liturgy as alienating and disempowering. The *mujerist* theology has also entered into a specific critique of the notion of sin, as it assaults Hispanic women from many sources. Sin is seen as a function of the oppressing community, both social and ecclesial, as it imposes oppressive structures of passivity, objectification and racist stereotyping against Hispanic women. Contrariwise, salvation is experienced as a growing sense of self-worth, which *mujerist* theologians call 'being created in the image of God'.[20] The ongoing task of *mujerist* theology is to define the preferred future for Hispanic women, and to struggle to make their 'eschatological glimpses' their whole horizon.[21]

All of these feminist theologies are directed toward change, toward a conversion of sensibilities and self-awareness in the individual, and toward a struggle against the unjust dimensions of church and society with regard to women's lives. This strong ethical dimension in feminist theology needs to be examined, however briefly, as it is one of the most creative challenges of Christian feminism to the community. In Christianity, much of the burden of ethics fell on the weaker members of the community, as we have seen. Even the biblical challenges to love, endurance and forbearance were directed primarily to slaves, women and the weaker members of the patriarchal community. Since it was the powerful that were formulating such ethical demands, it is not surprising that the biblical injunctions against unjust power and dominance became muted over the centuries and the emphasis was placed on service, self-sacrificing love and forgiveness. All forms of feminist theology have critiqued this ethical emphasis, both in its traditional forms and in the forms in which it continues to be preached today. What is offered here is a kind of smorgasbord of approaches and conclusions in a discipline that is growing daily.[22]

Since women were considered to be the moral inferiors of men throughout most of Christian history, traditional ethics have led to a kind of 'moral madness' for women. Even when more modern ethical theories were formulated in the late twentieth century by men and for men, using only the resources of male experience, women were considered morally inferior to the extent that they differed from the scholarly conclusions about their supposed moral journeys. Traditional ethicists, while accepting the inferiority of women as a starting point, were most troubled by the 'emotionality' of women, which supposedly prevented women from true moral discernment, and by the supposed tendency of women to focus on the particular rather than the abstract and universal. Women, besides, were without power and therefore could not be effective in any real moral sense. With this circular form of reasoning, women were more or less excluded from the moral domain, except for the traditional responsibilities of service and care, which arose from their 'nature' as women.

Initially, a kind of 'feminine' ethics aimed to supply what was missing in this traditional format. It made women visible in the ethical debate and gave true moral value to the aspect of relationships, care, service and love. It also focused on the need for passionate commitment in the moral life, thus emphasising the need for emotionality in ethics. Ethical scholars in this tradition drew attention to the gendered differences between the ethical thought and lives of women and men, as a result of their differing historical experiences, and not because of any supposed natural demands. Feminine ethicists wanted to raise to consciousness the values associated traditionally with the lives of women, values included in the phrase 'maternal thinking'.

The advantages of 'feminine ethics' are obvious in that they draw attention to an ethical dimension that, for the first time in Christian history, can now speak from the heart of women's experience. The dangers are equally obvious in that such ethical qualities could be – and are – co-opted by male ecclesiastical thinkers to reinforce traditional 'feminine' values of subordination and obedience.

Feminist ethical thinking has gone hand in hand with Christian feminist analysis from the start, in that ethical change was at the core of feminism. More recently, however, a more focused feminist ethics is occurring with real challenges to traditional modes that are altering the very foundations of the traditional ethical systems. Feminist ethics start from an explicitly political stance, where the key ethical act demands first of all the analysis of women's historical oppression. Feminist ethics overlaps at many points with feminine ethics, but is much more cautious about the emphasis on womanly caring, and wishes to subject all such ethical conclusions to a contextual analysis that will move them beyond the stereotypical. Feminist ethicists explore whether or not women's proficiency in caring is a result of their historically inferior status. They point out that, in a situation of unequal power, the powerless are required to be more sensitive and more compliant. They ask whether women's caring and nurturing skills are simply the survival skills of an oppressed group living in close proximity with the oppressor. They question the demands of mothering as an institutionalised structure, imposed on women from outside, and often over-riding her own preferences. Feminist ethicists also explore the stance and vested interests of the ethicist, who though traditionally presumed to be objective, has been distinctly not so in historical perspective. Such feminist ethicists are wary of positing deep differences between women and men with regard to such qualities as caring. Women value care, they point out, because men value women according to the care they are given. Feminist ethicists examine the contexts of and motives for care and suggest that there are occasions when it is morally preferable to withhold care, depending on the operative power structures.

Feminist ethics is totally committed to the elimination of the subordination of women, and therefore sees much traditional ethics as immoral in its intent and effects. Christian feminist ethicists also point out that for those in a subordinate position, as Third World feminists also ceaselessly point out, what is 'natural' and what is 'revealed' can look very different. Women, gay people, the poor, people of colour, indigenous people and the very earth itself have suffered as a result. The dominant also bear the ethical scars of their lives and choices, as do the dominant structures. It will be impossible, therefore, just to readjust the structures of power and dominance in order to include women, because this will never lead to ethical equality for all. All Christian feminist ethicists point out that the tradition itself holds within it the necessary resources for an ethical reconstruction of Christianity. Among these resources are: the redefinition of God by the life of Jesus in terms of accessibility and relationship; the life and liberating praxis of Jesus, who freed people to reach across boundaries to the untouchables and to redefine the meaning of the neighbour; the extension of the gospel invitation to include all slaves, women, lepers, Romans, Samaritans, tax-collectors and whoever society needs to name as the 'sinner'; the death of Jesus as resulting from his loyalty to this perspective; the concept of grace as living freely the reality of being both guest and host, resident and pilgrim; the concept of hope in its subversive dimension of expecting the unexpected; and the concept of love in all its potential for mutuality, outrage at injustice and interpersonal development.

As with all feminist methodology, the critique of the traditional ethical constructs is one of the starting places for the creation of a new ethical perspective. Among these critiques, the following would rank as fundamental. Traditional ethics has been fundamentally authoritarian, that is it has used power to bolster its authority, from the power of God's sanctions to the use of sometimes-extreme violence. There has never been a place for the voice of the weak. Traditional ethics has also been sexist and has reinforced sexism in the implementation of its decisions. The main emphasis has always been put on the passive virtues of submission, patience, resignation, acceptance of one's lot, and obedience. There has always been a reductionist quality to traditional ethics in its promotion of a passive longing rather than a subversive hope, and a reduction of the struggle for justice to prayer for future reward. In the past, sin was often reduced to an offence against those in power by individual persons, and the oppressive structures themselves were not regarded as sinful. With dramatic consequences for women, traditional ethical thinking focused in a fixated way on controlling women's sexuality. Feminist ethicists have remarked that if contraceptives had been showered down on Hiroshima, there would have been a universal cry of outrage. With this fixation, the traditional ethical perspective prevented creativity, risk, and real self-actualisation. This lack of personal growth was also partly a result of the emphasis on law rather than on the development of a mature conscience, again, with more direct consequences for women, for whom obedience was seen as a 'natural' state.

Feminist ethicists differ vastly in their analysis and in their conclusions, but there are several areas of agreement and some common principles. The starting point, as always, is with reflection on the concrete experience of women, never before seen as an ethical resource. This experience takes place in particular historical, cultural, religious, and personal contexts that are essential to the ethical analysis. One of the main ethical tasks is to sort out one's loyalties and decide whose side we stand on. The goal of feminist ethics is to be loyal to women in a way that is consistent with loyalty to all. This emphasis on loyalty is directly contrary to much traditional emphasis on reconciliation, where often there was an attempt to enforce reconciliation of justice with injustice on the basis of power. The disastrous consequences of such an approach can be seen in the last decade in the proliferation of stories of clerical sexual abuse, where the inequality of power in the relationships prevented the abuse of the weaker from being heard. Feminists always question the source of ethical claims, whether it is experience, the law, the Bible, Natural Law, tradition or simply custom. The source of the claim bears testimony on the ethical weight of the claim. This is a particularly important criterion in the Christian tradition, where often all ethical demands were perceived to be of equal weight as part of God's law. The principle of integrity is essential to feminist ethics, where decisions must be rooted in personal conscience and must be open to new alternatives. For feminist ethicists, then, the feminist community has become an ethical norm, where truth telling, personal integrity, the congruence of speech and action, and the recognition of the connectedness of all created reality are fundamental.

Feminist ethicists have targeted some ethical areas as deserving of particular attention. Among these are the Christian teaching on love, the question of violence against women and the issues of ecology. These issues will merely be identified here as they are multi-dimensional and interwoven with areas of justice, international law, Christian moral teaching and socio-cultural dynamics. There is no doubt that love is seen as central to the Christian message, above all *agape*, which is the chosen name to express the particular dynamics of gospel love. Christian feminists feel the need to unmask agape.[23] They point out that the core of agape is regard for the other, leading to self- sacrifice and self-giving. As we have seen, this is a particular part of the Roman Catholic reasoning about the ordination of women, where the self-giving love of women is part of the definition of love and the core meaning of a woman's life. The Christian norm, then, has been seen as an equivalency between love and sacrifice, especially in personal relationships. Mothers are supposed to be especially equipped with this gift, and its lack in them is equivalent to bad motherhood. In the context of personal relationships, agape is always seen in opposition to *eros*, and this opposition plays a very large part in Christian sexual ethics. The model of agape is the image of the crucified Christ, which acts as a judgement on all self-assertion, and expectation of a returned love. It is the disinterested nature of such love that has been key to the Christian tradition.

Feminists hold up the love of friendship, which is mutual and rooted in regard both for the self and the other, and this has been accepted by most people as a model for both private and public love. All traditional ethicists agree that the public expression of agape would be impossible in the public arena where competition reigns supreme. Most traditional theologians follow the conclusion of Rheinhold Niebuhr who called agape the 'impossible possibility'. For public life, a kind of justice or balance between competing interests is seen as the operative norm, and there are endless chunks of proverbial wisdom about the hardness of heart needed to survive in the 'marketplace'. Agape, then has been sidelined to the private sphere where women are seen to operate, and so agape has become the virtue for women and 'justice' the virtue for men. The traditional reasoning has added that the self-love of women and the particularities of her life require agape as a corrective. There is, of course, the Christian tradition of trinitarian mutuality, but the maleness of the imagery gives this a particularly contradictory overtone, making it usable neither by men nor by women.

Feminist ethicists, starting from the work of Valerie Saiving in the sixties, point out that this traditional understanding of agape may constitute the worst sin of women, namely self-denial and self-giving. It had always been taught that pride was the root of all sin, but feminists posit that this may be true of men, but it is not the truth about women. They point out that many women live for others to a degree that is damaging to them. Women do not wish to get rid of self-sacrifice, but emphasise the need for a mature self to be present first, and there is never a situation where all self-development can be sacrificed. Feminists go on to point out that agape is not an appropriate model of love for the oppressed, where basic needs are not being met. It is easy to see why the love of friendship has become a norm for Christian feminist ethics.

Anyone familiar with the history of Christianity will not be surprised that violence against women has become a major issue within feminism. Not only has violence against women been endemic in the tradition, it has been identified throughout the twentieth century as part of the daily life of women around the globe. The varieties and forms of this violence are horrific and seemingly endless in their ability to shock women into an awareness of the fragility of the advantages won by women throughout the last century. This violence is cultural, militaristic, trans-national and domestic. It is no respecter of persons and happens in every country to women at all socio-economic levels. Violence is not exclusive to the Christian tradition, of course, but seems to multiply in religions across the globe as the fundamentalist strains of religions increase in number and visibility, and as these religions appeal to what they call 'traditional family values'. This violence is structurally normative in patriarchal cultures and is not the result of occasional drunken binges or unbalanced behaviour. Whether such violence is aimed at producing the acceptable face of femaleness, that is docility and invisibility, or whether it is part of the obliteration of a nation or culture through genocide, no daily newspaper has failed to produce examples of such violence in any one week in the history of news reporting. That does not mean that violence against women produces shock waves of outrage and disgust, except for particularly horrific examples, but that the sheer volumes of examples demand some recognition. Without a doubt the volume of this violence is a direct result of the Christian and other religious approbation of the 'feminine' as the norm for women's behaviour. The details of this are by now familiar and do not need to be repeated here. Closely linked with violence against women in the ideology of patriarchy is violence against children, especially the sexual abuse of children of all ages.

Christian feminist theological analysis of such violence points to four main strands of thought.[24] First is the Greco-Roman influence on the Judaeo-Christian scriptures, and especially on particular sections of these scriptures such as the household codes in the Pauline and deutero-Pauline traditions. These scriptures have made the politics of patriarchal subordination normative in the West, applying them to all women and to slaves, barbarians, refugees, and prisoners of war and all powerless people of both sexes throughout history. All this violence is seen to have divine sanction from an almighty ruling Father, and his earthly representatives. For women, in particular, this violence is linked with the sinfulness of women inherited from Eve's deception. This is carried further in the cultural and legal patterns of blaming the victims of rape or battering, and the interiorised dispositions of women, who accept responsibility for such behaviour as being 'their own fault'. This also has its roots in the 'love patriarchy' tradition of the scriptures, where the burden of loving and of maintaining just relationships is placed on the weaker member of the relationship, whether that is slave or wife. Thirdly the Christian theological tradition of atoning for sin through the spilling of innocent blood and through undeserved suffering has placed a powerful religious weight on such violence, by focusing not on the one who perpetrates the violence, but on the 'victim'. Some feminist theologians have spoken of the 'divine child-abuse' evident in the crucifixion, and in the teaching that Jesus had to die for our sins. Feminists insist on the socio-political analysis of the suffering and death of Jesus and emphasise that his death was the result of his loyalty to his teaching on liberation. Finally, as we have seen above in the very brief exploration of the meaning of agape for women, such teaching lays a cruel burden of victimhood on women, in teaching that non-resistance to such violence is a more Christian form of behaviour. Canonised saints such as Maria Goretti further this teaching and suggest that the violence of rape is a less horrific prospect, if it can result in canonisation.

Feminist ethicists work to suggest an alternative mode of being for women in such volumes as *Women Resisting Violence: Spirituality for Life*. This is definitely not an attempt to 'spiritualise' the issue of violence, but to provide avenues toward a re-construction of the central Christian teachings about love, suffering, and forgiveness, and to articulate an alternative liberative praxis for women and all the oppressed. The above volume is a record of the meeting of feminist theologians in Costa Rica in

1994 on the topic that was used as the title of the volume. In the final statement of the gathering, an alternative theo-ethical discourse was outlined. Following are some of the points made in this statement. Accountability and responsibility for all levels of complicity with oppressive systems should inform our praxis and our theologising. Involvement in liberative praxis to end violence against women should be considered a precondition of theological work and its constant companion. Identification of women's bodies as the symbol of sinfulness has to be explicitly rejected. Systemic violation of the earth and its creatures has to be denounced as evil and sinful. Resisting violence is a deeply spiritual work interwoven with the struggle for life. Violence against women thrives on silence. For this reason, action for transformation should include making women's voices heard.[25]

From much of the preceding it is obvious that there is an intrinsic connection between violence against women and violence against the earth. Both arise from one understanding of the Natural Law tradition, in which 'man' was given power to dominate nature for 'his' own purposes. The use by feminists of words like rape to describe the devastation of the earth's fruitfulness, can therefore be easily connected to the rape of women. Both have the same rationale in domination by apparent right, often seen as a religious right. Ecofeminism is the name given to the feminist tradition that undertakes to unmask the many varieties of domination that comprise this enterprise, and the sources and methods of such domination. There have been many false twists and turns in the journey toward an adequate analysis of the woman-nature connection, but the solution seems to lie in the development of covenantal ethics. This is an ethical perspective that gives us a vision of an integrated community of humans, animals, and land that seeks to live by a spirituality and code of continual rest, renewal, and the restoration of just, sustainable relations between humans and all of creation. Rosemary Radford Ruether points out that such a covenant can be complemented by our heritage of sacramental cosmology, and by our dialogue with similar traditions from all parts of the globe.[26]

The development of this thought has led to an ecological spirituality where there is an amazement and admiration for the unity and solidarity of all life. The cycle of life through the seasons is experienced as holy, healing and renewing, and as a 'cosmic dance' celebrating the connections between people, the earth and all its inhabitants. What holds true for the earth and its beauty also holds true for corporeality. It is from this tradition that a new reverence for the sacredness of sexuality arises, not so much in connection with procreation, as in recognising the vitality and joy of all life forces and their connection with the God/ess.[27]

To conclude this chapter on a global ethical vision, two women are presented who encompass in their life's work, in two very different ways, many of the themes of this chapter. These are Mother Teresa of Calcutta and Dorothy Day. Both women seem to tower over the whole of the second half of the twentieth century. It is unlikely that they ever met, and probably would not have liked nor agreed with each other. One, Mother Teresa, is reported to be on a fast track for canonisation; the other will more than likely never be canonised, nor would her followers ever seek such a finalisation of the meaning of her life. One seems to embody what the feminists call the 'ethics of care', the other dedicated her whole life to the ethics of justice. Neither woman could be called feminist, and Mother Teresa is on record as disagreeing with the whole feminist enterprise.

Mother Teresa of Calcutta was born Agnes Gonxha Bojaxhiu on 27 August, 1910 in Skopje, Macedonia, the youngest of three children. Her family was Albanian and Catholic, and part of the successful merchant class. Her father, a local politician, died suddenly when she was only nine years of age, and her mother took up a sewing career in order to raise her family. The family was pious and charitable, so it came as no surprise when Agnes expressed a wish to join a convent. In September, 1928, she left for the Loreto Convent in Rathfarnham, Dublin. Within three months, now called Sister Teresa, she was on her way to Darjeeling in India to be trained as a missionary in the Loreto community. After teacher-training and final profession, Sister Teresa was named head-teacher of a school in Calcutta for middle-class Bengali girls. Nearby lay one of the largest of the Calcutta slums, and under the direction of the Belgian Jesuit, Father Henry, Mother Teresa's thoughts were being drawn more and more in that direction. On 10 September, 1947, Mother Teresa felt called to make the decision that would change her life radically, and make her name a household word through the remainder of the twentieth century. At the age of thirty-eight, Mother Teresa left the Loreto community to begin her life among the poor of Calcutta. She was trained as a nurse and was soon joined by a small group of local women. Their ministry of care for the poor, sick and dying street-people of Calcutta is simply described, but its effects electrified the world. In October 1950, the Community of the Sisters of Charity was approved by Rome, with its significant fourth vow of devoting themselves to the service of the poor. The work of the sisters struck a chord not only in India, but also all over the world, and postulants flocked to the community. Eventually, the community spread worldwide and the name and face of Mother Teresa became a familiar one. She met with the high and mighty as well as the poor and lowly and it was no surprise when she was awarded the Nobel Peace prize in 1979. Against her own wishes, she was re-elected as Superior in 1992, but was finally replaced in March 1997. She died in September 1997, and her funeral was seen as an event of world importance.

Mother Teresa was an uncompromising and sometimes controversial figure on the religious scene of the late twentieth century. There was unmitigated admiration for her work with the sick and dying in the slums of Calcutta. She had never changed her methodology of face-to-face ministry to these poorest of the poor. Her religious community was organised and run on very traditional lines, and again, there was no doubting the commitment needed to follow the strict regime she laid down for her followers. Mother Teresa travelled widely all over the world, speaking to small groups and world bodies, meeting the poor and the Presidents, seeking money and support for her work. Some criticism was voiced about the donors of some of this money. They were among the most unprincipled and brutal dictators on the world scene at the time. Such criticism, however, meant nothing to her, and it is likely that she did not understand its implications. Even though her message was always the same and expressed in simple terms, Mother Teresa could be depended on to side with the ecclesiastical authorities on the controversial issues of the day, especially with regard to the sexuality and roles of women.

Mother Teresa is a unique character in the history of Christian women. For the most part, these women had to walk a fine line between the implementation of their vision and the demands of church authorities. Mother Teresa, however, seemed to fit perfectly into the current ecclesiastical vision of the role of women. She lived the ethics of care to perfection and inspired millions. She did not, like the women religious founders of previous ages, tackle the authorities about the causes of the suffering or the economic realities, which made the slums of Calcutta inevitable. This was never part of her mission. It is likely that Mother Teresa will be named a saint before the twenty-first century is much older, and when that happens, it will be greeted with acclamation by the vast majority of believing Catholics. In an age when there were few models of sanctity, she provided a shining example of the traditional ecclesiastical model of the Christian woman. It is, however, a contradictory model, and its implications for the future of women in Christianity are not promising.[28]

Dorothy Day was also a controversial figure, but for entirely different reasons. She also engaged in a hands-on face to face ministry with the poorest of the poor in the large cities of the United States, but Dorothy Day never feared to confront the authorities, whether secular or ecclesiastical, in pursuit of a just and peaceful society. Dorothy Day was born in Brooklyn on 8 November, 1897, just a few blocks from the Brooklyn Bridge. Her father was a journalist in the field of his passion, horseracing.

Her mother, Grace, was really the mainstay of the family, and despite several moves and often the experience of real poverty, Dorothy remembers her childhood as happy. She was the middle of five children, but was closest to her sister Della, who remained a life-long companion. At the age of sixteen, Dorothy set out for the University of Illinois, where, as she tells us, she 'ceased to believe'. For just under twenty years, Dorothy's life was one of drifting from job to job and from romance to romance. She was involved in journalism, nursing, the anti-war movement, and the suffragist movement and was powerfully attracted to communism. She experienced several spells in jail for a variety of 'offences' committed in her anti-war work, and seemed for a while to have adopted an amoral attitude toward sexuality. The darkest moment in this period occurred when she had an abortion in May 1919, and from this point, her life began to be a search for some inner focus that would unify her being. In the spring of 1920, she married and set out with her new husband for Europe. The marriage only lasted as long as the European tour, that is, less than a year. By June of 1920, Dorothy was pregnant again and was full of 'blissful joy'. It seemed that this pregnancy helped her to deal with her guilt over the abortion. At the age of twenty-nine, she gave birth to her daughter Tamar, which was for her a 'terrible joy'. From this moment her life turned toward the Catholic Church and she began to take instructions to become a Catholic.

Dorothy's attraction to communism arose from her opposition to capitalism and its mistreatment of the poor. She began to work with the poor, but even after her baptism in 1927, she still felt that she was adrift and without any real vocation. It was the rather mysterious meeting with Peter Maurin in 1932 that changed the direction of her life. He offered to teach her how to be a Catholic and she must have been among the most willing students. From that time forward all of Dorothy Day's energies went into the working out of their vision of pacifism and work with the poor. Maurin suggested that she found a Catholic Labour newspaper, and eventually *The Catholic Worker* saw the light of day on Mayday, 1933. It was an extraordinary success, and by December 1964, sixty thousand copies were being printed.

The Catholic Worker was the seed ground for all the other developments in the joint mission of Peter Maurin and Dorothy Day. Houses of hospitality were spreading throughout the cities of North America in order to implement their shared vision, which could be summed up in the short phrase: 'Feed the poor for Christ's sake.' Dorothy was a voracious reader and a prolific writer and the pen became another mighty instrument for the dissemination of their philosophy of personalism. Dorothy Day hated the impersonal welfare that was grudgingly meted out to the poor and she was determined to put a human face on her work of feeding the poor. Her absolute pacifism during the Second World War led to endless confrontation, but she refused to budge. She could not understand how anyone could elaborate a theory of war from the New Testament. Dorothy died on 29 November, 1980 and her funeral was attended by people from all races and all walks of life. Dorothy Day mixed with the poorest of the poor as well as the mighty of the land. She was an utterly devoted Catholic, but when her work for peace or justice for the poor was obstructed, she allowed nothing and nobody to stand in her way.

Dorothy Day's life was an exhausting round of travelling, organising, looking for funding for her many enterprises, and endless meetings with the people who flocked to the houses of hospitality for food for body and soul. There is no doubt that her life was governed by an ethic of justice that was among the most radical to be elaborated in North America. It is doubtful if she knew the great tradition of women, which she continued, women, who, throughout the history of Christianity had but one goal, namely the public exercise of compassion. They and Dorothy shared the same vision, expressed by Dorothy in her radical motto: 'To bring Christ back to earth.'

Conclusion

It is difficult to conclude two thousand years of the history of Christian women, partly because the story continues, and partly because the story continues unchanged in so many ways. It is true that the Christian women of today live in entirely different contexts, but it is also true that the Christian content of the lives of today's women is still moulded by and rooted in the male-dominated tradition that was familiar to women Christians of all preceding centuries. There is, however, a parallel Christian tradition, the story of women Christians, and that is the story attempted in these three volumes. No one knows better than the author how little of this story has been told, and how difficult it is to take the proper perspective that will most faithfully represent the Christian content of women's lives through the centuries.

There is a tradition of WomanChristianity that runs on a parallel track to the official, institutional Christian story. It is a different tradition that has kept alive many elements of the Christian vision that are otherwise forgotten. It is the story of Christianity as lived from the outside, from the margins, from the perspective of those members who were, for the most part, not considered to be full members with all the privileges enjoyed by men. This is the story of those who, for most of the story, are not heard, who could not preach, whose Christian insights were not considered necessary, who risked their lives even in the act of thinking independently. It is the story of the millions of women whose grief at the death of children and whose joy at the birth of live children were equally considered inessential to the forming of Christian meaning. It is the story of women Religious who had to strive ceaselessly for the right to engage in the public exercise of compassion, to which they felt called. It is the story of thousands executed as witches and heretics, for no other reason than that they were women. It is the story of millions denied an education, and therefore denied the opportunity to hand on their history, to reflect publicly on their lives, to name the God of their being.

And yet ... there remains the testimony of Woman-Christianity. There are women, and many more than these volumes can even indicate, who found the courage and ingenuity to record their thoughts in ways that are still accessible to us. For many of these women, writing theology, or recording their mystical experiences, or entering into correspondence in challenging and critical ways with the powerful political and religious leaders of their day, or handing on their teaching to later generations, the very act of writing was dangerous, unconventional and disobedient. Some covered their activity by appealing to the irresistible power of God's direct command. Some engaged in rhetorical self-diminishment in order to deflect the anger and retribution of their male superiors. A few stood boldly by their own insights and sought no approbation other than the testimony of their own conscience. Such a woman was Marguerite Porete, the Beguine mystic who was burnt at the stake in Paris on 1 June, 1310. Her book, *The Mirror of Simple Souls*, survived to open for us a gateway to her brilliant mystical life.

WomanChristianity has left us a record of how these women saw themselves and approached their God. For Marguerite, her life flowed into God as the Seine flowed into the sea, so that, in the end, no one could tell where divine and human began or ended. For Julian of Norwich, God was only, always, and everywhere Love, and one could never conclude from her writings to the existence of a sinful ancestor called Eve, or a sinful condition like original sin. The religious experience of having been created, and living her life as the image of a graceful God was not a theological problem for Julian. The women of Helfta learned to 'laugh and leap in ordered dance' as they celebrated the experience of being bathed in the 'flowing light of the Godhead'. All, without exception, believed that the goal of their Christian life was the 'public exercise of compassion'. Catherine of Siena literally sped around Europe trying to convince political and church leaders that this should be their goal also. Her failure to convert their hearts is said to have led to her early death as a result of her own broken heart. Hundreds of women founders of Religious communities expended their life energy trying to convince church leadership that their call to serve the poor was not a danger to humanity, but a genuine expression of gospel living.

Among the women were those who would today be considered unbalanced, but then, today's women have not had to live in social and ecclesial conditions that considered women, by definition, to be unbalanced. Among the women were those, like Hildegard of Bingen, who would have to be considered among the geniuses of any age. Among the women were those not yet out of their teens, like Joan of Arc, who were burnt as heretics for not fitting into the conventional image of womanhood. Among the women were thousands, again like Joan of Arc, who were executed unjustly and in error, for a sin projected upon them by a false and fearful clergy.

Finally, the feminist challenge to Christianity, which has gained momentum since the nineteenth century, must be seen both as one of the greatest challenges in Christian history and one of the most remarkable opportunities offered to the Christian Church for revitalising its life, by fully incorporating more than half of its membership who have been deliberately side-lined. The global expression of feminist theology and spirituality is characterised by a sense of commitment, spiritual joy, and vivid energy, as well as by the mourning of remembered pain, so that one is awe-struck by its power. It is a power that cannot fail to survive.

Bibliography

Advisory Council for the Church's Ministry, *The Ordination of Women to the Priesthood*, Church Information Office, 1972.

Anderson, Anne and D'Angelo, Mary Rose, *Crossroads in Theology: Essays for Ellen M. Leonard, CSJ*, Toronto Journal of Theology, Vol. 16, No.1, Spring 2000.

Anderson, Bonnie S., and Zinsser, Judith P., *A History of Their Own: From PreHistory to the Present*, Volume II, Harper & Row, 1988.

Andolsen, Barbara Hilkert, Gudorf, Christine E., and Pellauer, Mary D., Editors, *Women's Consciousness, Women's Conscience: A Reader in Feminist Ethics*, Harper & Row, 1985.

Armstrong, Karen, *The Battle for God: Fundamentalism in Judaism, Christianity and Islam*, HarperCollinsPublishers, 2000.

Armstrong, Karen, *The End of Silence: Women and Priesthood*, Fourth Estate, 1993.

Aslanbeigui, Nahid, Pressman Steven and Summerfield, Gale, *Women in the Age of Economic Transformation*, Routledge, 1994.

Barstow, Anne Llewellyn, *Witchcraze: A New History of the European Witch Hunts*, Pandora, 1994.

Beard, Mary R., *Woman as Force in History*, Collier Books, 1946.

Beattie, Tina, *Eve's Pilgrimage: A Woman's Quest for the City of God*, Burns & Oates, 2002.

Behr-Siegel, Elisabeth, *The Ministry of Women in the Church*, Oakwood Publications, 1991.

Borresen, Kari Elisabeth, Editor, *The Image of God: Gender Models in Judaeo-Christian Tradition*, Fortress Press, 1991.

Bridenthal, Renate and Koonz, Claudia, Editors, *Becoming Visible: Women in European History*, Houghton Mifflin Company, 1977.

Briggs, Robin, *Witches & Neighbours*, Fontana Press, 1996.

Brown, Joanne Carlson and Bohn, Carole R. Editors, *Christianity, Patriarchy, and Abuse: A Feminist Critique*, The Pilgrim Press, 1989.

Brownmiller, Susan, *Femininity*, Linden Press, 1984.

Bruce, Michael & Duffield, G. E., Editors, *Why Not?: Priesthood & the Ministry of Women*, The Marcham Manor Press, 1972.

Byrne, Lavinia, *Woman at the Altar: The Ordination of Women in the Roman Catholic Church*, Mowbray, 1994.

Cady, Susan, Ronan, Marian and Taussig, Hal, *SOPHIA: The Future of Feminist Spirituality*, Harper & Row, 1986.

Carmody, Denise L., *Christian Feminist Theology*, Blackwell, 1995.

Carr, Anne and Schüssler Fiorenza, Elisabeth, Editors, *Motherhood: Experience, Institution, Theology*, Concilium, Volume 206, T. & T. Clark, 1989.

Carr, Anne and Van Leeuwen, Mary Stewart, Editors, *Religion, Feminism, and the Family*, Westminster John Knox Press, 1996.

Chadwick, Owen, *The Reformation*, Penguin books, 1972.

Chopp, Rebecca S., *Saving Work: Feminist Practices of Theological Education*, Westminster John Knox Press, 1985.

Christ, Carol P. and Plaskow, Judith, *Womanspirit Rising: A Feminist Reader in Religion*, Harper and Row, 1979.

Cixous, Helene and Clement, Catherine, *The Newly Born Woman*, University of Minnesota Press, 1975.

Clifford, Anne M., *Introducing Feminist Theology*, Orbis Books, 2001.

Coles, Robert, *Dorothy Day: A Radical Devotion*, Addison-Wesley Publishing Company Inc, 1987

Collins, Adele Yarbro, Editor, *Feminist Perspectives on Biblical Scholarship*, Scholars Press, 1985.

Collins, Kenneth J., *Exploring Christian Spirituality: An Ecumenical Reader*, Baker Books, 2000.

Cooey, Paula M., Eakin, William R., and McDaniel, Jay B., Editors, *After Patriarchy: Feminist Transformations of the World Religions*, Orbis Books, 1991.

Cooey, Paula M., Farmer, Sharon A., and Ross Mary Ellen, Editors, *Embodied in Love: Sensuality and Relationship as Feminist Values*, Harper & Row, 1987.

Cover, Jeanne IBVM, *Love, the Driving Force: Mary Ward's Spirituality: Its Significance for Moral Theology*, Marquette University Press, 1998.

Cragg, Gerald R., *The Church and the Age of Reason 1648-1789*, Penguin Books, 1970.

Daly, Lois K., Editor, *Feminist Theological Ethics: A Reader*, Westminster John Knox Press, 1994.

Daly, Mary, *Beyond God the Father: Toward a Philosophy of Women's Liberation*, Beacon Press, 1973.

Daly, Mary, *The Church and the Second Sex*, Beacon Press, 1985.

Danylewycz, Marta, *Taking the Veil: An Alternative to Marriage, Motherhood and Spinsterhood in Quebec, 1840-1920*, McClelland and Stewart, 1987.

Diamond, Irene and Orenstein, Gloria Feman, Editors, *Reweaving the World: The Emergence of Ecofeminism*, Sierra Club Books, 1990.

Donovan, Josephine, *Feminist Theory*, Continuum, 2000.

Duby Georges and Perrot, Michelle, General Editors, *A History of Women, Volume V: Toward a Cultural Identity in the Twentieth Century*, The Belknap Press of Harvard University Press, 1994.

Duby, Georges and Perrot, Michelle, General Editors, *A History of Women, Volume III: Renaissance and Enlightenment Paradoxes*, The Belknap Press of Harvard University Press, 1993.

Duby, Georges and Perrot, Michelle, General Editors, *A History of Women, Volume IV: Emerging Feminism from Revolution to World War*, The Belknap Press of Harvard University Press, 1993.

Duck, Ruth C., *Gender and the Name of God: The Trinitarian Baptismal Formula*, The Pilgrim Press, 1991.

Eck, Diana L. and Jain, Devaki, Editors, *Speaking of Faith: Global Perspectives on Women, Religion, and Social Change*, New Society Publishers, 1987.

Ellis, John Harvard, *The Works of Anne Bradstreet in Prose and Verse*, Peter Smith, 1962.

Fabella, Virginia and Torres, Sergio, Editors, *Doing Theology in a Divided World*, Orbis Books, 1985.

Fabella, Virginia, M .M. and Oduyoye, Mercy Amba, Editors, *With Passion and Compassion: Third World Women Doing Theology*, Orbis Books, 1988.

Flannery, Austin, OP, *Vatican Council II: The Conciliar and Post Conciliar Documents*, Dominican Publications, 1975.

Fraser, Antonia, *Marie Antoinette*, Weidenfeld and Nicholson, 2001.

Fraser, Antonia, *The Weaker Vessel: Woman's Lot in Seventeenth-Century England*, Methuen, 1984.

Gagan, Rosemary R., *A Sensitive Independence: Canadian Methodist Women Missionaries in Canada and the Orient, 1881-1925*, McGill-Queen's University Press, 1992.

Gilligan, Carol, *In a Different Voice: Psychological Theory and Women's Development*, Harvard University Press, 1982.

Ginzburg, Carlo, *Ecstasies: Deciphering the Witches' Sabbath*, Penguin Books, 1991.

Haddad, Yvonne Yazbeck and Findly, Ellison Banks, Editors, *Women, Religion, and Social Change*, State University of New York Press, 1985.

Halkes, Catherina J. M., *New Creation: Christian Feminism and the Renewal of the Earth*, SPCK, 1991.

Hampson, Daphne, Editor, *Swallowing a Fishbone: Feminist Theologians Debate Christianity*, SPCK, 1996.

Hampson, Daphne, *Theology and Feminism*, Basil Blackwell, 1990.

Hastings, Adrian, Editor, *A World History of Christianity*, Cassell, 1999.

Hayes, Alan and Urquhart, Diane, Editors, *The Irish Women's History Reader*, Routledge, 2001.

Heyward, Carter, *Our Passion for Justice: Images of Power, Sexuality, and Liberation*, The Pilgrim Press, 1984.

Higgins, Michael W. and Letson, Douglas R., *Power & Peril: The Catholic Church at the Crossroads*, HarperCollinsPublishersLtd, 2002.

Hogan, Linda, *Confronting the Truth: Conscience in the Catholic Tradition*, Darton, Longman & Todd, 2001.

hooks, bell, *Ain't I A Woman: Black Women and Feminism*, South End Press, 1981.

Hufton, Olwen, *The Prospect Before Her: A History of Women in Western Europe, 1500-1800*, Alfred A. Knopf, 1996.

Jedin, Hubert, Editor, *History of the Church, Volume IX: The Church in the Industrial Age*, Burns & Oates, 1981.

Jedin, Hubert, Editor, *History of the Church, Volume V: Reformation and CounterReformation*, A Crossroad Book, 1980.

Jedin, Hubert, Editor, *History of the Church, Volume VI: The Church in the Age of Absolutism and Enlightenment*, Burns & Oates, 1981.

Jedin, Hubert, Editor, *History of the Church, Volume VII: The Church Between Revolution and Restoration*, Crossroad, 1981.

Jedin, Hubert, Editor, *History of the Church, Volume VIII: The Church in the Age of Liberalism*, Crossroad, 1981.

Jedin, Hubert, Editor, *History of the Church, Volume X: The Church in the Modern Age*, Burns & Oates, 1981.

Jewett, Paul K., *The Ordination of Women*, William B. Eerdmans Publishing Company, 1980.

Johnson, Paul, *A History of Christianity*, Penguin Books, 1976.

Johnson, Paul, *A History of the Modern World: From 1917 to the 1980s*, Weidenfeld and Nicholson, 1983.

Jordan, Constance, *Renaissance Feminism: Literary Texts and Political Models*, Cornell University Press, 1990.

Karlsen, Carol F., *The Devil in the Shape of a Woman: Witchcraft in Colonial New England*, Vintage Books, 1989.

Kavanaugh, Kieran, OCD and Rodriguez, Otilio, OCD, Translators, *Teresa of Avila: The Interior Castle*, The Classics of Western Spirituality, Paulist Press, 1979.

Kelleher, Margaret, *The Feminization of Famine: Expressions of the Inexpressible?* Cork University Press, 1997.

Kelly, Linda, *Women of the French Revolution*, A Hamish Hamilton Paperback, 1987.

Kemp, Sandra and Squires, Judith, Editors, *Feminisms*, Oxford University Press, 1997.

Kienzle, Beverly Mayne and Walker, Pamela J., *Women Preachers and Prophets Through Two Millennia of Christianity*, University of California Press, 1998.

Kimel, Alvin F. Jr., Editor, *Speaking the Christian God: The Holy Trinity and the Challenge of Feminism*, William B. Eerdmans, 1992.

King, Ursula, Editor, *Feminist Theology from the Third World*, SPCK/Orbis Press, 1994.

King, Ursula, Editor, *Religion and Gender*, Blackwell, 1995.

King, Ursula, Editor, *Women in the World's Religions: Past and Present*, Paragon House, 1987.

King, Ursula, *Women and Spirituality: Voices of Protest and Promise*, Second Edition, MacMillan, 1993.

Kolbenschlag, Madonna, Editor, *Women in the Church 1*, Pastoral Press, 1987.

Küng, Hans, *Christianity: The Religious Situation of Our Time*, SCM, 1994.

Lerner, Gerda, *The Creation of Feminist Consciousness: From the Middle Ages to Eighteen-seventy*, Oxford University Press, 1993.

Levack, Brian P., *The Witch-Hunt in Early Modern Europe*, Longman, 1995.

Littlehales, Margaret Mary, *Mary Ward: Pilgrim and Mystic*, Burns & Oates, 1998.

Loades, Ann, Editor, *Feminist Theology: A Reader*, SPCK, 1990.

Luddy, Maria and Murphy, Cliona, Editors, *Women Surviving: Studies in Irish Women's History in the 19th and 20th Centuries*, Poolbeg, 1990.

MacCurtain, Margaret and O'Dowd, Mary, Editors, *Women in Early Modern Ireland*, Wolfhound Press, 1991.

MacHaffie, Barbara J., *HerStory: Women in Christian Tradition*, Fortress Press, 1986.

MacHaffie, Barbara J., *Readings in HerStory: Women in Christian Tradition*, Fortress Press, 1992.

Mananzan, Mary John, et al, *Women Resisting Violence: Spirituality for Life*, Orbis Books, 1996.

Manning, Joanna, *Is the Pope Catholic?: A Woman Confronts her Church*, Malcolm Lester Books, 1999.

Marek, George R., *The Bed and the Throne: The Life of Isabella d'Este*, Harper & Row, 1976.

Martin, Francis, *The Feminist Question: Feminist Theology in the Light of Christian Tradition*, William B. Eerdman, 1994.

Mauffette-Leenders, Louise and Maigler, Gloria, *Women of Zana*, Heart-Links, 2001.

Mayeskie, Mary Anne, *Women Models of Liberation*, Sheed and Ward, 1988.

McAlister, Linda Lopez, Editor, *Hypatia's Daughters: Fifteen Hundred Years of Women Philosophers*, Indiana University Press, 1996.

McFague, Sallie, *Metaphorical Theology: Models of God in Religious Language*, Fortress Press, 1982.

McFague, Sallie, *Models of God: Theology for an Ecological, Nuclear Age*, Fortress Press, 1987.

McManners, John, Editor, *The Oxford Illustrated History of Christianity*, Oxford University Press, 1992.

McNamara, Jo Ann Kay, *Sisters in Arms: Catholic Nuns Through Two Millennia*, Harvard University Press, 1996.

Meer, Haye van der SJ, *Women Priests in the Catholic Church?* Temple University Press, 1973.

Micks, Marianne H. and Price, Charles P., Editors, *Towards a New Theology of Ordination: Essays on the Ordination of Women*, Virginia Theological Seminary, 1976.

Milcent, Paul, *Jeanne Jugan: Humble, so as to Love More*, Darton, Longman and Todd, 1980.

Miles, Rosalind, *The Women's History of the World*, Paladin, 1988.

Milhaven, Annie Lally, *The Inside Stories: 13 Valiant Women Challenging the Church*, Twenty-Third Publications, 1987.

Miller, William D., *Dorothy Day: A Biography*, Harper & Row, 1982.

Monks of Solesmes, Editors, *The Woman in the Modern World*, St Paul Editions, 1958.

Moore, Peter, Editor, *Man, Woman & Priesthood*, SPCK, 1978.

Mowry LaCugna, Catherine, *Freeing Theology: The Essentials of Theology in Feminist Perspective*, HarperSanFrancisco, 1993.

Murphy, Cullen, *The World According to Eve: Women and the Bible in Ancient Times and Our Own*, The Penguin Press, 1999.

Neill, Stephen, *A History of Christian Missions*, Penguin Books, 1975.

Nichols, John A. and Shank, Lillian Thomas, *Peace Weavers: Medieval Religious Women*, Volume Two, Cistercian Publications, 1987.

Noddings, Nel, *Women and Evil*, University of California Press, 1989.

Ó Murchú, Diarmuid, *Reclaiming Spirituality*, Gill and MacMillan, 1997.

O'Dwyer, Peter, O Carm, *Mary: A History of Devotion in Ireland*, Four Courts Press, 1988.

O'Grady, Selina and Wilkins, John, Editors, *Spiritual Stars of the Millennium*, Continuum, 2001.

O'Hara Graff, Ann, Editor, *In the Embrace of God: Feminist Approaches to Theological Anthropology*, Orbis Books, 1995.

Ozment, Steven, *Magdalen & Balthasar*, Simon and Schuster, 1986.

Ozment, Steven, *Protestants: The Birth of a Revolution*, Image Books, 1991.

Peers, E. Allison, Editor and Translator, *Ascent of Mount Carmel by St John of the Cross*, Image Books, 1958.

Pelikan, Jaroslav, Flusser, David and Lang, Justin, *Mary: Images of the Mother of Jesus in Jewish and Christian Perspective*, Fortress Press, 1986.

Philips, John A., *Eve: The History of an Idea*, Harper and Row, 1984.

Plant, Judith, *Healing the Wounds: The Promise of Ecofeminism*, New Society Publishers, 1989.

Plaskow, Judith and Christ, Carol P., Editors, *Weaving the Visions: Patterns in Feminist Spirituality*, Harper & Row, 1989.

Procter-Smith, Marjorie, *In Her Own Rite: Constructing Feminist Liturgical Tradition*, Abingdon Press, 1990.

Purcell, Mary, *To Africa with Love: The Biography of Mother Mary Martin*, Gill and MacMillan, 1987.

Quigley, Florence, CND, *In the Company of Marguerite Bourgeoys*, Novalis, 1982.

Ramshaw-Schmidt, Gail, *Christ in Sacred Speech: The Meaning of Liturgical Language*, Fortress Press, 1986.

Report of the Archbishops' Commission, *Women and Holy Orders*, Church Information Office, 1966.

Riley, Maria, *Transforming Feminism*, Sheed & Ward, 1989.

Rose, Mary Beth, Editor, *Women in the Middle Ages and the Renaissance: Literary and Historical Perspectives*, Syracuse University Press, 1986.

Ross, Susan A., *Extravagant Affections: A Feminist Sacramental Theology*, Continuum, 2001.

Ruether, Rosemary & McLaughlin, Eleanor, *Women of Spirit: Female Leadership in the Jewish and Christian Traditions*, Simon and Schuster, 1979.

Ruether, Rosemary Radford and Keller, Rosemary Skinner, General Editors, *Women and Religion in America*, Volume 3, 1900-1968, Harper & Row, 1986.

Ruether, Rosemary Radford, *Christianity and the Making of the Modern Family: Ruling Ideologies, Diverse Realities*, Beacon Press, 2000.

Ruether, Rosemary Radford, *New Woman, New Earth: Sexist Ideologies and Human Liberation*, A Crossroad Book, 1975.

Ruether, Rosemary Radford, *Sexism and God-Talk: Toward a Feminist Theology*, Beacon Press, 1983.

Ruether, Rosemary Radford, *Women and Redemption: A Theological History*, Fortress Press, 1998.

Russell, Letty M., Editor, *Feminist Interpretation of the Bible*, The Westminster Press, 1985.

Ryan, Frances DC, and Rybolt, John E. CM, Editors, *Vincent de Paul and Louis de Marillac: Rules, Conferences, and Writings*, The Classics of Western Spirituality, Paulist Press, 1995.

Schüssler Fiorenz, Elisabeth and Copeland, M. Shawn, Editors, *Feminist Theology in Different Contexts*, Concilium 1996/1, SCM Press/Orbis Books, 1996.

Schüssler Fiorenza, Elisabeth and Carr, Anne, Editors, *Women, Work and Poverty*, Concilium, Volume 194, T. & T. Clark, 1987.

Schüssler Fiorenza, Elisabeth and Copeland, Mary Shawn, Editors, *Violence Against Women*, Concilium, 1994/1, SCM Press/Orbis Books, 1994.

Schüssler Fiorenza, Elisabeth, *Bread Not Stone: The Challenge of Feminist Biblical Interpretation*, Beacon Press, 1984.

Schüssler Fiorenza, Elisabeth, Editor, *Searching the Scriptures: A Feminist Introduction*, Crossroad, 1993.

Schüssler Fiorenza, Elisabeth, Editor, *Searching the Scriptures: A Feminist Commentary*, Crossroad, 1994.

Schüssler Fiorenza, Elisabeth, *In Memory of Her: A Feminist Theological Reconstruction of Christian Origins*, Crossroad, 1983.

Second Report by the House of Bishops, *The Ordination of Women to the Priesthood*, General Synod of the Church of England, 1988.

Sharma, Arvind, Editor, *Women in World Religions*, State University of New York Press, 1987.

Sheldrake, Philip, *Spirituality and History: Questions of Interpretation and Method*, Crossroad, 1992.

Shogan, Debra, Editor, *A Reader in Feminist Ethics*, Canadian Scholars' Press, 1993.

Snyder, C. Arnold and Hecht, Linda A. Huebert, Editors, *Profiles of Anabaptist Women: Sixteenth Century Reforming Pioneers*, Wilfrid Laurier University Press, 1996.

Snyder, Mary Hembrow, *The Christology of Rosemary Radford Ruether: A Critical Introduction*, Twenty-Third Publications, 1988.

Sobel, Dava, *Galileo's Daughter: A Drama of Science, Faith and Love*, Fourth Estate, 1999.

Spender, Dale, Editor, *Feminist Theorists: Three Centuries of Key Women Thinkers*, Pantheon Books, 1983.

Spretnak, Charlene, Editor, *The Politics of Women's Spirituality: Essays by Founding Mothers of the Movement*, Anchor books, 1994.

Swidler, Leonard and Swidler, Arlene, Editors, *Women Priests: A Catholic Commentary on the Vatican Declaration*, Paulist Press, 1977.

Tamez, Elsa, Editor, *Through Her Eyes: Women's Theology from Latin America*, Orbis Books, 1989.

Tarnas, Richard, *The Passion of the Western Mind*, Ballantine Books, 1991.

Tavard, George H., *Woman in Christian Tradition*, University of Notre Dame Press, 1973.

Thibert, Peronne Marie VHM, Translator, *Francis de Sales, Jane de Chantal: Letters of Spiritual Direction*, The Classics of Western Spirituality, Paulist Press, 1988.

Thrall, M. E., *The Ordination of Women to the Priesthood, Studies in Ministry and Worship*, SCM Press Ltd, 1958.

Torjesen, Karen Jo, *When Women Were Priests: Women's Leadership in the Early Church and the Scandal of their Subordination in the Rise of Christianity*, HarperSanFrancisco, 1993.

Torres, Sergio and Eagleson, John, Editors, *The Challenge of Basic Christian Communities*, Orbis Books, 1981.

Townes, Emilie, M, Editor, *Embracing the Spirit: Womanist Perspectives on Hope, Salvation and Transformation*, Orbis Books, 1997.

Valiulis, Maryann Gialanella and O'Dowd, Mary, *Women and Irish History*, Wolfhound Press, 1997.

Vidler, Alec R., *The Church in the Age of Revolution*, Penguin Books, 1971.

Walker, Alice, *The Color Purple*, Washington Square Press, 1992.

Walrond-Skinner, Sue, Editor, *Crossing the Boundary: What Will Women Priests Mean?* Mowbray, 1994.

Ward, Margaret, *Unmanageable Revolutionaries: Women and Irish Nationalism*, Brandon, 1983,

Ware, Kallistos, et al, *Women and the Priesthood*, St Vladimir's Seminary Press, 1973.

Warner, Marina, *Alone of All Her Sex: The Myth and Cult of the Virgin Mary*, Vintage, 2000.

Warner, Marina, *Monuments and Maidens: The Allegory of the Female Form*, Picador, 1985.

Washbourn, Penelope, *Becoming Woman: The Quest for Wholeness in Female Experience*, Harper and Row, 1977.

Weaver, Mary Jo, *New Catholic Women: A Contemporary Challenge to Religious Authority*, Harper & Row, 1985.

Webster, Margaret, *A New Strength, A New Song: The Journey to Women's Priesthood*, Mowbray, 1994.

Weir, Alison, *The Six Wives of Henry VIII*, Pimlico, 1992.

Welch, Sharon D., *Communities of Resistance and Solidarity: A Feminist Theology of Liberation*, Orbis Books, 1985.

Wetter, Immaculata IBVM, *Mary Ward's Apostolic Vocation*, The Way, Supplement 17, Autumn, 1972.

White, Michael, *The Pope and the Heretic: A True Story of Courage and Murder at the Hands of the Inquisition*, Little, Brown and Company, 2002.

Wijngaards, John, *The Ordination of Women in the Catholic Church: Unmasking a Cuckoo's Egg Tradition*, Darton, Longman & Todd, 2001.

Williams, Delores S., *Sisters in the Wilderness: The Challenge of Womanist God-Talk*, Orbis Books, 1993.

Winter, Miriam Therese, Lummis, Adair, and Stokes, Allison, *Defecting in Place: Women Claiming Responsibility for Their Own Spiritual Lives*, Crossroad, 1994.

Wolski Conn, Joann, Editor, *Women's Spirituality: Resources for Christian Development*, Second Edition, Paulist Press, 1996.

Young, Pamela Dickey, *Feminist Theology/Christian Theology: In Search of Method*, Fortress Press, 1990.

Notes

CHAPTER ONE

1. Joan Kelly-Gadol, 'Did Women Have a Renaissance?' pp 137-164 in *Becoming Visible: Women in European History*, Edited by Renate Bridenthal and Claudia Koonz, Boston, 1977.

2. There is a huge volume of recent literature on Christine de Pizan. See the bibliography, for example, in *Hypatia's Daughters: Fifteen Hundred Years of Women Philosophers*, Edited by Linda Lopez McAlister, p 66. The translation of the main work used here, *The Treasure of the City of Ladies*, Penguin, 1985, is easily available.

3. *City of Ladies*, Chapter 1.

4. Ibid., Chapter 44.

5. See especially Gerda Lerner, *The Creation of Feminist Consciousness: From the Middle Ages to Eighteen-seventy*, Oxford, 1993, especially Chapters Two and Three.

6. For a most readable account of the renaissance popes, see *Vicars of Christ: The Dark Side of the Papacy*, by Peter de Rosa, Poolbeg Press, 1999.

7. *The Bed and the Throne: The Life of Isabella d'Este*, by George R. Marek, New York, 1976.

8. Ibid., p 90ff.

9. Ibid., p 182.

10. Letter of Isabella to her niece, one of the best descriptions of a Renaissance ceremony. Marek, p 227-228.

11. For the full religious significance of these events, see Karen Armstrong, *The Battle for God: Fundamentalism in Judaism, Christianity and Islam*, HarperCollins, 2001, p 3ff.

12. For a brief account of Isabella's life, see Antonia Fraser, *The Warrior Queens*, Viking, 1988, pp 182-202. For a fuller account, see F. Fernandez-Armesto, *Ferdinand and Isabella*, London, 1975.

13. Fraser, p 183.

14. Alison Weir, *The Six Wives of Henry VIII*, Pimlico, 1991, p 296-297.

15. For a much fuller account of these and other debates, see Gerda Lerner, *The Creation of Feminist Consciousness: From the Middle Ages to Eighteen- seventy*, Oxford University Press, 1993, pp 146ff.

16. Lerner, p 148.

17. Ibid.

18. See the brief but apt summation of the life of Erasmus in *Spiritual Stars of the Millennium*, Continuum, 2001, pp 56-58.

19. Constance Jordan, *Renaissance Feminism*, Cornell University Press, 1990, p 58.

20. Ibid., p 60.

21. Erasmus, *The Institute of Christian Marriage*, written in 1526. See excerpts in Jordan, pp 60ff.

22. One of the earliest explorations of these texts from a feminist perspective was that of Karen Armstrong in 1986 in *The Gospel According to Woman: Christianity's Creation of the Sex War in the West*, pp 93ff. Elm Tree Books.

23. *Malleus Maleficarum*, 4, translated by Montague Summers, London, 1928.

24. 'The Woman/The Witch: Variations on a Sixteenth-Century Theme' (Paracelsus, Wier, Bodin), by Gerhild Scholz Williams, pp 119-137 in *The Crannied Wall: Women, Religion and the Arts in Early Modern Europe*, edited by Craig A. Monson, The University of Michigan Press, 1992.

25. *Witchcraze: A New History of the European Witch Hunts*, Pandora, 1994, p 5. See the bibliography for a complete list of recent works on the subject.

26. Barstow, pp 143-145.

CHAPTER TWO

1. For two accessible and quite different accounts of the Protestant Reformation, see Owen Chadwick, *The Reformation*, Volume Three, *The Pelican History of the Church*, Penguin Books, 1979, and Steven Ozment, *Protestants: The Birth of a Revolution*, Image Books, 1993.

2. Quoted in 'Great Reasoners in Scripture: The Activities of Women Lollards, 1380-1530', by Claire Cross, pp 359-380, in *Medieval Women*, edited by Derek Baker, Oxford, 1978.

3. Ibid., p 376.

4. For a general history of women preachers throughout Christianity, see *Women Preachers and Prophets through Two Millennia of Christianity*, edited by Beverly Mayne Kienzle and Pamela J. Walker, University of California Press, 1998. Eamon Duffy gives abundant information about the activities of women in these early reform years in *The Stripping of the Altars: Traditional Religion in England 1400-1580*, Yale University Press, 1992.

5. The substance of this chapter owes much to the works mentioned above by Steven Ozment and Owen Chadwick.

6. The manuscript was translated by Walter Klassen, and will soon be published by Pandora Press, with an introduction by Mary T. Malone.

7. For this whole section, see Malone's introduction, note 6, above.

8. For Hoffman, see *Profiles of Anabaptist Women: Sixteenth Century Reforming Pioneers*, edited by C. Arnold Snyder and Linda A. Huebert Hecht, Wilfrid Laurier Press, 1996.

9. What we know of Ursula Jost is to be found in 'Ursula Jost and Barbara Rebstock of Strasbourg', in *Profiles*, pp 273ff.

10. Julian of Norwich, *Revelations of Divine Love*, Showing 5.

11. Jane Dempsey Douglass, 'Women and the Continental Reformation', pp 292-318 in *Religion and Sexism: Images of Women in the Jewish and Christian Traditions*, edited by Rosemary Radford Ruether, Simon and Schuster, 1974.

12. 'Maria and Ursula van Beckum' in *Profiles*, pp 352-358. There are several examples of the courage of Anabaptist women in *Profiles* and they deserve to be better known and remembered.

13. 'An Extraordinary Lay Leader: The Life and Work of Helene of Freyberg, Sixteenth Century Noblewoman and Anabaptist from the Tirol', *The Mennonite Quarterly Review* 66 (July 1992) pp 312-341, by Linda Huebert Hecht. By the same author, see also 'Women and religious change: The significance of Anabaptist women in the Tirol, 1527-29', *Studies in Religion/Sciences Religieuses*, Vol. 21, No. 1, 1992, pp 57-66.

14. Hecht, 'An Extraordinary Lay Leader...' p 322.

15. Jane Dempsey Douglass, p 309ff.

16. Malone, *Women and Christianity, Volume Two, From 1000 to the Reformation*, Chapter Two.

17. Douglass, p 293ff.

18. The title of Knox's work, *The First Blast of the Trumpet Against the Monstrous Regiment of Women* leaves no doubt as to where his sympathies lie.

19. See Sherrin Marshall Wyntjes, 'Women in the Reformation Era' pp 165-191 in *Becoming Visible: Women in European History*, edited by Renate Bridenthal and Claudia Koonz, Houghton Mifflin Company, 1977.

20. *Magdalena and Balthasar: An Intimate Portrait of Life in 16th Century Europe Revealed in the Letters of a Nuremberg Husband and Wife*, Steven Ozment, Simon and Schuster, 1986.

21. Ozment, p 137.

22. ibid., p 143.

23. ibid., p 164.

24. ibid., p 110.

25. ibid., pp 28-29.

26. ibid., pp 61-63.

27. Ibid., p 94.

28. Ibid., pp 100-102.

CHAPTER THREE

1. There is a good overview of the pre-reformed state of the Catholic Church in Hubert Jedin, *History of the Church, Volume V, Reformation and Counter Reformation*, by Erwin Iserloh, Joseph Glazik and Hubert Jedin, The Seabury Press, 1980. See especially Part Two, 'Catholic Reform and Counter Reformation', p 431ff.

2. Peter de Rosa, *Vicars of Christ: The Dark Side of the Papacy*, has a very redable account of this period. See chapter seven, 'The Inevitable Reformation'. The Burckhardt quotation is on p 121.

3. De Rosa, pp 123-125, 172-173, 191-197; and also Jedin, op. cit. p 451ff.

4. Owen Chadwick, *The Reformation*, Pelican History of the Church, Volume Three, Penguin Books, 1976, p 270ff.

5. Jedin, p 465f.

6. *Journal of the Council for 3 March 1546*, by Secretary Massarelli. Quoted in *How to Read Church History*, Volume 2: From the Reformation to the Present Day, Jean Comby with Diarmaid MacCulloch, SCM, 1989, p 26.

7. *A World History of Christianity*, Edited by Adrian Hastings, Cassell, 1999. See especially Chapter 7, 'Reformation and Counter-reformation' by Andrew Pettigree, pp 238-281.

8. See the discussion of the effects of the Counter-Reformation on women in Jo Ann Kay McNamara, *Sisters in Arms: Catholic Nuns through Two Millennia*, Harvard University Press, 1996, especially pp 489ff.

9. For the purposes of this chapter, I have concentrated on *Interior Castle*, which Teresa herself seems to have regarded as a kind of summing up of her previous works, *The Book of Her Life*, and *The Way of Perfection*. The edition I used is in *The Classics of Western Spirituality*, translated by Kieran Kavanaugh, OCD and Otilio Rodriguez, OCD, with an Introduction by Kieran Kavanaugh and Preface by Raimundo Panikkar, Paulist Press, 1979.

10. The phrase comes from Marie Anne Mayeskie, 'Teresa of Avila: Restless Gadabout', in *Women Models of Liberation*, Collins, 1988, pp 110-155.

11. Letter 224, quoted in Mayeskie, p 125.

12. E. Allison Peers has translated and edited much of John of the Cross. See, for example, *Ascent of Mount Carmel*, translated and edited by E. Allison Peers, Image Books, 1958. For a very brief and concise statement about John of the Cross, see Rowan Williams, in *Spiritual Stars of the Millennium*, edited by Selina O'Grady and John Wilkins, Continuum, 2001. For an excellent contemporary interpretation of the dark night of the soul, see 'Impasse and Dark Night' by Constance Fitzgerald, in *Women's Spirituality: Resources for Christian Development*, Edited by Joann Wolski Conn, Paulist Press, 1996.

13. See the introduction to *Interior Castle*, pp 6-29. See also the three articles on Teresa in *Peace Weavers: Medieval Religious Women*, edited by John A. Nichols and Lillian Thomas Shank, Cistercian Studies,1987: 'Teresa of Jesus: The Saint and her Spirituality', by Laurin Hartzog, pp 317-330; 'The Foundations of Mystical Prayer: Teresa of Jesus', pp 331-344; 'St Teresa of Avila: A Guide for Travel Inward', pp 345-352.

14. Sixth Dwelling, 7, 6 and 15.

15. Seventh Dwelling 1, 2.

16. Ibid., 1, 8.

17. Ibid., 4,15.

18. *A Woman of Genius: The Intellectual Autobiography of Sor Juana Ines de la Cruz*, translated by Margaret Sayers Peden, Second Edition, Lime Rock Press, 1987; *A Sor Juana Anthology*, translated by Alan S. Trueblood, Cambridge University Press, 1988. See also Donald Beggs, 'Sor Juana's Feminism: From Aristotle to Irigaray', in *Hypatia's Daughters: Fifteen Hundred Years of Women Philosophers*, edited by Linda Lopez McAlister, Indiana University Press, 1996, pp 108-127.

19. Sor Juana, *Response*, 1691. Quoted in McNamara, op. cit. note 8, p 539.

20. See Beggs, op. cit. for the philosophical interpretation of Sor Juana's work and for this final quotation, p 108.

CHAPTER FOUR

1. For a complete overview of the Catholic reform see Hubert Jedin, Editor, *History of the Church*, Volumes V and VI: *Reformation and Counter-Reformation*, Seabury Press, 1980, and *The Church in the Age of Absolutism and Enlightenment*, Burns & Oates, 1981.

2. See Owen Chadwick, *The Reformation*, for a good description of these events. The quotation from Clement VIII is on p 167.

3. Gerald R. Cragg, *The Church & the Age of Reason 1648-1789*, Pelican History of the Church, Volume Five, p 9.

4. Dava Sobel, *Galileo's Daughter: A Drama of Science, Faith and Love*, Fourth Estate, 1999.

5. See *A History of Women*, Volume Three, *Renaissance and Enlightenment Paradoxes*, edited by Natalie Zemon Davis and Arlette Farge, Harvard University Press, 1993. See especially Chapter 4, 'A Daughter to Educate', by Martine Sonnet, pp 101-131, and Chapter 5, 'Virgins and Mothers between Heaven and Earth', by Elisja Schulte van Kessel, pp 132-166.

6. There is a good general description of Angela's work in Jo Ann Kay McNamara's *Sisters in Arms: Catholic Nuns through Two Millennia*, Harvard University Press, 1996, pp 457ff. See also Ruth P. Liebowitz, 'Virgins in the Service of Christ: The Dispute over an Active Apostolate for Women during the Counter-Reformation', in Rosemary Ruether and Eleanor McLaughlin, *Women of Spirit: Female Leadership in the Jewish and Christian Traditions*, pp 132-152, Simon and Schuster, 1979. I owe a special debt of gratitude to Maire O'Donohoe for sharing with me her 1999 paper on the life and work of Angela Merici.

7. Olwen Huften, *The Prospect Before Her: A History of Women in Western Europe 1500-1800*, Alfred A. Knopf, 1996, p 377.

8. Quoted in *Women Preachers and Prophets through Two Millennia of Christianity*, by Beverley Mayne Kienzle and Pamela J. Walker, University of California Press, 1998, p 212.

9. Ibid., p 215.

10. Ibid., p 217.

11. Ibid., p 218.

12. I depend in large part in this section on the following works by Mary Ward's contemporary followers: *Mary Ward: Pilgrim and Mystic*, Margaret Mary Littlehales, Burns and Oates 2001; 'Mary Ward's Apostolic Vocation', in *The Way*, Supplement 17, Autumn 1972, pp 69-91; and, with special thanks to the author, *Love, the Driving Force: Mary Ward's Spirituality*, Jeanne Cover, IBVM, Marquette University Press, 1998.

13. Littlehales, pp 18-22.

14. Littlehales, p 69.

15. Littlehales, p 130.

16. Littlehales, p 213.

17. Cover, op. cit., p 17.

18. The Classics of Western Spirituality series has published the letters of spiritual direction of Jane and Francis translated by Peronne Marie Thibert, V.H.M., Paulist Press, 1988, with very good introduction to both lives. See also *Les Dévotes: Women and Church in Seventeenth Century France*, by Elizabeth Rapley, McGill-Queen's University Press, 1990, especially pp 34ff; 'Two Faces of Christ: Jeanne de Chantal', by Wendy Wright, *Peace Weavers: Medieval Religious Women*, Vol. 2, Cistercian Publications, 1987, pp 353-364. For Francis de Sales, see *Library of St Francis de Sales*, translated and edited by H. B. Mackey, London, 1873-1910. For Jane de Chantal, see *The Spirit of Saint Jane Frances de Chantal as Shown in her Letters*, translated by the Sisters of the Visitation, Longmans, Green and Co., 1922; and *Saint Jane Frances de Chantal: Her Exhortations, Conferences and Instructions*, Loyola University Press, 1928.

19. Classics, Introduction, p 25-27.

20. *Les Dévotes*, p 34ff.

21. Ibid., p 37.

22. Ibid., p 38.

23. Ibid., p 39, and see note 70, p 215.

24. Classics, Introduction, p 31.

25. Classics, Introduction, p 34ff.

26. See below, chapter nine.

27. The Classics of Western Spirituality has published an excellent volume in *Vincent de Paul and Louise de Marillac: Rules, Conferences, and Writings*, Paulist Press, 1995. This is the source of much of the material for this section. See also *Les devotes*, pp 78ff for a good analysis of the contribution of Vincent and Louise.

28. Classics, pp 80ff.

29. *Les Devotes*, p 83.

30. Classics, p 52.

31. Classics, p 87.

CHAPTER FIVE

1. For a general over view of this period see Hubert Jedin, *History of the Church*, Volume VI, *The Church in the Age of Absolutism and Enlightenment*, Burns & Oates, London, 1981. See also, Gerald R. Cragg, *The Church & the Age of Reason 1648-1789*, Volume Four, *The Pelican History of the Church*, Penguin Books, 1970. For an introduction to the missions see Stephen Neill, *A History of Christian Missions,* Volume Six, *The Pelican History of the Church*, Penguin Books, 1964. The most accessible book on women of this period is Elizabeth Rapley, *Les Dévotes: Women & Church in Seventeenth Century France*, McGill-Queen's University Press, 1990.

2. Cragg, p 24ff.

3. Neill, p 170ff.

4. Cragg, p 174ff.

5. *HerStory: Women in the Christian Tradition*, pp 80-83, by Barbara J. MacHaffie, Fortress Press, 1986.

6. It is probable that, as Anglican clergy seem to have accompanied Frobisher's expeditions, an Anglican Communion service had been celebrated sometime in the 1570s.

7. Neill, p 200ff.

8. McNamara, pp 470-471.

9. Ibid., p 479ff.

10. For an excellent brief description of Marie de l'Incarnation and the other women described in this chapter, see Prudence Allen, RSM, 'Six Canadian Women: Their Call, Their Witness, Their Legacy', pp 246-258 in *The Canadian Catholic Review*, Volume 5, Number 7, July/August, 1987.

11. Allen, p 250.

12. Kienzle and Walker, p 217.

13. Ibid., p 220.

14. Rapley, p 101ff.

15. Rapley, p 101ff.

16. Rapley, p 104.

17. Ibid.

18. Quoted from Marguerite's writing in Rapley, p 106.

19. Allen, p 252.

20. Allen, p 249.

21. Allen, pp 248-253.

22. Allen, pp 247-252.

23. Allen, p 250.

24. See below, Chapter Seven.

25. Rapley, p 143.

26. Ibid.

27. Rapley, p 151

28. Rapley, p 162.

CHAPTER SIX

1. For an overview of the eighteenth century see Gerald R. Cragg, *The Church & the Age of Reason 1648-1789*, Volume Four, *The Pelican History of the Church*, Penguin Books, 1970; Adrian Hastings, editor, *A World History of Christianity*, especially Chapter 12 by Mary Heimann, 'Christianity in Western Europe from the Enlightenment', Cassell, 1999. For the effects of the Enlightenment on women, see *A History of Their Own: Women in Europe*, Volume 11, by Bonnie S. Anderson and Judith P. Zinsser, Harper and Row, 1988, especially Part VII, 'Women of the Salons and Parlors', pp 103ff; *A History of Women*, Volume IV, *Emerging Feminism from Revolution to World War*, edited by Genevieve Fraisse and Michelle Perrot, Harvard University Press, 1993; Gerda Lerner, *The Creation of Feminist Consciousness: From the Middle Ages to Eighteen-seventy*, Oxford University Press, 1993, especially chapters nine and ten; Olwen Hufton, *The Prospect Before Her: A History of Women in Western Europe 1500-1800*, Alfred A. Knopf, 1996.

2. Anderson and Zinsser, pp 114-116.

3. Rousseau's masterpiece (*sic*) on education, *Emile*, was long regarded as an enlightened volume in educational circles of the eighteenth century and later. Such statements indicate how little of his educational philosophy was directed to the betterment of women. Op. cit., p 118-119.

4. Peter de Rosa, *Vicars of Christ: The Dark Side of the Papacy*, Poolbeg, 1988, p 232ff. Cragg, p 193ff.

5. Stephen Neill, *A History of Christian Missions*, Volume Six, *The Pelican History of the Church*, Penguin Books, 1964, pp 221ff.

6. Cragg, p 234ff.

7. Cragg, pp 235ff.

8. 'Damaris Cudworth Masham: A Seventeenth Century Feminist Philosopher', by Lois Frankel in *Hypatia's Daughters: Fifteen hundred Years of Women Philosophers*, edited by Linda Lopez McAlister, Indiana University Press, 1996, pp 128-138.

9. 'Now Foolish, Then Wise: Belle van Zuylen's Game with Sexual Identity', by Joke J. Hermsen, pp 165-180 in McAlister.

10. 'Reason and Sensibility: The Ideal of Women's Self-Governance in the Writings of Mary Wollstonecraft', by Catriona Mackenzie, pp 181-203 in McAlister. Also Anderson and Zinsser, pp 123ff.

11. Anderson and Zinsser, p 124.

12. Ibid., p 123.

13. Ibid., p 124.

14. Ibid., pp 125-126

15. Heimann, op. cit., p 471.

16. Richard Tarnas, *The Passion of the Western mind: Understanding the Ideas That Have Shaped Our World View*, Ballantine Books, 1991, especially pp 285ff. It is obvious to even the most casual reader of Tarnas that it is the male western mind that is the subject of Tarnas' inquiry.

17. My use of the word *sic* and the use of apostrophes around the word

'man' are not in Tarnas, but are designed to illustrate that Tarnas is speaking specifically about the male of the species. Women are specifically excluded from his account, as he says in a special note on the subject, pp 468-469.

18. Barbara J. MacHaffie, *HerStory: Women in Christian Tradition*, Fortress Press, 1986, p 78. I follow MacHaffie's material in large part in this section.

19. Ibid., p 87. See also MacHaffie, *Readings in HerStory*, Fortress Press, 1992, for selected writings illustrating the work of these women. Sarah Edwards' ecstasy is described on p 105ff.

20. p 107ff.

21. Pythia Press, London, 1989. Extracts quoted in *Readings in Herstory*, p 110ff.

22. Elaine C. Huber, "A Woman Must Not Speak': Quaker Women in the English Left Wing', pp 153-181 in *Women of Spirit: Female Leadership in the Jewish and Christian Traditions*, edited by Rosemary Ruether & Eleanor McLaughlin, Simon and Schuster, 1979.

23. *Readings*, p 111-112.

24. Ruether & McLaughlin, p 166.

25. Ibid., p 162-165.

26. Ibid., pp 166-178.

27. Catherine F. Smith, 'Jane Lead: The Feminist Mind and Art of a Seventeenth-Century Mystic', in Ruether & McLaughlin, op. cit., pp 183-203.

28. p 199.

1. The general description of church and society in this chapter owes much to the following volumes: Alec R. Vidler, *The Church in an Age of Revolution*, Volume Five, *The Pelican History of the Church*, 1971; Paul Johnson, *A History of Christianity*, Penguin Books, 1978; John McManners, Editor, *The Oxford Illustrated History of Christianity*, Oxford University Press, 1992; Hubert Jedin, Editor, *History of the Church*, Volume VII, *The Church Between Revolution and Restoration*; Volume VIII, *The Church in the Age of Liberalism*; Volume IX, *The Church in the Industrial Age*. Volumes VII and VIII published by Crossroads, New York, 1981, Volume IX, published by Burns & Oates, London, 1981; Adrian Hastings, Editor, *A World History of Christianity*, Cassell, 1999; and Hans Küng, *Christianity: The Religious Situation of our Time*, SCM Press, 1995.

2. Vidler, pp 14ff

3. Johnson, pp 375ff.

4. For this whole period, see *A History of Women*, Volume IV, *Emerging Feminism from Revolution to World War*, Harvard University Press, 1993, especially Chapter 2, 'The French Revolution as the Turning Point', pp 33-47, by Elisabeth G. Sledziewski.

5. *History*, p 41.
6. Linda Kelly, *Women of the French Revolution*, Hamish Hamilton, 1987, pp 35ff.
7. Ibid., pp 37-38.
8. Ibid., p 125.
9. Mary T. Malone, *Who Is My Mother? Rediscovering the Mother of Jesus*, Wm. C. Brown, 1984, chapters five and six.
10. Marina Warner, *Alone of All Her Sex: The Myth and Cult of the Virgin Mary*, Vintage Books, 1976, pp 334ff.
11. Ibid., p 335.
12. Ibid., p 336ff.
13. *Moral Monopoly: The Catholic Church in Modern Irish Society*, Gill and Macmillan, 1987, especially, Chapter 8, 'The Irish Mother', pp 187-214.
14. Ibid., pp 110ff.
15. Ibid., p 134ff.
16. Ibid., p 213.
17. Quoted from George W. Burnap (1802-1850), pastor of the First Unitarian Church in Baltimore, from a work of 1840 in Barbara J. MacHaffie, *Readings in HerStory: Women in Christian Tradition*, Fortress Press, 1992, p 115. See also Barbara J. MacHaffie, *HerStory: Women in Christian Tradition*, Fortress Press, 1986.
18. *HerStory*, pp 99f.
19. *Readings*, p 125.
20. *A History of Women*, Volume IV, pp 323ff.
21. Ibid., p 166ff for the Catholic model, and pp 199ff for the Protestant.

CHAPTER EIGHT

1. Rosalind Miles, *The Women's History of the World*, Paladin Books, 1988, p 221.
2. *A History of Women*, Volume Four, *Emerging Feminism from Revolution to World War*, pp 482ff, edited by Genevieve Fraisse and Michelle Perrot, Harvard University Press, 1993, and Volume Five, *Toward a Cultural Identity in the Twentieth Century*, edited by Francoise Thebaud, Harvard University Press, 1994. See also Gerda Lerner, *The Creation of Feminist Consciousness: From the Middle Ages to Eighteen-seventy*, Oxford University Press, 1993, and Bonnie S. Anderson and Judith P. Zinsser, *A History of Their Own: Women in Europe From Prehistory to the Present*, Volume Two, Harper and Row, 1988.
3. Renate Bridenthal and Claudia Koonz, Editors, *Becoming Visible: Women in European History*, Houghton Mifflin Company, 1977, pp 327ff.
4. Gerda Lerner, Introduction, p 9.
5. Gerda Lerner, *The Grimke Sisters*, US, 1967; Marie Anne Mayeskie, 'The Rays of her Candle: Sarah Grimke', in *Women: Models of Liberation*, pp 156174, Collins Fount Paperbacks, 1988; and Frank G. Fitzpatrick, 'From Shackles to Liberation: Religion, the Grimke Sisters and Dissent', pp 433-455 in *Women, Religion and Social Change*, edited by Yvonne

Yasbeck Haddad and Ellison Banks Findley, State University of New York Press, 1985.

6. Fitzpatrick, p 435.

7. Ibid., p 437.

8. The letter is quoted in MacHaffie, *Readings*, pp 124-128.

9. Quoted in Mayeskie, p 164.

10. Fitzpatrick, pp 444ff.

11. Elisabeth Gossman, 'History of Biblical Interpretation by European Women', pp 27-40 in *Searching the Scripture*, Volume 1, *A Feminist Introduction*, edited by Elisabeth Schüssler Fiorenza, Crossroads, 1993.

12. Elisabeth Schüssler Fiorenza, 'Transforming the Legacy of The Women's Bible' in *Searching*, pp 1-24.

13. Carolyn De Swarte Gifford, 'Politicizing the Sacred Texts: Elizabeth Cady Stanton and The Women's Bible', pp 52-63 in *Searching*.

14. *Searching*, Introduction, pp 12-19, and Karen Baker-Fletcher, 'Anna Julia Cooper and Sojourner Truth: Two Nineteenth-Century Black Feminist Interpreters of Scripture', pp 41-51.

15. Karen Baker-Fletcher, p 49.

16. Quoted in Rosalind Miles, op. cit., p 232. For an excellent analysis of the interweaving of feminism and racism, see *Ain't I a Woman: Black Women and Feminism*, bell hooks, South End Press, 1981.

17. Quoted in Maria Riley, *Transforming Feminism*, Sheed & Ward, 1989, pp 16-17.

18. The phrase is used by Jo Ann McNamara in describing the debilitating effects of Canon Law on Religious communities of women particularly in the early twentieth century. *Sisters in Arms: Catholic Nuns Through Two Millennia*, Harvard University Press, 1996, p 613.

19. Mary Ewens, OP, 'Removing the Veil: The Liberated American Nun' pp 255-278 in *Women of Spirit: Female Leadership in the Jewish and Christian Traditions*, edited by Rosemary Ruether & Eleanor McLaughlin, Simon and Schuster, 1979.

20. For a good survey of this period, see Mary Jo Weaver, *New Catholic Women: A Contemporary Challenge to Traditional Religious Authority*, Harper and Row, 1985, especially pp 17-42.

21. Ellen Leonard, *Unresting Transformation: The Theology and Spirituality of Maud Petre*, University of America Press, 1992, passim.

22. Paul Johnson, *A History of Christianity*, Penguin books, 1976.

23. The literature on the ordination of women is enormous. Here we just mention a few to illustrate the development of the issues involved: *The Ordination of Women to the Priesthood*, Studies in Ministry and Worship, by M. E. Thrall, SCM Press, 1958; *Women and Holy Orders*, Report of the Archbishops' Commission, Church Information Office, 1966; *The Ordination of Women to the Priesthood*, Church Information Office1972; *Why Not? Priesthood and the Ministry of Women*, edited by Michael Bruce & G. E. Duffield, Marcham Manor Press, 1972; Haye van der Meer, SJ, *Women Priests in the Catholic Church: A Theological Invest-*

igation, Temple University Press, 1973; *Inter Insigniores*: Declaration on the Admission of Women to the Ministerial Priesthood, Rome, 1976; *Commentary on Inter Insigniores*, Rome, 1977; *Women Priests: A Catholic Commentary on the Vatican Declaration*, edited by Leonard Swidler and Arlene Swidler, Paulist Press, 1977; *Man, Woman, Priesthood*, edited by Peter Moore, SPCK, 1978; *The Ordination of Women*, Paul K. Jewett, William B. Eerdmans Publishing Company, 1980; *Women and the Priesthood*, edited by Thomas Hopko, St Vladimir's Seminary Press, 1983; *The Ordination of Women to the Priesthood: A Second Report*, General Synod of the Church of England, 1988; *The Ministry of Women in the Church*, Elisabeth Behr-Siegel, Oakwood Publications, 1991; *The End of Silence: Women and the Priesthood*, Karen Armstrong, Fourth Estate, 1993; *A New Strength, A New Song: The Journey to Women's Priesthood*, Mowbray, 1994; *Crossing the Boundary: What Will Women Priests Mean?*, edited by Sue Walrond-Skinner, Mowbray, 1994; *Women at the Altar: The Ordination of Women in the Roman Catholic Church*, Lavinia Byrne, Mowbray, 1994; *Ordinatio Sacerdotalis*, Rome, 1994; *Ad Tuendam Fidem*, Rome, 1998; *Commentary on Ad Tuendam Fidem*, Rome, 1998; *The Ordination of Women in the Catholic Church: Unmasking a Cuckoo's Egg Tradition*, John Wijngaards, Darton, Longman, Todd, 2001. And for a vast quantity of information on the documentary tradition underlying the current Roman Catholic approach, see www.womenpriests.org

24. MacHaffie, *HerStory*, pp 134ff.

25. Betty Friedan, *The Feminine Mystique*, Norton, 1963 and Pope John XXIII, *Pacem in Terris*, Rome, 1963.

26. Armstrong, p 186.

27. Webster, *A New Strength, A New Song*, pp 204-205.

28. *Origins*, July 17, 1986. See also, Mary T. Malone, 'The Case for Ordination', in *Grail: An Ecumenical Journal*, Vol. 4, Issue 2, pp 9-20.

29. Rosemary Radford Ruether provides a brief summary of the work of these women scholars in *Women and Redemption: A Theological Vision*, Fortress Press, 1998. To prevent repetition, the books will be included in the bibliography.

30. 'Transforming the Legacy of *The Woman's Bible*', pp 1-24 in *Searching the Scriptures*, Volume One, *A Feminist Introduction*, p 11, Crossroad, 1993.

31. *Sexism and God-talk: Toward a Feminist Theology*, Beacon Press, 1983.

32. *SHE WHO IS: The Mystery of God in Feminist Theological Discourse*, Crossroad, 1992.

33. Kari Elisabeth Borresen, Editor, *The Image of God: Gender Models in Judaeo-Christian Tradition*, Fortress Press, 1995.

34. Catharina Halkes, *New Creation: Christian Feminism and the Renewal of the Earth*, SPCK, 1989.

35. Ann O'Hara Graff, Editor, *In the Embrace of God: Feminist Approaches to Theological Anthropology*, Orbis Books, 1995.

36. Catherine Mowry LaCugna, Editor, *Freeing Theology: The Essentials of Theology in Feminist Perspective*, HarperSanFrancisco, 1993.

CHAPTER NINE

1. *A History of the Modern World: From 1917 to the 1980s,* Weidenfeld and Nicholson, 1983.

2. Ibid., p 13.

3. On the advice of the Nuncio, Eugenio Pacelli, later Pope Pius XXII.

4. Paul Johnson, *A History of Christianity*, Penguin Books, 1976, p 502.

5. *Mater et Magistra*, 1961 and *Pacem in Terris*, 1963.

6. For a good introduction to twentieth-century spirituality, see Philip Sheldrake, *Spirituality and History: Questions of Interpretation and Method*, Crossroad, 1992.

7. For an excellent and revealing interpretation of the fundamentalist traditions of Judaism, Christianity and Islam, see Karen Armstrong, *The Battle for God*, HarperCollins, 2001.

8. Austin Flannery, OP, *Vatican Council II: The Conciliar and Post Conciliar Documents*, Dominican Publications, 1975.

9. *The Church and the Second Sex: With the Feminist Postchristian Introduction and New Archaic Afterwords,* The Twenty-fifth Anniversary Edition, Beacon Press, 1985.

10. The traditional sources of this spirituality are described in the previous volumes of this series. Here it is only necessary to refer to the writings of two popes as exemplars of this teaching: Pius XII in *The Woman in the Modern World*, selected and arranged by the monks of Solesmes, St Paul Editions, 1959. This book is intended 'for the conscientious teenage girl, for the active working miss, for the dedicated housewife, for the loving Christian mother, and for all guidance counsellors of women'. The writings of John Paul II are replete with this spirituality for women, with some contemporary variations. See especially *Mulieris dignitatem*, 1988, *Ordinatio Sacerdotalis*, 1994, and *Letter to Women* in preparation for the Beijing Women's International Conference, 1995.

11. Quoted in John Wijngaards, *The Ordination of Women in the Catholic Church*, Darton, Longman & Todd, 2001, p 119.

12. Ibid., p 119–120.

13. From a huge volume of literature, see the following: Jeanne Achterberg, *Woman as Healer*, Shambala, 1990; Anne E. Carr and Elisabeth Schüssler Fiorenza, Editors, *The Special Nature of Women*, SCM, 1991; Susan Griffin, *Woman and Nature*, The Women's Press, reprinted 1994; James B. Nelson and Sandra P. Longfellow, *Sexuality and the Sacred*, John Knox Press, 1994; Eileen Sutcliffe and Lorna Rowsell, *Eve Returns Adam's Rib*, Loraleen Enterprises, 2002.

14 Susan A. Ross, *Extravagant Affections: A Feminist Sacramental Theology*, Continuum, 2001.

15. I want to distinguish here between my use of the word 'feminine' as it has been used historically in the Catholic tradition, and the psycho-

logical use of the word in the Jungian sense by practitioners such as
Marion Woodman. See e.g. *To Be a Woman: the Birth of the Conscious
Feminine*, edited by Connie Zweig, Jeremy P. Tarcher, Inc. 1990.

16. One of the most accessible descriptions of these groups is in *Beyond
Patching: Faith and Feminism in the Catholic Church*, Sandra Schneiders,
Paulist Press, 1991. For a more extended study see Rosemary Tong,
Feminist thought: A Comprehensive Introduction, Routledge, 1994.

17. Ibid., pp 29ff. See also Mary Jo Weaver, *New Catholic Women: A
Contemporary Challenge to Traditional Religious Authority*, Harper and
Row, 1985, especially pp 180-213.

18. *Defecting in Place: Women Claiming Responsibility for Their Own Spiritual
Lives*, Crossroad, 1994.

19. *Beyond God the Father: Toward a Philosophy of Women's Liberation*,
Beacon Press, 1973.

20. Schneiders, p 34.

21. See *Sexism and God-Talk: Toward a Feminist Theology*, Beacon Press,
1983, especially pp 116-138, and see also *The Christology of Rosemary
Radford Ruether: A Critical Introduction*, by Mary Hembrow Snyder,
Twenty-Third Publications, 1988.

22. An excellent anthology illustrating the abundance of feminist scholarship on this subject is *In the Embrace of God: Feminist Approaches to
Theological Anthropology*, edited by Ann O'Hara Graff, Orbis Books, 1995.

23. Schneiders, p 75.

24. *Sexism and God-Talk*, pp 18-19.

25. Sandra Schneiders, *Beyond Patching*, pp 106ff.

26. Autobiographical Preface to the 1975 edition of *The Church and the
Second Sex*, p 5.

27. Daphne Hampson, *Theology and Feminism*, Blackwell, 1990, p 41. See
also *Swallowing a Fishbone: Feminist Theologians Debate Christianity*, edited
by Daphne Hampson, SPCK, 1996.

28. Carolyn Osiek, *Beyond Anger: On Being a Feminist in the Church*,
Paulist Press, 1968.

29. Catherine Mowry LaCugna, *God For Us: The Trinity and Christian
Life*, HarperCollins, 1991; Sallie McFague, *Models of God: Theology for an
Ecological, Nuclear Age*, Fortress Press, 1987; Elizabeth A. Johnson, *SHE
WHO IS: The Mystery of God in Feminist Theological Discourse*, Crossroad,
1992.

30. See Susan Cody, Marian Ronan, Hal Taussig, *Sophia: The Future of
Feminist Spirituality*, Harper and Row, 1986.

31. 'God in Communion with Us: The Trinity', p 106 in *Freeing Theology*.

32. *Models of God*, pp 69ff for the world as God's body, and pp 78ff for
the imagery of mother, lover and friend.

33. See especially Elizabeth Johnson, *SHE WHO IS*, pp 262ff.

34. 'A Theological Case for God-She: Expanding the Treasury of
Metaphor', in *Commonweal*, 29 January 1993, pp 9-14.

35. Ibid., p 12.

CHAPTER TEN

1. See especially the final chapter of *The Oxford Illustrated History of Christianity*, edited by John McManners, Oxford University Press, 1992: 'The Future of Christianity', by John Taylor, pp 628-663.

2. Ursula King has edited a collection of readings from Third World feminists that gives a flavour of this diversity and commonality: *Feminist Theology from the Third World*, SPCK/Orbis Press, 1994. Much of the following is based on this volume.

3. See for example *Doing Theology in a Divided World*, edited by Virginia Fabella and Sergio Torres, Orbis Books, 1985; *With Passion and Compassion: Third World Women Doing Theology*, edited by Virginia Fabella, MM, and Mercy Amba Oduyoye, Orbis Books, 1988; and *Through Her Eyes: Women's Theology from Latin America*, edited by Elsa Tamez, Orbis Books, 1989.

4. 'The Struggle about Women's Theological Education' by Mercy Amba Oduyoye and Roina Fa'Atauva'A, in Ursula King, op. cit., p 170.

5. See also Dorothy Ramodibe, 'Women and men building together the Church in Africa', in *With Passion and Compassion*, p 15; and Rosemary Radford Ruether, *Women and Redemption: A Theological History*, Fortress Press, 1998, pp 254ff.

6. See the sections on Asian feminist theology in the above publications as well as *Any Room for Christ in Asia?* edited by Leonardo Boff and Virgil Elizondo, Orbis Books 1993; *We Dare to Dream: Doing Theology as Asian Women*, edited by Virginia Fabella and Sun Ai Lee-Park, Orbis, 1990; and Chung Hyun Kyung, *Struggle to Be the Sun Again: Introducing Asian Women's Theology*, Orbis, 1990.

7. Quoted in Ruether, pp 265-266.

8. Ibid., pp 269ff.

9. See the text in Ursula King, pp 392-394.

10. To the works listed in note 6 above, add, Ivone Gebara and Maria Clara Bingemer, *Mary, Mother of God, Mother of the Poor*, Orbis Books, 1989.

11. Ursula King, pp 183-188.

12. Ibid., pp 308ff.

13. To the volumes noted above, add bell hooks, *Ain't I a Woman: Black Women and Feminism*, South End Press, 1981; Emilie M. Townes, *Embracing the Spirit: Womanist Perspectives on Hope Salvation & Transformation*, Orbis Books, 1997; Delores S. Williams, *Sisters in the Wilderness: The Challenge of Womanist God-Talk*, Orbis Books, 1993.

14. Ruether, p 230.

15. hooks, pp 7, 15, 137ff.

16. Williams, pp 4-8, 236ff.

17. Ruether, pp 229ff has a good analysis of womanist theology in the context of the history of feminist theology.

18. Alice Walker, *The Color Purple*, and Zora Neale Hurston, *Their Eyes Were Watching God*.

19. Cheryl Townsend Gilkes, 'A Conscious Connection to All that Is' in *Embracing the Spirit*, p 292.

20. Ada Maria Isasi-Diaz and Yolanda Tarango, *Hispanic Women: Prophetic Voices in the Church*, Harper and Row, 1988; and *En la Lucha, Elaborating a Mujerista Theology*, Fortress Press, 1993. See also the analysis of Ruether, pp 234ff.

21. Ada Maria Isasi-Diaz, 'The Task of Hispanic Women's Liberation Theology – Mujeristas: Who We Are and What We Are About', in Ursula King, pp 88-102.

22. See especially Lois K. Daly, Editor, *Feminist Theological Ethics: A Reader*, Westminster John Knox Press; Paula M. Cooey, Sharon A. Farmer and Mary Ellen Ross, *Embodied Love: Sensuality and Relationship as Feminist Values*, Harper and Row, 1987; Ann O'Hara Graff, *In the Embrace of God: Feminist Approaches to Theological Anthropology*, Orbis Books, 1995; Linda Hogan, *Confronting the Truth: Conscience in the Catholic Tradition*, Darton, Longman & Todd, 2001; Mary John Mananzan et al, Editors, *Women Resisting Violence: Spirituality for Life*, Orbis Books, 1996; Elisabeth Schüssler Fiorenza and Mary Shawn Copeland, Editors, *Violence Against Women*, SCM/Orbis, 1994; Catherine J. M. Halkes, *New Creation: Christian Feminism and the Renewal of the Earth*, SPCK, 1989; Rosemary Radford Ruether, *Christianity and the Making of the Modern Family: Ruling Ideologies, Diverse Realities*, Beacon Press, 2000.

23. For one example of this discussion, see Barbara Hilkert Andolsen, 'Agape in Feminist Ethics', in Lois K. Daly, pp 146-159.

24. Joanne Carlson Brown and Carole R. Bohn, Editors, *Christianity, Patriarchy and Abuse: A Feminist Critique*, The Pilgrim Press, 1989; Elisabeth Schüssler Fiorenza and Mary Shawn Copeland, *Violence Against Women*, SCM/Orbis, 1994; Mary John Mananzan et al, *Women Resisting Violence: Spirituality for Life*, Orbis 1996; and Margaret Kelleher, *The Feminization of Famine: Expressions of the Inexpressible*, Cork University Press, 1997.

25. *Women Resisting Violence*, pp 183-184.

26. 'Ecofeminism: first and third world Women', pp 27-35 in *Women Resisting Violence*.

27. Catherina Halkes, pp 108ff.

28. There is an extensive web site on Mother Teresa, maintained by her followers and admirers, with up-to-date information on the development of the community and the state of the canonisation process.

29. There is a vast library on Dorothy Day. I have depended on William D. Miller, *Dorothy Day: A Biography*, Harper and Row, 1982 and Robert Coles, *Dorothy Day: A Radical Devotion*, Addison-Wesley Publishing Company, 1987.

Index of People and Places